THE
EVERYTHING®

Slow Cooker Cookbook
2ND Edition

Dear Reader,

Like you, one of my everyday realities is that I have to get meals on the table—somehow. Because with just a little planning ahead I can practically fix it and forget it until it's time to serve the meal, the slow cooker is one of the easiest ways to go about getting that done. Hopefully with the help of my book, you too will come to appreciate that the slow cooker is the perfect countertop appliance for creating and cooking an endless assortment of family-friendly dishes.

Unless stated otherwise, the recipes in this book were tested using the Cuisinart four-quart Programmable Slow Cooker. (See Appendix B for additional equipment.)

This is my fourth *Everything®* cookbook. I truly enjoy finding innovative methods for fixing and adapting traditional methods to create tasty food. I'm fortunate that I then get to pass that information along through the recipes in my cookbooks.

My sincere wish is that your time spent cooking will be more enjoyable because I've helped make the food that comes out of your kitchen not only delicious but also easier to prepare.

Pamela Rice Hahn

Welcome to the EVERYTHING® Series!

These handy, accessible books give you all you need to tackle a difficult project, gain a new hobby, comprehend a fascinating topic, prepare for an exam, or even brush up on something you learned back in school but have since forgotten.

You can choose to read an *Everything*® book from cover to cover or just pick out the information you want from our four useful boxes: e-questions, e-facts, e-alerts, e-ssentials. We give you everything you need to know on the subject, but throw in a lot of fun stuff along the way, too.

We now have more than 400 *Everything*® books in print, spanning such wide-ranging categories as weddings, pregnancy, cooking, music instruction, foreign language, crafts, pets, New Age, and so much more. When you're done reading them all, you can finally say you know *Everything*®!

QUESTIONS?
Answers to
common questions

FACTS
Important snippets
of information

ALERTS!
Urgent
warnings

ESSENTIALS
Quick
handy tips

PUBLISHER Karen Cooper

DIRECTOR OF INNOVATION Paula Munier

MANAGING EDITOR, EVERYTHING SERIES Lisa Laing

COPY CHIEF Casey Ebert

ACQUISITIONS EDITOR Katie McDonough

SENIOR DEVELOPMENT EDITOR Brett Palana-Shanahan

EDITORIAL ASSISTANT Hillary Thompson

Visit the entire Everything® series at *www.everything.com*

THE
EVERYTHING®
SLOW COOKER
COOKBOOK

2ND Edition

Easy-to-make meals that
almost cook themselves!

Pamela Rice Hahn

Avon, Massachusetts

To all my visitors at CookingWithPam.com!

An Everything® Series Book.
Everything® and everything.com® are registered trademarks of F+W Media, Inc.

Published by Adams Media, a division of F+W Media, Inc.
57 Littlefield Street, Avon, MA 02322. U.S.A.
www.adamsmedia.com

ISBN 10: 1-59869-977-6
ISBN 13: 978-1-59869-977-7

Printed in the United States of America.

J I H G F E D C B A

Library of Congress Cataloging-in-Publication Data
is available from the publisher.

This publication is designed to provide accurate and authoritative information with regard to the subject matter covered. It is sold with the understanding that the publisher is not engaged in rendering legal, accounting, or other professional advice. If legal advice or other expert assistance is required, the services of a competent professional person should be sought.

—From a *Declaration of Principles* jointly adopted by a Committee of the American Bar Association and a Committee of Publishers and Associations

Many of the designations used by manufacturers and sellers to distinguish their products are claimed as trademarks. Where those designations appear in this book and Adams Media was aware of a trademark claim, the designations have been printed with initial capital letters.

This book is available at quantity discounts for bulk purchases.
For information, please call 1-800-289-0963.

Contents

Acknowledgments

For their help and support, I would like to thank everyone at Adams Media. For all of their hard work and perseverance, I would like to thank my agents Sheree Bykofsky and Janet Rosen. Special thanks also go to my daughter, Lara Sutton; her husband, Randy; and the other joys in my life: Taylor, Charles, and Courtney; Ann, Andrew, Dennis, and Tony Rice; my mother; my nephew Brian Teeters; and Eric J. Ehlers, David Hebert, Star Geisz, everybody at ProudPatriots.org, and my other online friends.

Introduction

The recipes in this book were created for use in today's world—with an emphasis on making as much of that food as possible using a slow cooker.

The slow cooker makes it possible for you to prepare great-tasting food in ways that save you time and effort. Take a quick look at this book and you'll see that there are recipes for food that can take you from breakfast to lunch to dinner, and through all points in between.

While every effort was made to create foolproof recipes for this book, it's impossible to anticipate every factor that can affect cooking times. For example, a slow cooker sitting on a kitchen counter next to a drafty window on a sub-zero, windy winter day is going to take longer to come to temperature than one sitting in direct sunlight in the summer. Regardless of the cooking method, ingredients at room temperature will cook faster than those just out of the refrigerator, and even faster than those fresh from the freezer.

Convenience isn't a constant either. A slow cooker isn't conducive to making a meal in a hurry. On the other hand, the oven isn't always practical in the summer, and, when there are other chores to be done around or away from the house, the stovetop certainly isn't practical even for the most organized master at multitasking. Different methods will suit your needs at different times. But when you plan ahead and allow for the extra cooking time that a slow cooker requires, it lets you avoid adding heat to the kitchen from using the oven and the necessity of standing over (or at least staying close by) the stove to keep an eye on various pots and pans.

Just like when you fix something using any other cooking method, adapting a recipe for the slow cooker doesn't mean that there is only one correct way to fix each dish. For that reason, this book also includes side-bars that have bonus recipes, tips, and suggestions on how to alter some of the recipes.

Last, but not least, it is also worth noting that the exact measurement for salt is seldom given in this book. The author prefers to add as little white sea salt as possible during the cooking process, and then have gray sea salt available at the table to season the food. (It's no coincidence that the author also wrote *The Everything*® *Low-Salt Cookbook*.) Therefore, unless otherwise indicated, when a recipe calls for salt, sea salt was used to test the recipe.

Chapter 1
Good Food Without the Fuss

Who wouldn't want to come home to an already-prepared home-cooked meal? It's not just a fantasy of tired cooks, a slow cooker can make it possible. Just gather the ingredients, load up your slow cooker, and then go on with your busy life, while your slow cooker prepares a meal to perfection. This chapter will cover some basic slow cooker methods, give you some handy tips, and teach you some easy ways to modify slow cooker recipes.

Slow Cooker Cooking

Throughout this book, you'll encounter cooking terms usually associated with other methods of cooking. While the slow cooker does provide an easy way to cook foods, there are simple tricks you can employ to let your slow cooker mimic those other methods. Cooking methods terms you'll find in this book include the following:

- **Baking** usually involves putting the food that's in a baking pan or ovenproof casserole dish in a preheated oven; the food cooks by being surrounded by the hot, dry air of your oven. (In the case of a convection oven, it cooks by being surrounded by circulating hot, dry air.) In the slow cooker, food can be steam-baked in the cooker itself, or you can mimic the effect of baking at a low oven temperature by putting the food in a baking dish and resting that dish on a cooking insert or rack.
- **Braising** usually starts by browning a less expensive cut of meat in a skillet on top of the stove and then putting the meat with a small amount of liquid in a pan with a lid or covering and slowly cooking it. Braising can take place on the stovetop, in the oven, or in a slow cooker. The slow-cooking process tenderizes the meat. Incidentally, the liquid that's in the pan after you've braised meat often can be used to make a flavorful sauce or gravy.
- **Poaching** is accomplished by gently simmering ingredients in broth, juice, water, wine, or other flavorful liquid until they're cooked through and tender.
- **Sautéing** is the method of quickly cooking small or thin pieces of food in some oil or butter that has been brought to temperature in a sauté pan over medium to medium-high heat. Alternatively, you can sauté in a good-quality nonstick pan without using added fat; instead use a little broth, nonstick cooking spray, or water in place of the oil or butter. As mentioned later in this chapter, another alternative is to steam-sauté food in the microwave.
- **Steaming** is the cooking method that uses the steam from the cooking liquid to cook the food. (None of the recipes in this book call for steaming food in a perforated basket suspended above simmering

liquid, the method most often associated with steaming. Instead, steaming ingredients or vegetables directly in a covered container placed in the microwave is sometimes suggested.)

- **Stewing** is similar to braising in that food is slowly cooked in a liquid; however, stewing involves a larger liquid-to-food ratio. In other words, you use far more liquid when you're stewing food. It is the method often associated with recipes for the slow cooker. Not surprising, this method is most often used to make stew.

Tempering is the act of gradually increasing the temperature of one cooking ingredient by adding small amounts of a hotter ingredient to the first. For example, tempering beaten eggs by whisking small amounts of hot liquid into them before you add the eggs to the cooking pan lets them be mixed into the dish; tempering prevents them from scrambling instead.

Equipment Considerations

Your cooking equipment can make a difference in how easy it is to prepare foods. Buy the best you can afford. Better pan construction equals more even heat distribution, which translates to reduced cooking time and more even cooking.

Better doesn't always have to be the newest and most expensive pan on the market. The stovetop pan named in a recipe is only a suggestion. Cooks used to working with a well-seasoned cast-iron skillet may prefer using that instead of a nonstick skillet. That's okay. Use whatever pan you believe will help you achieve the result called for in the recipe.

A slow cooker is one of the easiest fix-it-and-forget-it options for today's busy cook. You add the ingredients, usually simply in the order that they're listed in the ingredients list, turn the cooker to the desired setting, and come back several hours later to a fully cooked dish.

The most efficient slow cookers have a removable stoneware cooking pot or crock. The stoneware is good at holding the heat. The food stays warm when you remove the crock and serve the meal directly from it. A stoneware crock is also easier to clean because it can go into the dishwasher.

Programmable slow cookers like Cuisinart's 4-quart and 6½-quart slow cookers let you start the cooking process at one temperature and will then automatically switch to a different setting according to how you've programmed the cooker. For example, if you haven't had time to thaw the foods you're putting in the cooker, you have the option of starting it out on high for a couple of hours, and then switching it to low heat for the appropriate number of hours. When the cooking time is completed, the cooker automatically switches to the "keep warm" setting, which holds the food at serving temperature until you're ready to serve it.

The option of having a "keep warm" setting is an important one for foods that can scorch or take on an unpleasant taste or texture if they're cooked too long. For that reason, even if you don't buy a slow cooker with all the bells and whistles, at least look for one that lets you set a cooking time and then automatically switches over to a warm setting when the cooking time is done.

Help ensure that meat cooked in the slow cooker is done to your liking by using a thermometer with a probe that goes into the food and is attached to a programmable unit that sits outside the slow cooker (see Appendix B for suggestions). The thermometer's display unit should show the current internal temperature and have an alarm that goes off when the meat reaches the correct internal temperature.

There are a number of factors that can affect cooking time, such as the temperature of the food when you add it to the slow cooker. Another important consideration is the size and shape of meat, the amount of fat and bone, and whether or not the meat was aged. The best way to ensure that meat is cooked to your liking is to use the suggested cooking time given in a recipe as a gauge to time when you can have your meal ready to serve, and set a programmable thermometer so you'll know when it's actually ready. As a general rule, internal meat temperatures indicate:

- 130°F to 140°F for medium rare
- 145°F to 150°F for medium
- 155°F to 165°F for well done

For example, referring to those temperature suggestions will prevent you from ending up with pork loin that's too dry. Any recipe that calls for you to shred the meat or cook until the meat is tender generally means that you'll cook the meat beyond those cooking temperature.

Most recipes calling for meat to be combined with other ingredients take into consideration that the meat may be cooked beyond the temperature that would be ideal had it been cooked by itself. In casseroles and other dishes in which the meat is cooked together with other food, the dish isn't done until all of the food is cooked. Even so, using a probe thermometer lets you know that the meat has cooked to the temperature at which it is safe to serve. Or it can let you know when you should remove meat such as a pork loin, wrap it in foil, and maintain its temperature in a warm oven while you wait for the other ingredients to cook through.

Foods cooked on top of the stove usually need a little more attention than those made using other methods. This is especially true if you're not used to using your stove. Use the heat settings suggested in the recipes, but until you become familiar at what temperatures are required to achieve the desired affect (like browning meat), plan on babysitting the pan on the stove. Accidentally burning food can not only ruin a meal, it can cause an even bigger disaster by causing a fire.

As you prepare the dishes in this cookbook, make notes in the margins about which ones you and your family preferred. If you think a recipe would benefit by adding a bit more seasoning, then note that too. Making such notes now will mean that someday, when you're ready to write out recipe cards, you'll be able to have an entire slow cooker section in the recipe box.

The cooking vessels you use will make a difference, too. Food will burn more easily in an inexpensive discount-store nonstick skillet than it will in heavier cast-iron, multiclad stainless, or hard anodized steel cookware. How well your cooking pan conducts the heat will make a difference on how high you set the burner temperature. But with some practice, you'll soon learn the perfect heat settings for each of your pans: It might take a medium-high setting to sauté food in an inexpensive skillet and lots more stirring to prevent the food from burning, but you can accomplish the same task in your triple-ply nonstick stainless steel skillet over medium-low heat and with less frequent stirring.

On the flipside, a heavier pan will retain the heat longer once it's removed from the burner than will an inexpensive skillet, so to prevent it from overcooking, food cooked to perfection in a heavier pan must be moved to the slow cooker more quickly. This is especially true of foods like gravy that tend to thicken the longer they sit. For example, a loose gravy meant to be added to the slow cooker can turn from a succulent liquid to one big lump if it stays on the heat too long, even when that heat is only that retained by the skillet.

FACT

Once you've moved the meat and other ingredients you've cooked in the pan and rid the pan of any excess remaining fat, you *deglaze* it by putting it over a medium-high heat and then adding enough cooking liquid to let you scrape up any browned bits stuck to the bottom of the pan. Doing this step before you add the other ingredients for your sauce or gravy gives more flavor and color to the result.

The stovetop cooking steps called for in the slow cooker recipes don't have to be intimidating. Once you become familiar with the quirks associated with how each of your pans performs on your particular stovetop, you'll begin to intuit how much time will be needed to sauté or brown foods before you add them to the slow cooker.

Slow Cooker Tips

Unless stated otherwise, the recipes in this book are for a 4-quart slow cooker. Also, unless indicated otherwise in the recipe instructions, all dishes tested for this book were cooked on low. Even though the high setting is only around 300°F, temperatures of slow cookers can vary.

The advantage to using a slow cooker is that you add the food to it and then let it do its work. In theory you can cook a dish in half the time on high, but cooking on high means that you need to check on the food to make sure it isn't scorching or boiling dry. Each time you raise the lid of your slow cooker, you increase the cooking time, so the need to fuss over the food decreases some of the time advantage you might gain by cooking on high. There's also the possibility that an extended cooking time on high can cause other unpleasant things to happen, like cheese separating into an oily mess or pasta (like the macaroni in macaroni and cheese) overcooking into a soft gooey mass.

Be sure to read the instruction manual that came with your slow cooker. It'll provide slow-cooking tips plus important information on the correct handling of the crock, the cooking insert, and the cooking timer settings.

The heating elements for a slow cooker are across the bottom of the slow cooker and up the sides. The ceramic crock insert is effective at conducting that heat so that the food cooks slowly and properly, but it isn't perfect. Until you become very familiar with the quirks of your slow cooker, cooking on low is the safest bet for ensuring the food turns out the way you want it.

Many slow cooker recipes can be changed from cooking on low to cooking on high by simply dividing the cooking time in half. It's trickier with pork, especially when cooking with a sugar-based or fruit sauce. If the dish scorches, the whole taste will change, so unless you can carefully monitor the cooking process, it's better to cook pork dishes on low.

Cooking with a slow cooker becomes even easier when you add Reynolds Slow Cooker Liners. The liners are made of food-safe, heat-resistant nylon. Unless you accidentally pierce the liner with a fork or other sharp utensil while you're transferring the food from the slow cooker to the plate, they make slow cooker cleanup fast and easy because, once the contents in the liner have cooled sufficiently, you can simply lift it out of the slow cooker and throw it away. The inside of the crock stays clean, which lets you avoid the soaking and scrubbing that used to be associated with slow cooking. You simply place the liner in the slow cooker crock, add the ingredients, cook according to the recipe instructions, throw the liner away when you're done, and wipe down the slow cooker and wash the lid.

Don't Be Afraid to Take Short Cuts and Improvise

Throughout this book there are recipe steps and sidebar suggestions that explain how there are times you can take shortcuts without compromising a recipe. Straying from the recipe may seem like a daunting task at first, but once you understand the logic behind such shortcuts, you'll begin to look on them as alternative measures rather than total improvisations. Before you know it, you'll be adding a little bit of this and a little bit of that like the best of them. For example:

- **Use broth bases or homemade broth:** Use of a broth base or home-made broth lets you eliminate the need to sear meat and sauté vegetables. In addition, broth bases can be made double strength, which saves you the time of reducing broth and you avoid that briny, overly salty taste associated with bouillon cubes. Bases also take up less storage space. It usually only takes ¾ to 1 teaspoon of broth mixed together with a cup of water to make 1 cup of broth. A 16-ounce container of base, for example, is enough to make 6 gallons of broth. (Try finding room for 6 gallons of broth in your refrigerator or pantry!)
- **Replace each peeled, cored, and seeded apple with ¼ cup unsweetened applesauce:** Because the applesauce is already cooked down, you have the advantage that you can taste the dish near the end of the cooking time and add more if you think it's called for. (Or, even if you've used the apples as called for in the recipe, that already cooked-down advantage means that you can

add in some unsweetened or sweetened applesauce near the end of the cooking time if you think the dish would benefit from some additional apple flavor or sweetness.)

- **Use a microwave-safe measuring cup:** Rather than dirtying a microwave-safe bowl and a measuring cup, planning the steps so that you add the ingredients to a microwave-safe measuring cup means you can use it to sauté or steam onions or other vegetables called for in the recipe. This makes it easier to pour the results into the slow cooker and you end up with fewer dishes to wash.

- **Steam-sauté vegetables in the microwave:** Sautéing vegetables in the microwave has the added advantage of using less oil than it would take to sauté them in a pan. Or you can compromise further and eliminate the oil entirely and substitute broth if you prefer. Just because a recipe suggests sautéing the onions in a nonstick skillet doesn't mean that you can't use the alternative microwave method, or vice versa. Use the method that is most convenient for you.

- **Take advantage of ways to enhance or correct the flavor:** Like salt, a little bit of sugar can act as a flavor enhancer. The sweetness of sugar, honey, applesauce, or jelly can also be used to help tame an overly hot spicy dish or curry. Just start out adding a little bit at a time; you want to adjust the flavor without ending up with a dish with a cloying result.

There are other times you may need to adjust some of the recipe instructions. For example, if you have fresh herbs on hand, it's almost always better to use those instead of dried seasoning; however, if you substitute fresh herbs, don't add them until near the end of the cooking time. Also keep in mind that you need to use three times the amount called for in the recipe. In other words, if the recipe specifies 1 teaspoon of dried thyme, you'd add 1 tablespoon (3 teaspoons) of fresh thyme.

A practical and budget-friendly shortcut is to have cooked meat on hand to add to a recipe. Shred or cube leftover chicken or other meat and then freeze it in cup-size portions so that it's already measured for future use. If the meat was highly seasoned, just be sure to indicate that on the freezer label so that you don't completely alter the intended flavor of the dish. For example, unless your intention is to create an original fusion-style dish, you don't want to accidentally add Jerk Chicken to Chicken Alfredo.

If you're using the frozen meat to replace raw meat called for in the recipe, chances are you can add it straight from the freezer to the slow cooker and not greatly affect the cooking time. If the meat is thawed, or it's seafood (which should be thawed), you'll want to wait until near the end of the cooking time to add it so that you don't overcook the meat.

QUESTIONS

Once I remove the meat from a slow-cooked chicken, can I use the bones again to make chicken broth?
It's not recommended. When you cook chicken in the slow cooker, those bones have already flavored the water or other liquid in which you cooked the chicken. Unlike beef bones that benefit from being browned, overcooked chicken bones can adversely affect the taste of the broth.

There are practical reasons given for some cooking steps, such as browning ground beef so that you can then drain and discard the excess fat before you add the meat to the slow cooker. That fat not only adds calories, it can give the entire dish a fatty flavor that you may not like. If you need to introduce fat into or back into a dish, it's much better to use fat with better flavor, such as butter, extra-virgin olive oil, or bacon.

On the other hand, skipping other steps, like sautéing onion, carrot, celery, or bell pepper before you add them to the slow cooker, won't ruin the taste of the food; you'll just end up with a dish that tastes good instead of great. When time is an issue, there may be times when good is good enough. And that's okay. The slow cooker police won't show up and arrest you—and, even though they may not always specifically express their appreciation, your family will still enjoy the meal.

Chapter 2
Beverages

Spiced Cherry Punch

An ounce of tart cherry juice concentrate is added to 7 ounces of water to make a cup of cherry juice. The apple and orange juices in Spiced Cherry Punch add natural sweetness, but you can also stir in some sugar to taste if you prefer a sweeter punch.

Serves 14

Ingredients:
8 cups (2 quarts) apple cider or apple juice
½ cup tart cherry juice concentrate
3 cups water
2 cups orange juice
1½ teaspoons whole allspice berries
1½ teaspoons whole cloves
2 (3-inch) cinnamon sticks
Optional: 1 tablespoon aromatic bitters
Optional: Cinnamon sticks for garnish
Optional: Dark rum or other adult beverage

1. Add the apple cider or apple juice, tart cherry juice concentrate, water, and orange juice to a 4-quart slow cooker.

2. Add the allspice berries and whole cloves to a muslin spice bag or a piece of cheesecloth that has been rinsed and wrung dry; secure with a piece of kitchen twine and add to the juices in the cooker.

3. Add the cinnamon sticks. Stir in the aromatic bitters if using. Cover and cook until very hot but not boiling, or 2 hours on high or 4 hours on low.

4. Remove the spices in the muslin bag or cheesecloth and cinnamon sticks from the cooker. The punch can be kept at serving temperature by setting the slow cooker on low, keeping in mind that the flavors will become more concentrated the longer the punch is uncovered and on the heat. Serve in punch glasses or mugs garnished with cinnamon sticks if desired. Have dark rum or other adult beverage available for those who wish to add it to the punch.

Tart Cherry Juice Concentrate
Tart cherry juice concentrate is available at most natural food stores or online through Michigan producers like Brownwood Acres Foods, Inc. (www.brownwoodacres.com) and King Orchards (www.mi-cherries.com).

Wassail

To make a nonalcoholic version of this recipe, substitute additional apple juice for the sherry and ale.

Serves 20

Ingredients:
6 cups apple juice
2 cups cranberry juice or
    lemonade
6 cups orange juice
¼ cup brown sugar
1 cup water
2 cups semisweet sherry
2 (12-ounce) bottles of ale
4 (3-inch) cinnamon sticks
1 orange
1 teaspoon whole cloves
1 lemon
12 whole allspice berries
1 tablespoon chopped
    candied ginger
Optional: 1 tablespoon
    aromatic bitters

1. Add the apple juice, cranberry juice or lemonade, orange juice, brown sugar, water, sherry, ale, and cinnamon sticks to a 4-quart slow cooker.

2. Stud the orange with the whole cloves, cut the orange and lemon into quarters and remove any seeds, and add to the slow cooker.

3. Add the allspice berries and candied ginger to a muslin spice bag or a piece of cheesecloth that has been rinsed and wrung dry; secure with a piece of kitchen twine and add to the juices in the cooker. Stir in the bitters if using.

4. Cover and cook on low for 4 hours. Remove cinnamon sticks, spice bag, and orange and lemon wedges before serving.

Slow-Cooking Alcoholic Beverages
If you're in a hurry and want to bring an alcoholic punch to temperature quicker, you can begin the slow-cooking process on high; however, be sure to watch the punch carefully and be sure that you switch the cooker to low before the liquids come to a boil.

Rich and Indulgent Hot Chocolate

Serves 8

Ingredients:
2 cups heavy cream
6 cups whole milk
Optional: 2 (3-inch)
    cinnamon sticks
1 (12-ounce) package
    semisweet chocolate
    chips
1 tablespoon vanilla
Optional: Marshmallows

*If you prefer to indulge in a darker chocolate beverage, substitute 12
ounces of chopped bittersweet chocolate for the chocolate chips.
You can let the milk mixture come to temperature for up to 6 hours
on low before you add the chocolate and serve this drink.*

1. Add the cream and whole milk to the slow cooker; stir to combine. Add the cinnamon sticks if using. Cover and cook long enough to bring the milk mixture to temperature: approximately 3 hours on low or 1½ hours on high.

2. If a "skin" has developed on the milk, skim it off and discard. Whisk in the chocolate until melted. Stir in the vanilla. Ladle into mugs and serve immediately. Top each mug with marshmallows if desired.

Low-Fat Hot Chocolate

Serves 12

Ingredients:
12 cups water
5 cups nonfat dry milk
¾ cup cocoa
1 cup sugar
Optional: 2 teaspoons mint or
    almond extract

*For a richer drink, unwrap 24 York peppermint patties (a 12-ounce package)
and add them 2 hours into the cooking time; stir until they're melted into
the drink. Cover and continue to cook until ready to serve.*

Add the water to the slow cooker; cover and cook on low while you mix together the dry milk, cocoa, and sugar in a bowl. Whisk the dry ingredients into the water. Add extract if using. Cover and cook on low for 3 to 4 hours.

German Mulled Wine

To add a touch more sweetness to this drink, sprinkle a few pieces of cinnamon red hot candies into each serving.

1. Add the cider, wine, and honey to a slow cooker.

2. Put the cloves, allspice berries, and lemon zest in a muslin spice bag or a piece of cheesecloth that has been rinsed, wrung dry, and secured with a piece of kitchen twine; add to the slow cooker along with the cinnamon sticks.

3. Cover and cook on low for 3 to 4 hours.

According to Your Personal Sweet Tooth
While honey adds an extra flavor dimension to the German Mulled Wine drink, you can omit adding it during the slow-cooking portion of this recipe. You can then sweeten the finished drink using honey, sugar, brown sugar, or sugar substitute according to your personal taste and preference.

Serves 12

Ingredients:
5 cups apple cider
5 cups burgundy wine
½ cup honey
1 teaspoon whole cloves
12 whole allspice berries
Zest of 1 lemon
2 (3-inch) pieces stick
   cinnamon

Hot Mommas

For a cocktail with a kick, add ½ teaspoon or more of the hot pepper sauce and double the amount of horseradish that you stir into this drink. It can be served as a satisfying start to a winter morning brunch or along with the appetizers at a buffet or dinner party.

Serves 8

Ingredients:
5 cups tomato juice or vegetable juice cocktail
3 cups beef broth
Hot pepper sauce, to taste
2 teaspoons celery seeds
1 tablespoon prepared horseradish
1 tablespoon Worcestershire sauce
1 cup vodka
1 tablespoon fresh lime juice
Optional: Celery sticks
Optional: Lime wedges

1. Add the tomato juice or vegetable juice cocktail, broth, pepper sauce, and celery seeds to a slow cooker. Stir to combine. Cover and cook on low for 4 hours or until very hot.

2. Just before serving, stir in the horseradish, Worcestershire sauce, vodka, and lime juice. Taste for seasoning and add additional horseradish, Worcestershire sauce, and hot pepper sauce if desired. Ladle into large mugs and garnish with celery sticks and lime wedges if desired.

Cup of Soup
Omit the vodka from the Hot Mommas recipe and you end up with warm mugs of spicy soup that you can serve alongside toasted cheese or roast beef sandwiches.

Hot Cranberry-Pineapple Punch

If you prefer, you can omit the brown sugar and water called for in the Hot Cranberry-Pineapple Punch and sweeten it with 2 cups of apple juice instead.

1. Add the cranberry juice, pineapple juice, brown sugar, and water to the slow cooker.

2. Break the cinnamon sticks into smaller pieces and add them along with the whole cloves to a muslin spice bag or wrap them in cheesecloth tied shut with cotton string or kitchen twine. Add to the slow cooker. Cover and cook on low for 1 hour.

3. Uncover and stir until the brown sugar is dissolved into the juice. Cover and cook for another 7–8 hours.

4. Uncover the cooker and remove the spice bag or cheesecloth; holding over the slow cooker, squeeze to extract the seasoned juice. To serve, ladle into heatproof mugs and add vodka to taste to each serving.

Chilled Cranberry-Pineapple Punch
After slow cooking, allow the punch to cool to room temperature and then chill until needed. Add 3–4 cups lemon-lime soda or Mountain Dew. Serve in punch cups or in tall glasses over ice, garnished with a maraschino cherry.

Yield: About 18–22 cups

Ingredients:
8 cups cranberry juice
8 cups unsweetened
     pineapple juice
2 cups brown sugar, packed
2 cups water
2 (3-inch) cinnamon sticks
2 teaspoons whole cloves
Optional: 3–4 cups vodka

Hot Buttered Rum

Time the cooking of this drink so that you can stir in the rum and let it "mull" for 20 minutes before serving.

1. Add the butter and 2 cups of the water to the slow cooker. Cover and cook on high for ½ hour or until the butter is melted.

2. Stir in the brown sugar, and then add the remaining water, salt, nutmeg, cloves, and cinnamon. Cover and cook on low for 2 to 4 hours.

3. Twenty minutes before serving, stir in the rum; cover and cook for 20 minutes. To serve, ladle into small heatproof mugs.

Irish Coffee

The coffee, which is best made using medium-roast beans, can be made ahead and added to the slow cooker two hours before you plan to serve dessert.

1. Add the chilled coffee to the slow cooker. Cover and cook on low for 1 hour. If you're using fresh-brewed coffee, you can skip this step.

2. Stir in the sugar until it's dissolved; cover and cook on low for 1 hour. To serve, ladle into heatproof mugs. Add whiskey to taste and garnish with a dollop of whipped cream.

Mexican Hot Chocolate

This drink is rich enough that you can use half whole milk and half water or all low-fat milk. You can serve this drink with a complete southwestern-style breakfast. A simpler, yet delicious alternative is to dunk buttered slices of toast made from homemade bread into the drink.

Serves 16

Ingredients:
1 gallon milk
1⅓ cups dark brown sugar
1 cup masa harina (corn flour)
7 tablespoons cornstarch
4 ounces bittersweet chocolate, chopped
2 (3-inch) cinnamon sticks
3 tablespoons vanilla
Optional: Ground cinnamon

1. Add 3 cups of the milk to the slow cooker. Add the brown sugar, masa harina, and cornstarch to a bowl and mix well, and then whisk into the milk in the slow cooker. Whisk in the remaining milk. Cover and cook on high for 30 minutes to bring to a simmer.

2. Add the chocolate and whisk until it's melted and combined with the milk mixture. Add the cinnamon sticks. Cover and cook on low for approximately 2 hours, stirring occasionally; the drink is done when it is thickened and lightly coats the back of a spoon. Just before serving, stir in the vanilla. Ladle into mugs and garnish with ground cinnamon if desired.

Chocolate Chips Instead
You can substitute semisweet chocolate chips for the chopped bittersweet chocolate. If you do, reduce the amount of brown sugar to ¾ cup. Taste the drink for sweetness midway through the cooking time and add more sugar if desired.

Chai Tea

Serves 12

Ingredients:
5 cups water
6 slices fresh ginger
1 teaspoon whole cloves
2 (3-inch) pieces stick
    cinnamon
1½ teaspoons freshly ground
    nutmeg
½ teaspoon ground
    cardamom
1 cup sugar
12 tea bags
6 cups milk

*Store any leftover tea in a covered container in the refrigerator. It
can be reheated, but leftover tea is best served over ice.*

1. Add the water to the slow cooker. Put the ginger and cloves in a muslin
   spice bag or a piece of cheesecloth that has been rinsed, wrung dry,
   and secured with a piece of kitchen twine; add to the cooker along
   with the cinnamon, nutmeg, and cardamom. Cover and cook on low
   for 4 to 6 hours or on high for 2 to 3 hours.

2. Stir in the sugar until it's dissolved into the water. Add the tea bags and
   milk; cover and cook on low for ½ hour. Remove and discard the spices
   in the muslin bag or cheesecloth, cinnamon sticks, and tea bags. Ladle
   into tea cups or mugs to serve.

Sweet Tip
*If you prefer, you can omit adding the sugar during the cooking process
and allow each drinker to add sugar or sugar substitute to his or her
serving according to taste.*

Cappuccino

Simmering the cinnamon in milk adds a more subtle, yet distinctive flavor to this drink than what's achieved by just sprinkling cinnamon on top of the frothed milk.

Serves 10

Ingredients:
2 cups milk
2 (3-inch) sticks cinnamon
8 cups hot coffee or espresso

1. Add the milk and cinnamon sticks to the slow cooker. Cover and cook on low for 2 hours; keep the milk on the warm setting until ready to serve.

2. Remove the cinnamon sticks. Add the coffee to the slow cooker. Use an immersion blender to add froth to the drink. Ladle into mugs. Repeat using the immersion blender, if necessary, to create more froth between ladling out the servings.

Frothy Milk

If you prefer, you can skip adding the coffee or espresso to the slow cooker. Instead, use an immersion blender to froth the milk in the slow cooker, repeating as necessary as you top individual servings of the coffee or espresso with frothed milk ladled into the drinks according to taste. This method works better if you or another guest's preference is to sweeten the drink; stir in the sugar or sweetener to taste, and then top with the froth.

Mocha

If you prefer lower-fat mocha, replace the cream with milk.

Add the coffee and cream to a slow cooker. Stir to combine. Cover and cook on low for 3 to 6 hours. If a "skin" has developed on top from the cream, skim it off and discard. Whisk in the chocolate chips until melted. Ladle into mugs and serve immediately.

Chocolate Chips Substitute

In the mocha recipe, you can use ½ cup cocoa and 1 cup sugar or the all-natural sugar substitute Whey Low (www.wheylow.com) instead of the chocolate chips. Mix the cocoa and sugar or Whey Low together in a bowl, and then whisk it into the hot coffee and cream mixture. You can serve it immediately or let the coffee, cream, cocoa, and sugar or Whey Low cook covered on low for an additional hour or two.

Serves 12

Ingredients:
10 cups coffee
2 cups heavy cream
1 (12-ounce) bag semisweet
    chocolate chips

Chapter 3
Appetizers and Party Fare

Sassy and Sweet Chicken Wings

Serves 12

Ingredients:
4 pounds chicken wings
2 cups Brooks Rich & Tangy
  Ketchup
1 (12-ounce) can Coca-Cola

*For larger servings or to increase the number of servings, substitute
4 pounds of chicken drumettes (the meatiest pieces of the
chicken wings) for the whole chicken wings.*

Add the chicken wings and ketchup to the slow cooker in alternating layers. Pour the cola over the chicken and ketchup. Cover and cook on low for 6–8 hours. Uncover and continue to cook on low until sauce is thickened. To serve, reduce the heat setting of the slow cooker to warm.

Tangy Substitutions

An alternative to using Brooks Rich & Tangy Ketchup is to substitute 1 cup of regular ketchup and 1 cup of chili sauce.

Hot Fudge Fondue

Yield: About 4 cups

Ingredients:
2 sticks (1 cup) butter
1 cup heavy cream
½ cup light corn syrup
Pinch salt
1 pound (16 ounces)
  semisweet chocolate
  chips
1 tablespoon vanilla extract

*Leftover hot fudge fondue can be stored in a covered container in the refrigerator
for up to 3 weeks. Reheat to serve, whisking in additional cream if needed.*

1. Add the butter, cream, corn syrup, and salt to the slow cooker. Cover and cook on low for 1 hour. Uncover and stir with a silicone-coated whisk or heatproof spatula, cover, and cook for another hour. Uncover and stir or whisk until the sugar is completely dissolved.

2. Add the chocolate chips and vanilla. Stir or whisk until the chocolate is completely melted and incorporated into the fondue. Reduce the heat setting of the slow cooker to warm.

Fabulous Fondue

For six servings, cut the recipe in half and prepare in a small (1½-quart) slow cooker. To make it easier for your guests to access the fondue and to ensure that it is maintained at the proper temperature to prevent the cheese from separating, transfer the prepared fondue to an electric fondue pot.

Serves 12

Ingredients:
2 cloves of garlic, peeled and
    cut in half
2 cups evaporated milk
1 cup dry white wine or
    sparkling white grape
    juice
1 teaspoon hot pepper sauce,
    or to taste
¼ cup all-purpose flour
1 teaspoon dry mustard
4 cups Swiss cheese, cubed
4 cups fontina cheese, cubed
Optional: Salt and freshly
    ground black pepper

1. Rub the inside of the slow cooker crock with the cut cloves of garlic. (For a stronger garlic flavor, leave the garlic in the cooker and use a slotted spoon to remove them just before serving.) Add the milk, wine or sparkling grape juice, and hot pepper sauce to the slow cooker.

2. Add the flour and dry mustard to a large zip-closure bag. Seal and shake to mix well. Add the cheese cubes to the bag; seal the bag and shake well to coat the cheese cubes in the flour. Pour the contents of the bag into the slow cooker and stir to combine. Cover and cook on low for 4 hours or until heated through and the cheese has melted.

3. Whisk the fondue to incorporate the melted cheese fully into the liquid. Taste for seasoning and add more hot sauce, and/or salt and freshly ground pepper if desired.

Fabulous Fondue Serving Suggestions

Cheese fondue is traditionally served with bread cubes that are each pierced with a fondue fork and dipped into the fondue. Steamed or roasted asparagus spears and raw or cooked baby carrots, broccoli florets, cauliflower florets, cucumber or pickle slices, radishes, snow peas, and sweet bell pepper strips are also delicious dipped in a savory fondue sauce.

Butterscotch Caramel Sauce

Yield: About 6 cups

Ingredients:
½ cup (1 stick) butter
2 cups heavy cream
4 cups brown sugar
2 tablespoons fresh lemon
   juice
Pinch sea salt
1 tablespoon vanilla

*For a delicious butterscotch caramel cake, pour this sauce
over a warm sheet cake that you've poked holes in.*

1. Add the butter, cream, brown sugar, lemon juice, and salt to the slow cooker. Cover and cook on high for an hour or until the butter is melted and the cream begins to bubble around the edges of the crock. Uncover and stir.

2. Cover and cook on low for 2 hours, stirring occasionally. Uncover and cook on low for 1 more hour or until the mixture coats the back of the spoon or the sauce reaches its desired thickness. Stir in the vanilla.

Peanut Butter Fondue

Serves 20

Ingredients:
2 sticks (1 cup) butter
1 cup light corn syrup
2 (14-ounce) cans sweetened
   condensed milk
2 cups light brown sugar
Pinch salt
1 cup peanut butter

*Leftover peanut butter fondue can be stored in a covered container in the
refrigerator for up to 3 weeks. Alternatively, it can be poured into a buttered pan,
allowed to cool, and then cut it into pieces of peanut butter fudge.*

1. Add the butter, corn syrup, condensed milk, brown sugar, and salt to the slow cooker. Cover and cook on low for 1 hour. Uncover and stir with a heatproof spatula, cover, and cook for another hour. Uncover and stir or whisk until the sugar is completely dissolved.

2. Add the peanut butter. Cover and cook on low for 15 minutes to ½ hour to soften the peanut butter. Stir or whisk until the peanut butter is blended with the condensed milk mixture. Reduce the heat setting of the slow cooker to warm.

Party-Pleasing Chicken Livers

The resulting sauce will be a bit sweeter, but if you prefer not to use white wine you can substitute an equal amount of red currant or apple jelly or apple juice.

1. Add the diced bacon and onion to the slow cooker. Cover and cook on high for ½ hour or until fat begins to be rendered and the onions are transparent.

2. Cut the chicken livers into bite-size pieces. Add the flour, salt, and pepper to a large zip-closure bag. Seal and shake to mix. Add the chicken livers to the bag and toss to coat them with the seasoned flour.

3. Add the broth, soups, mushrooms, and wine to the slow cooker. Stir to combine. Add the chicken livers and fold them into the soup mixture. Cover and cook on low for 6–8 hours. Serve on buttered toast points.

Serves 18

Ingredients:
6 slices bacon, diced
6 green onions with tops, chopped
2 pounds chicken livers
1 cup all-purpose flour
1 teaspoon salt
¼ teaspoon freshly ground black pepper
2 cups chicken broth
1 (10½-ounce) can condensed cream of mushroom soup
1 (10½-ounce) can condensed cream of chicken or celery soup
2 (4-ounce) cans sliced mushrooms, drained
½ cup dry white wine

Chili-Cheese Dip

You can substitute 3¾ cups homemade chili for the canned chili. For a thicker dip to serve with tortilla chips or celery sticks, stir in a pound of cooked and drained ground beef. This dip also makes a delicious topper for baked potatoes.

Add the chili and cheese to a slow cooker. Cover and, stirring the mixture every half hour, cook on low for 2 to 3 hours or until the cheese is melted. To serve, reduce the heat setting of the slow cooker to warm.

Serves 12

Ingredients:
1 (15-ounce) can chili
1 pound Velveeta cheese, cut into cubes

Retro Meatballs

Serves 8

Ingredients:

2 tablespoons extra virgin
    olive oil or vegetable oil
2 pounds frozen precooked
    meatballs
1 (12-ounce) jar chili sauce
1 cup grape jelly

*This recipe is an adaptation of an appetizer recipe popular in the 1960s.
You can ladle the meatballs directly from the slow cooker and then
provide toothpicks to make them easier for your guests to eat.*

1. Add the oil to the bag of frozen meatballs; close and toss to coat the meatballs in the oil. Add to the slow cooker. Cover and cook on high for 4 hours. (To prevent the meatballs on the bottom of the cooker from burning, carefully stir the meatballs every hour to rearrange them in the cooker.)

2. In a measuring cup or bowl, mix the chili sauce together with the grape jelly. Pour over the meatballs in the slow cooker. Cover and cook on low for 2 hours or until the sauce is heated through and thickened. To serve, reduce the heat setting of the slow cooker to warm.

In a Hurry Retro Meatballs

Preheat the oven to 425°F. Arrange the oil-coated frozen meatballs on a baking sheet; bake for 30 minutes, use tongs to turn the meatballs, and continue to bake for 15–30 minutes or until warmed through. Add the meatballs to the slow cooker and continue with Step 2 of the Retro Meatballs recipe.

Mexican Dip

This recipe makes enough dip to feed a hungry crowd, which makes it popular for a snack following a youth group meeting or at a Super Bowl party. Warm up leftover Mexican Dip and use it as the dressing for a taco salad or as a baked potato topper.

Add all ingredients to the slow cooker. Stir to combine. Cover and cook on low for 4–6 hours, stirring every 30 minutes until cheese is melted. Once cheese is melted, taste for seasoning and add more salsa if desired. To serve, reduce the heat setting of the slow cooker to warm.

Processed Cheese
Processed cheeses like Velveeta and American cheese will stand up to long periods of heat without separating.

Serves 24

Ingredients:
3 pounds lean ground beef, cooked and drained
1 large sweet onion, peeled and diced
1 (15-ounce) can refried beans
1 (10½-ounce) can condensed tomato soup
1 package taco seasoning
1 cup salsa
2 pounds Velveeta cheese, cut into cubes

Parmesan Artichoke Dip

For a more savory dip, reduce the amount of mayonnaise to 2 cups and then stir in 2 cups of room temperature sour cream immediately before serving. For fewer servings, cut the recipe in half and reduce the cooking time.

1. Drain and chop the artichoke hearts. Add to the slow cooker along with the mayonnaise, cream cheese, Parmesan-Reggiano cheese, garlic, dill, and pepper. Stir to combine. Cover and cook on low for 2 hours; uncover and stir well.

2. Re-cover and cook on low for an additional 2 hours or until the cheese is melted completely and the dip is heated through. To serve, reduce the heat setting of the slow cooker to warm. Serve with crackers, toast points, pita crisps, or crusty rye or country whole grain bread.

Serves 24

Ingredients:
2 (13½-ounce) jars of marinated artichoke hearts
4 cups mayonnaise
2 (8-ounce) packages of cream cheese, cubed
12 ounces (3 cups) freshly grated Parmesan-Reggiano cheese
4 cloves of garlic, peeled and minced
1 teaspoon dried dill
Freshly ground black pepper or white pepper to taste

Welsh Rarebit

Serves 8

Ingredients:
2½ cups beer
2 tablespoons butter
Hot sauce, to taste
Worcestershire sauce, to taste
2 pounds (4 cups) medium or
    sharp Cheddar cheese,
    grated
2 tablespoons all-purpose
    flour
2 teaspoons dry mustard
2 large eggs
Optional: Paprika

Welsh Rarebit can be served as a party dip or spooned over toast points and then dusted with paprika. It's also good served as part of a breakfast buffet to be spooned over scrambled eggs or egg-topped English muffins.

1. Pour 2 cups of the beer and the butter, hot sauce, and Worcestershire sauce into the slow cooker. Cook uncovered on high for ½ hour.

2. Put half of the grated cheese and the flour in a zip-closure bag. Shake well to coat the cheese with flour, adding as much of the cheese to the bag as will fit and still allow room to mix it with the flour. Add all of the cheese-flour mixture and remaining cheese to the slow cooker. Cover and cook on low for 1 hour or until cheese is melted.

3. Add the dry mustard and the eggs to a bowl or measuring cup; whisk to combine. Whisk the remaining ½ cup of beer into the egg mixture and then slowly stir the egg mixture into the slow cooker. Cover and cook on low for ½ hour. To serve, reduce the heat setting of the slow cooker to warm. Dust servings with paprika if desired.

Leftover Welsh Rarebit
Refrigerate leftover Welsh Rarebit in a covered container for up to a week. Reheat slowly (so the cheese doesn't separate) and serve over steamed vegetables or as a baked potato topper.

Chapter 4
Snacks

Roasted Pistachios

Yield: 16 (1-ounce) servings

Ingredients:
1 pound raw pistachios
2 tablespoons extra-virgin
   olive oil or melted butter
Optional: 1 teaspoon sea salt,
   or to taste

Raw pistachios are available at Trader Joe's (www.traderjoes.com) or health food stores. Roasting your own lets you control the amount of salt on the nuts, which makes them a snack that perfectly matches your tastes.

Add the nuts, oil or butter, and salt, if using, to the slow cooker. Stir to combine. Cover and cook on low for 1 hour. Stir the mixture and, if using salt, taste for seasoning; add more salt and stir into the nuts if desired. Cover and cook for 2 more hours, stirring the mixture again after 1 hour. Store in an airtight container.

Putting Roasted Pistachios to Work
You can make 8 servings of a delicious coleslaw alternative by mixing together 3 very thinly sliced heads of fennel; ½ cup roasted, chopped pistachios, 3 tablespoons extra-virgin olive oil; 3 tablespoons freshly squeezed lemon juice; and 1 teaspoon finely grated lemon zest. Taste for seasoning and add sea salt, freshly ground black pepper, and additional lemon juice if desired. Serve immediately or cover and refrigerate up to 1 day.

Spiced Pecans

If spicy-hot Cajun seasoning isn't to your liking, you can use sweet-hot barbecue seasoning blend, savory Italian seasoning blend, or another seasoning mix instead.

Yield: 16 (1-ounce) servings

Ingredients:
3 pounds pecan halves
2 tablespoons extra-virgin olive oil or melted butter
2 tablespoons Cajun seasoning blend

1. Add the pecans, oil or butter, and Cajun seasoning blend to the slow cooker. Stir to combine. Cover and cook on low for 1 hour. Taste for seasoning, and add more Cajun spices if desired. Stir the mixture.

2. Cover and cook for 2 more hours, stirring the mixture again after 1 hour. Store in an airtight container.

Sugared Walnuts

Sugared walnuts are a snack that will satisfy any sweet tooth. Cooled sugared walnuts can be stored at room temperature in a covered container for up to 3 days.

Yield: 16 (1-ounce) servings

Ingredients:
1 pound walnut halves
1 stick (½ cup) butter, melted
⅔ cup pure cane or powdered sugar

1. Add the walnuts, butter, and sugar to the slow cooker. (If using powdered sugar, sift it to remove any lumps.) Stir to combine. Cover and cook on high for 15 minutes.

2. Reduce heat to low and cook uncovered for 2 hours, stirring occasionally. At the end of the cooking time, evenly spread the walnuts on a lined baking sheet until completely cooled.

Cinnamon and Sugar Nuts

Serves 24

Ingredients:
3 cups raw almonds, pecan
    halves, or walnut halves
3 tablespoons butter, melted
2 teaspoons vanilla
½ cup sugar
1 teaspoon cinnamon
Salt, to taste

*Not only a good snack, chopped Cinnamon and Sugar Nuts are
good sprinkled over French toast.*

1. Add all ingredients to the slow cooker. Stir to coat the nuts evenly. Cover and cook on low for 6 hours, stirring occasionally.

2. Uncover and continue to cook on low for another hour, stirring occasionally, to dry the nuts. Next, evenly spread the nuts on a lined baking sheet until completely cooled. Store in a covered container.

Butterscotch Caramel–Glazed Nuts

Serves 32

Ingredients:
4 cups raw almonds, pecan
    halves, or walnut halves
½ cup Butterscotch Caramel
    Sauce (See page 26)
Optional: 1½ teaspoons
    cinnamon

These nuts taste even better when tossed together with some popcorn.

1. Add all ingredients to the slow cooker. Stir to coat the nuts. Cover and cook on low for 3 hours, stirring at least once an hour.

2. Uncover and, stirring the mixture every 20 minutes, cook on low for 1 more hour or until the nuts are almost dry. Next, evenly spread the nuts on a lined baking sheet until completely cooled. Store in a covered container.

Low-Carb Snack Mix

For this recipe, use raw almonds, cashews, pecans, shelled pumpkin seeds, shelled sunflower seeds, walnuts, and raw or dry-roasted peanuts. The amounts you use of each kind of nut is up to you, although because of their size, ideally the recipe shouldn't have more than 1 cup of sunflower seeds.

1. Add all ingredients to the slow cooker. Stir to coat the nuts evenly. Cover and cook on low for 6 hours, stirring occasionally.

2. Uncover and continue to cook on low for another hour to dry the nuts and seeds, stirring occasionally, and then evenly spread them on a lined baking sheet until completely cooled. Store in a covered container.

Pepitas
Raw pumpkin seeds are also known as "pepitas" when sold in Latino food markets.

Yield: 24 (⅓-cup) servings

Ingredients:
4 tablespoons butter, melted
3 tablespoons Worcestershire sauce
1½ teaspoons garlic powder
2 teaspoons onion powder
Optional: Seasoned salt or sea salt, to taste
8 cups raw nuts

Party Seasoned Nuts

Whether or not you add salt to this recipe will depend on whether or not the nuts you use are already salted. Store leftovers in a covered container for up to a week or freeze them.

1. Add the butter and choice of seasoning to the slow cooker. Stir to combine. Add the nuts and stir to coat them with the seasoning. Cover and cook on high for ½ hour. Stir well. Cover and cook on high for an additional 30 minutes. Stir again.

2. Cover, reduce the heat to low, and continue to cook (and occasionally stir) for an additional 1–2 hours or until heated through.

Serves 16

Ingredients:
4 tablespoons butter, melted
3 tablespoons curry or chili powder, or taco seasoning
Salt, to taste
8 cups mixed nuts

Popular Party Mix

Yield: About 12 cups

Ingredients:
2 cups Rice Chex cereal
2 cups Wheat Chex cereal
2 cups Corn Chex cereal
4 cups Cheerios cereal
1 cup mini pretzels or thin
  pretzel sticks
1 cup peanuts
½ stick (¼ cup) butter, melted
1 tablespoon Worcestershire
  sauce
½ teaspoon garlic powder
¼ teaspoon onion powder
Optional: ¾ teaspoon fine sea
  salt or seasoned salt

*Not only is this snack a welcome crowd pleaser at just about
any party, it's fun to munch on at home, too.*

1. Add the cereal, pretzels, and peanuts to the slow cooker. Stir to mix. In a small bowl, mix together the butter, Worcestershire sauce, garlic powder, onion powder, and salt if using. Pour over the mixture in the slow cooker and stir to mix.

2. Cook uncovered on high for 1 hour, stirring frequently. Reduce heat to low and, stirring frequently, continue to cook for 1 hour or until the cereal is dry and crisp.

3. Divide the party mix evenly between 2 baking sheets and allow to cool completely. Store in a covered container for up to a week.

Party Mix Variations
One variation for party mix for which you have omitted the optional salt is to sprinkle it with freshly grated Parmesan-Reggiano cheese immediately after you spread it out on the baking sheets. If you prefer a more robust flavor, use hot sauce instead of Worcestershire sauce and use chili powder in place of the garlic and onion powders.

Chapter 5
Sauces and Condiments

Vodka Cream Sauce

Yield: About 3½ cups

Ingredients:
1 cup vodka
2 tablespoons olive oil
2 medium shallots, peeled
    and minced
3 cloves of garlic, peeled and
    minced
2 (28-ounce) cans crushed
    tomatoes in purée
1 teaspoon dried oregano
1 teaspoon sugar
Salt and freshly ground
    pepper, to taste
2 cups heavy cream

*If you prefer not to use vodka in this recipe, you can skip Step 1
and use ½ cup tomato sauce instead.*

1. Add the vodka to the slow cooker. Cook uncovered on high for 1 hour or until reduced by half.

2. Add the olive oil and minced shallots to a microwave-safe bowl. Cover and microwave on high for 1 minute. Uncover and stir in the garlic. Cover and microwave on high for 30 seconds. Add to the slow cooker along with the tomatoes, oregano, sugar, salt, and pepper. Stir to combine. Cover and cook on low for 10–12 hours.

3. Shortly before serving, stir the cream into the sauce. Cook uncovered on low until heated through. Taste for seasoning and, if necessary, add additional oregano, sugar, salt, and pepper if needed.

4. Any leftover sauce can be refrigerated in a covered container or frozen.

Serving Suggestion for Vodka Cream Sauce
Serve Vodka Cream Sauce over cooked penne pasta or fried eggplant. Top with freshly grated cheese if desired.

Hot Pickled Vegetables

You can adjust the vegetables that you use according to your tastes. Chop the vegetables and add some to give some kick to meatloaf or crab cakes. Dress with extra-virgin olive oil and serve antipasto-style or serve as a condiment for Mexican or Italian sandwiches.

Yield: About 4 quarts

Ingredients:
4 cups baby carrots
1 (7-ounce) jar of whole
    jalapeño peppers,
    undrained
1 large sweet onion, peeled
    and sliced
1 tablespoon vegetable oil
½ cup white wine vinegar
Salt and freshly ground black
    pepper, to taste
2 cups frozen green beans,
    thawed
1 cup frozen corn, thawed
1 cup frozen baby peas,
    thawed

1. Cut the baby carrots in half and add to the slow cooker along with the jar of jalapeño peppers, onion, oil, vinegar, and salt and pepper. Cook on low for 2 hours or until the carrots are crisp-tender.

2. Uncover and stir in the green beans, corn, and baby peas. Transfer to glass jars and allow to come to room temperature before storing in the refrigerator. Chill before serving.

Mild Pickled Vegetables
Substitute a jar of roasted red peppers for the jalapeño peppers. Chop the red peppers into bite-sized pieces and add them along with the juice from the jar to the slow cooker.

Sweet Pickled Vegetables

Yield: About 3 quarts

Ingredients:

2 teaspoons sea salt

2 cups Sucanat or raw pure
  cane sugar

1½ teaspoons cracked or
  freshly ground black
  pepper

½ teaspoon celery seed

1½ cups organic cider vinegar

1 (1-pound) bag of baby
  carrots

1 large sweet onion, peeled
  and diced

1 green bell pepper, cleaned
  and diced

1 yellow bell pepper, cleaned
  and diced

1 red bell pepper, cleaned
  and diced

2 stalks celery, finely diced

1 cup frozen corn, thawed

1 cup frozen green beans,
  thawed

You can substitute 2 cups of (white) cane sugar or 1½ cups of cane sugar and ½ cup light brown sugar for the Sucanat. Chopped sweet pickled vegetables are a delicious addition to salmon patties or chicken salad.

1. Add the salt, Sucanat or sugar, pepper, celery seed, and cider vinegar to the slow cooker. Cover and, stirring every 15 minutes, cook on high for an hour or until the sugar is dissolved.

2. Cut the baby carrots into four pieces each and add to the slow cooker. Cover, reduce the heat to low, and cook for 1 hour or until the carrots are crisp-tender.

3. Add the onion; green, yellow, and red peppers; celery; corn; and green beans to the slow cooker. Stir to combine with the carrots.

4. Transfer to glass jars and allow to come to room temperature before storing in the refrigerator. Chill before serving. Can be stored in the refrigerator for several weeks if the vegetables are completely submerged in the sweet vinegar.

Sweet Pickled Beets and Vegetables

Substitute 1 or 2 (11- to 16-ounce) cans of drained sliced beets for an equal amount of the diced peppers, corn, or green beans called for in this recipe.

Plum Sauce

Plum sauce is often served with egg rolls. It's also delicious if you brush it on chicken or pork ribs; doing so near the end of the grilling time will add a succulent glaze to the grilled meat.

1. Add the plums, onion, water, ginger, and garlic to the slow cooker; cover and, stirring occasionally, cook on low for 4 hours or until plums and onions are tender.

2. Use an immersion blender to pulverize the contents of the slow cooker before straining it or press the cooked plum mixture through a sieve.

3. Return the liquefied and strained plum mixture to the slow cooker and stir in sugar, vinegar, coriander, salt, cinnamon, cayenne pepper, and cloves. Cover and, stirring occasionally, cook on low for 2 hours or until the sauce reaches the consistency of applesauce.

Yield: 4 cups

Ingredients:
8 cups (about 3 pounds) plums, pitted and cut in half
1 small sweet onion, peeled and diced
1 cup water
1 teaspoon fresh ginger, peeled and minced
1 clove of garlic, peeled and minced
¾ cup granulated sugar
½ cup rice vinegar or cider vinegar
1 teaspoon ground coriander
½ teaspoon salt
½ teaspoon cinnamon
¼ teaspoon cayenne pepper
¼ teaspoon ground cloves

Homemade Ketchup

1. Add all ingredients, except paprika, to the slow cooker. Cover and, stirring occasionally, cook for 2–4 hours or until ketchup reaches desired consistency.

2. Turn off the slow cooker or remove the crock from the slow cooker and stir in the paprika. Allow mixture to cool, then put in a covered container (such as a recycled ketchup bottle). Store in the refrigerator until needed.

Ketchup with a Kick
If you like zesty ketchup, you can add crushed red peppers, Mrs. Dash Extra Spicy Seasoning Blend, or salt-free chili powder along with, or instead of, the cinnamon and other seasonings. Another alternative is to use hot paprika rather than sweet paprika.

Serves 32

Ingredients:
1 (15-ounce) can no-salt-added tomato sauce
2 teaspoons water
½ teaspoon onion powder
½ cup sugar
⅓ cup cider vinegar
¼ teaspoon sea salt
¼ teaspoon ground cinnamon
⅛ teaspoon ground cloves
Pinch ground allspice
Pinch nutmeg
Pinch freshly ground pepper
⅔ teaspoon sweet paprika

Easy Applesauce

Yield: About 4 cups

Ingredients:
10 medium apples
2 tablespoons fresh lemon
   juice
2 tablespoons water
Optional: 6-inch cinnamon
   stick
Optional: Sugar, to taste

Homemade applesauce is easy to make and tastes so much better than what you can get in the store. Choose the apples according to your preference. Combine varieties if you want. It freezes well, too, so you can make extra when apples are in season.

1. Peel, core, and slice the apples. Add to the slow cooker along with the lemon juice, water, and cinnamon stick if using; stir to mix.

2. Cover and cook on low for 5 hours or until the apples are soft and tender. For chunky applesauce, mash the apples with a potato masher. For smooth applesauce, purée in a food processor or blender, use an immersion blender, or press through a food mill or large mesh strainer. While applesauce is still warm, add sugar to taste if desired. Store covered in the refrigerator for up to 2 weeks or freeze.

Traditional Apple Butter

To ensure that the peels haven't been waxed, buy your apples directly from an orchard or at a farmer's market. (The natural pectin in the peels helps thicken the butter.) Don't forget to pick up some freshly pressed cider while you're there.

1. Core and quarter the apples. Add to the slow cooker. Stir in the zest and juice from the lemon, brown sugar, and cider. Add the cinnamon stick if using. Cover and cook on low for 10 hours or until the apples are soft and tender.

2. Uncover and, stirring occasionally, cook on high for an additional 8 to 10 hours or until the mixture has reduced to about 3 cups.

3. If used, remove and discard the cinnamon stick. Use a spatula to press the apple butter through a large mesh strainer to remove the peel. Ladle the warm apple butter into hot sterilized jars. Screw two-piece lids onto the jars. Allow to stand at room temperature for 8 hours; refrigerate for up to 6 months.

Yield: About 3 cups

Ingredients:
4 pounds (Jonathan, MacIntosh, or Rome) apples
1 lemon
1⅓ cups light brown sugar, packed
1 cup apple cider
Optional: 6-inch cinnamon stick

Peach Marmalade

As you'd expect, you can spread this on toast. It can also be used to turn an ordinary cracker into a delicious snack.

Yield: About 8 cups

2 pounds peaches, peeled and chopped
½ cup (about 6 ounces) dried apricots, chopped
1 (20-ounce) can pineapple tidbits, in unsweeted juice
2 medium oranges
1 small lemon
2½ cups granulated cane sugar
2 (3-inch) sticks cinnamon

1. Peel, pit, and chop the peaches and add to a food processor along with the apricots and can of pineapple tidbits and juice.

2. Remove the zest from the oranges and lemon; add to food processor or blender. Peel the oranges and lemon. Cut into quarters and remove any seeds; add to the food processor or blender. Pulse until entire fruit mixture is pulverized. Pour into the slow cooker.

3. Add the sugar to the slow cooker and stir to combine with the fruit mixture. Add the cinnamon sticks. Cover and, stirring occasionally, cook on low for 4 hours or until the mixture reaches the consistency of applesauce.

4. Unless you process and seal the marmalade in sterilized jars, store in covered glass jars in the refrigerator.

Innovative Peach Marmalade Uses
By keeping this marmalade the consistency of applesauce you have the added versatility of using it as a condiment to top cooked chicken breasts, easily mix it together with barbecue or chili sauce to create a sweet and spicy dipping sauce, or use it to replace applesauce in many recipes.

Traditional Barbecue Sauce

Use this sauce as you'd use any barbecue sauce, as a serving sauce served on the side, or as a dipping sauce. Most barbecue seasoning mixes contain salt, so salt isn't added to this recipe.

Add all ingredients to the slow cooker. Stir to mix. Cover and, stirring every 15 minutes, cook on high for 1 hour or until the mixture reaches a simmer. Reduce the heat to low and, continuing to stir every 15 minutes, cook uncovered 1 hour or until the sauce has reached desired thickness. Ladle into glass jars; cover and store in the refrigerator for up to 3 months.

Customizing Barbecue Sauce

You can change up the flavor of Traditional Barbecue Sauce by using a mix of prepared (yellow) mustard and Dijon or stone-ground mustard, adding red pepper flakes or some Mrs. Dash (Extra Spicy or Southwest Chipotle) seasoning, or substituting lemon juice for the vinegar.

Yield: About 2½ cups

Ingredients:
2 cups ketchup
¼ cup apple cider vinegar
¼ cup Worcestershire sauce
¼ cup light brown sugar, firmly packed
2 tablespoons molasses
2 tablespoons prepared mustard
1 tablespoon barbecue seasoning
½ teaspoon freshly ground black pepper
Optional: 2 teaspoons liquid smoke
Optional: 1 tablespoon hot sauce, or to taste

Blackberry Barbecue Sauce

Ingredients:
1 tablespoon vegetable oil
1 small sweet onion, peeled and diced
2 cloves of garlic, peeled and minced
¼ cup red wine
¼ cup apple cider vinegar
2½ pounds blackberries
¼ cup light brown sugar, packed
1 tablespoon Worcestershire sauce
1 lemon
Pinch salt
Pinch red pepper flakes

A red wine with a distinct berry aroma like Pinot Noir works best in this recipe. The sauce complements chicken, duck, or game hen.

1. Add the oil and onion to a microwave-safe bowl. Cover and microwave on high for 1 minute or until the onion is transparent.

2. Stir in the garlic; cover and microwave on high for 30 seconds.

3. Add the onion-garlic mixture to the slow cooker along with the wine, vinegar, blackberries, brown sugar, Worcestershire sauce, grated zest from the lemon, salt, and red pepper flakes. Stir to combine. Cover and cook on low for 8 hours or until thickened.

4. Stir in the lemon juice. Strain through a mesh strainer if desired. Can be refrigerated in covered containers for up to 2 weeks.

Change Things Up
Make a meatloaf using ground chicken or turkey, and instead of adding and glazing the meatloaf with ketchup, use Blackberry Barbecue Sauce.

Wine Vinegar–Based Barbecue Sauce

This sauce is thinner and more like a mop sauce than a traditional thick barbecue sauce. You can use it as a basting sauce for grilled tender cuts of meat. It's even good mixed into a glass of tomato juice or tomato soup.

Add all of the ingredients to the slow cooker. Stir to mix. Cover and, stirring every 15 minutes, cook on high for 1 hour or until the mixture has come to a simmer. Reduce heat to low and cook covered for an additional hour. Ladle cooled sauce into glass jars, cover, and store in the refrigerator. Keeps for 6 months or longer.

Pulled Venison

Vinegar-Based Barbecue Sauce is perfect for wild game. To remove any gamy taste, add a 4-pound venison roast to the slow cooker. Add enough water to cover the roast and ⅓ to 1 cup of cider vinegar; cook on low overnight. The next morning, pour off and discard that water and replace it with Vinegar-Based Barbecue Sauce. Cover and cook on low for 4 hours or until the meat is tender and pulls apart.

Yield: About 3 quarts

Ingredients:
½ cup brown sugar
½ cup Worcestershire sauce
½ cup Dijon mustard
1⅓ cup ketchup
⅛ cup freshly ground black pepper
1 tablespoon red pepper flakes, or to taste
1 quart (4 cups) red wine vinegar
2 ⅔ cups water
1⅓ cups white wine
Salt, to taste

Marinara Sauce

Yield: Sauce for 2 pounds
of pasta

Ingredients:

2 tablespoons extra-virgin
   olive oil

2 medium onions, peeled and
   diced

4 cloves of garlic, peeled and
   minced

1½ teaspoons dried oregano

⅛ teaspoon red pepper flakes

1 (6-ounce) can tomato paste

1 cup dry red wine

4 (28-ounce) cans crushed
   tomatoes with basil

½ cup (1 ounce) freshly grated
   Parmesan-Reggiano
   cheese

Optional: ¼ cup fresh basil,
   minced

Sea salt, to taste

1½ teaspoons sugar

You can serve Marinara Sauce separately or toss it with the pasta before bringing it to the table. Serve pasta along with a tossed salad, garlic bread, cooked meatballs, or Italian sausage, and have lots of freshly ground Parmesan-Reggiano cheese and a pepper grinder available.

1. Add the oil and onions to the slow cooker. Cover and, stirring occasionally, cook on high for 30–45 minutes or until onions are golden brown. Stir in the garlic, oregano, red pepper flakes, and tomato paste. Cover and cook on high for 15 minutes.

2. Stir in the wine and undrained tomatoes. Cover and cook on low for 4 hours or until sauce is no longer watery. Stir in the cheese, additional basil if using, salt, and sugar. Taste for seasoning and adjust if necessary.

Chapter 6
Breakfast and Brunch

Crustless Quiche Lorraine

Ham is often already salty, so take that into consideration when deciding how much salt you add to the egg mixture.

1. Spray the crock of the slow cooker with nonstick spray. If desired, remove the crusts from the toast. Butter each slice with 1 teaspoon of butter, tear the toast into pieces, and arrange the toast pieces butter side down in the slow cooker.

2. Spread half of the cheese over the toast pieces, and then spread the ham over the cheese, and top the ham layer with the remaining cheese.

3. In a bowl, beat the eggs together with the mayonnaise, mustard, and cream, and salt, pepper, and cayenne pepper if using. Pour the egg mixture into the slow cooker. Cover and cook on high for 2 hours or until the eggs are set.

Or, if you prefer . . .
Rather than using toast to create the crust for this quiche, instead melt the butter and toss it together with 4 small, crumbled buttermilk biscuits. Arrange the buttered buttermilk biscuit crumbs over the bottom of the slow cooker and then complete the recipe as described in Steps 2 and 3.

Brunch Casserole

You can substitute Worcestershire sauce for the steak sauce if you prefer. Because of the usually high sodium content in canned soup, this recipe doesn't call for added salt. Country hash browns are blended with onion and red and green bell peppers.

1. Brown the sausage links according to package directions. Cut into ½-inch pieces.

2. Treat the crock of the slow cooker with nonstick spray. Add the sausage, soup, milk, steak sauce, pepper, hash browns, and vegetables; stir to combine. Cover and cook for 6 hours on low.

3. Turn the cooker to warm. About 45 minutes before you'll be serving the casserole, sprinkle the Cheddar cheese over the cooked mixture in the slow cooker. After 30 minutes, uncover the casserole and let stand for 15 minutes before serving.

Vegetables in Cheese Sauce
Choose the frozen vegetables you use in the Brunch Casserole according to your tastes. A broccoli and cauliflower blend is good, as is the California Blend from Birds Eye that includes carrots.

Serves 8

Ingredients:
2 (7-ounce) packages brown-and-serve sausage links
Nonstick spray
1 (10¾-ounce) can condensed cream of potato soup
⅔ cup milk
2 teaspoons steak sauce
¼ teaspoon freshly ground black pepper
1 (28-ounce) package of frozen country hash browns, thawed
1 (9½-ounce) package frozen vegetables in cheese sauce, thawed
2 ounces (½ cup) Cheddar cheese, grated

Eggs Florentine

Freshly ground black pepper goes well in this dish. You can use up to a teaspoon in the recipe. If you prefer to go lighter on the seasoning to accommodate individual tastes, be sure to have a pepper grinder at the table for those who want to add more.

Serves 4

Ingredients:
Nonstick spray
9 ounces (2 cups) Cheddar
    cheese, grated
1 (10-ounce) package frozen
    spinach, thawed
1 (8-ounce) can sliced
    mushrooms, drained
1 small onion, peeled and
    diced
6 large eggs
1 cup heavy cream
½ teaspoon Italian seasoning
½ teaspoon garlic powder
Freshly ground black pepper,
    to taste

1. Treat the crock of the slow cooker with nonstick spray. Spread 1 cup of the grated Cheddar over the bottom of the slow cooker. Drain the spinach and squeeze out any access moisture; add in a layer on top of the cheese. Next add the drained mushrooms in a layer and then top them with the onion.

2. Beat together the eggs, cream, Italian seasoning, garlic powder, and pepper in a bowl or measuring cup. Pour over the layers in the slow cooker. Top with the remaining cup of Cheddar cheese.

3. Cover and cook on high for 2 hours or until eggs are set.

Cheese Performance
The oil content of cheese can vary, which can affect how the cheese will melt (or, worst case scenario, separate) in the slow cooker. The recipes in this book calling for Cheddar cheese were tested using Kraft medium Cheddar after one test using a national store brand Cheddar resulted in an unappetizing clump of food with an oil slick on top.

Breakfast Welsh Rarebit

Think of this as a German-style eggs Benedict. If you're serving it for brunch, when you make the Welsh Rarebit you can substitute beer for the milk.

Serves 4

Ingredients:
1 tablespoon butter, melted
Pinch cayenne pepper or hot sauce to taste
1 teaspoon Worcestershire sauce
1 cup whole milk
2 teaspoons cornstarch
1 teaspoon dry mustard
1 pound (4 cups) medium or sharp Cheddar cheese, grated
4 (thick) slices bread or English muffins, toasted
4 tomato slices
8 strips bacon, cooked and drained
4 poached or fried eggs

1. Add the butter to the slow cooker and stir in the cayenne pepper or hot sauce and Worcestershire sauce. Cover and cook on high for 15 minutes. Uncover, stir in the milk, and when the milk begins to bubble around the edges of the crock (reaches a simmer), lower the heat setting to low. (You must melt the cheese over a low temperature to prevent the cheese from separating into a greasy mess.)

2. Sift the cornstarch and dry mustard to remove any lumps; toss together with the grated cheese. Add the cornstarch- and mustard-coated cheese to the milk mixture. Cook uncovered, stirring occasionally, for 1 hour or until the cheese is melted.

3. Place the toast on individual plates; evenly ladle Breakfast Welsh Rarebit over the top of each slice.

4. Top each slice of toast with a tomato slice, criss-crossed bacon slices, and an egg. Top with more Breakfast Welsh Rarebit.

Luncheon Welsh Rarebit

Sauté a chopped, small onion and 8 ounces mushroom slices in butter, and stir into the Welsh Rarebit along with a 10½-ounce can of condensed cream of tomato soup; bring to temperature. To serve, arrange slices of hard-boiled egg over toast slices and top with a generous helping of the Luncheon Welsh Rarebit.

Bacon and Broccoli Crustless Quiche

Serves 6

Ingredients:
Nonstick spray
2 cups frozen broccoli cuts,
    thawed
8 ounces (2 cups) Colby
    cheese, grated
6 slices bacon, cooked
4 large eggs
2 cups whole milk
Salt and freshly ground black
    pepper, to taste
½ teaspoon Dijon mustard
1 tablespoon mayonnaise
Water

*This recipe requires a heatproof 1½- to 2-quart casserole dish that
can rest on the cooking rack in your slow cooker.*

1. Treat the casserole dish with nonstick spray. Arrange the broccoli cuts over the bottom of the dish, and top them with the grated cheese. Cut the bacon into pieces and sprinkle them evenly over the top of the cheese.

2. Add the eggs to a bowl or large measuring cup. Lightly beat the eggs and then stir in the milk, salt, pepper, mustard, and mayonnaise. Pour over the broccoli mixture in the casserole dish.

3. Place the casserole dish onto the cooking rack in the slow cooker. Pour water into the slow cooker so that it comes up and over the cooking rack and about an inch up the sides of the casserole dish. Cover and cook on low for 4 hours.

4. Turn off the slow cooker. Uncover and allow to cool enough to let you lift the casserole dish out of the cooker. Cut the crustless quiche into six wedges. Serve warm or at room temperature.

Cottage Cheese Casserole

This recipe is good made with Birds Eye Steamfresh asparagus, gold and white corn, and baby carrots vegetable blend. If you use a vegetable mixture without corn, omit the masa harina or cornmeal and use another ¼ cup of flour instead.

1. Treat a heatproof 1½- to 2-quart casserole dish that can rest on the cooking rack in your slow cooker with nonstick spray.

2. Add the eggs and whisk until fluffy. Stir in the cottage cheese. Add the flour, masa harina or cornmeal, salt, pepper, baking powder, and butter, and mix well. Fold the cheese and the vegetables into the egg–cottage cheese mixture. Stir in the onion, shallots or scallions, and sausage pieces if using.

3. Place the casserole dish onto the cooking rack in the slow cooker. Pour water into the slow cooker so that it comes up and over the cooking rack and about an inch up the sides of the casserole dish. Cover and cook on low for 4 hours.

4. Turn off the slow cooker. Uncover and allow to cool enough to let you lift the casserole dish out of the cooker. Cut the casserole into four pieces. Serve warm or at room temperature.

Serves 4

Ingredients:
Nonstick spray
4 large eggs
1 cup cottage cheese
⅛ cup unbleached all-purpose flour
⅛ cup masa harina or fine cornmeal
Salt and freshly ground black pepper, to taste
¼ teaspoon baking powder
⅛ cup (2 tablespoons) melted butter
8 ounces (2 cups) Cheddar cheese, grated
1 cup frozen vegetable mix, thawed
Optional: Chopped red onion, shallots, or scallions to taste
Optional: 4 brown-and-serve sausage links, cut into pieces

Banana Walnut Frittata

Serves 6

Ingredients:

1 tablespoon butter

1 (1-pound) loaf bread, cut
   into cubes

1 (8-ounce) package cream
   cheese

2 ripe bananas

1 cup walnuts, coarsely
   chopped

12 large eggs

¼ cup maple syrup

1 cup milk or heavy cream

¼ teaspoon salt

Optional: Additional maple
   syrup at serving

*You can add another flavor dimension to this dish by sprinkling some
cinnamon to taste over the banana layers. Another option is
to serve it with blueberry or strawberry syrup.*

1. At least 12 hours before you plan to begin cooking the frittata, ready the crock to the slow cooker by coating the bottom and sides with the butter. Place ⅓ of the bread cubes (about 4 cups) in the bottom of the crock. Cut the cream cheese into very small cubes and evenly spread half of them over the bread cubes. Slice one of the bananas, arrange the slices over the cream cheese layer, and sprinkle half of the walnut pieces over the banana. Add another 4 cups of bread cubes and create another cream cheese, banana, and walnut layer over the top of the bread. Add the remaining 4 cups of bread cubes to the cooker. Press the mixture down slightly into the crock.

2. Add the eggs to a bowl; whisk until frothy. Whisk in the syrup, milk or cream, and salt. Pour over the bread in the crock. Cover and refrigerate for 12 hours.

3. Remove the crock from the refrigerator and place in the slow cooker. Cover and cook on low for 6 hours. Serve with warm maple syrup if desired.

Or, if you prefer . . .
You can substitute 1 cup of blueberries, raspberries, or blackberries for the bananas and use toasted pecans instead of walnuts, or omit the nuts entirely.

Maple Syrup–Infused Slow-Cooked Oatmeal

Feel free to substitute other dried fruit according to your tastes such as a tropical mix of coconut, papaya, pineapple, and mango or strawberries and blueberries. It's even a way you can sneak some prunes into your diet.

1. Add the oats, water, apple juice, apples (cut with kitchen shears into small pieces), raisins, maple syrup, cinnamon, and salt to the slow cooker and stir to mix.

2. Cover and cook on the low-heat setting for 6 to 7 hours.

3. Serve the oatmeal warm topped with brown sugar or additional maple syrup; chopped nuts; and milk, half and half, or heavy cream.

Cooking Ahead
Once the oatmeal has cooled, divide any leftovers into single-serving containers and freeze. Later, transfer the frozen oatmeal to a microwave-safe container (or better yet: freeze it in a microwave-safe container and save yourself a step!) and put it in the microwave to defrost while you get ready to start your day. Cover the bowl with a piece of paper towel (to catch any splatters), then microwave on high for 1–2 minutes and enjoy!

Serves 8–10

Ingredients:
2 cups steel-cut Irish oats
5 cups water
1 cup apple juice
½ cup dried apples
¼ cup golden raisins
¼ cup maple syrup
1 teaspoon ground cinnamon
½ teaspoon salt
Optional: Brown sugar or maple syrup
Optional: Chopped toasted walnuts or pecans
Optional: Milk, half and half, or heavy cream

Sausage and Cheese Casserole

Serve this casserole with toasted whole-grain bread spread with some honey-butter and you have a comfort-food breakfast feast.

Serves 8

Ingredients:

1 tablespoon extra-virgin olive oil or vegetable oil

1 large onion, peeled and diced

1 green pepper, seeded and diced

1 pound ground sausage

4 cups frozen hash brown potatoes, thawed

Nonstick spray

8 large eggs

¼ cup water or heavy cream

Optional: A few drops hot sauce

Salt and freshly ground pepper, to taste

½ pound Cheddar cheese, grated

1. Preheat a deep 3½-quart nonstick sauté pan over medium-high heat and add the oil. Once the oil is heated, add the onion and pepper and sauté until the onion is transparent, or about 5 minutes. Add the sausage, browning (and crumbling) and cook for 5 minutes. Remove any excess fat, if necessary, by carefully dabbing the pan with a paper towel. Stir the hash browns into the sausage mixture, and then transfer the mixture to the slow cooker treated with nonstick spray.

2. Whisk together the eggs, water or heavy cream, hot sauce if using, and salt and pepper. Pour over the sausage–hash browns mixture in the slow cooker. Cover and cook on low for 4 hours.

3. Turn the cooker to warm. About 45 minutes before you'll be serving the casserole, sprinkle the Cheddar cheese over the cooked mixture in the slow cooker. After 30 minutes, uncover the casserole and let stand for 15 minutes before serving.

Feeding a Crowd
You can stretch this recipe to even more servings by increasing the amount of chopped peppers you sauté with the onion. In fact, a mixture of red, green, and yellow peppers makes for a delicious combo.

Bacon and Egg Casserole

*You can substitute 2 large peeled and diced potatoes
for the hash browns if you prefer.*

1. Ready the crock to the slow cooker by coating the bottom and sides with nonstick spray. Remove the crusts from the bread and cut the bread into cubes. Place ⅓ of the bread cubes (about 3 cups) in the bottom of the crock. Add the eggs to a bowl; whisk until frothy. Whisk in the milk or cream and salt. Pour ⅓ of the egg mixture over the bread in the crock.

2. Preheat a deep 3½-quart nonstick sauté pan over medium high heat. Cut the bacon into pieces and add to the skillet. Once the bacon begins to render its fat, add the onion; sauté until the onion is transparent and the bacon is cooked through. Remove any excess fat, if necessary, by carefully dabbing the pan with a paper towel. Stir the hash browns into the sausage mixture.

3. Evenly spread half of the bacon mixture over the top of the bread cubes in the slow cooker. Pour half of the remaining egg mixture over the bacon mixture, add another 3 cups of bread cubes, and pour the remaining bacon mixture over the top of the bread. Add the remaining 3 cups of bread cubes to the cooker. Press the mixture down slightly into the crock. Pour the rest of the egg mixture over the top. Cover and cook on low for 6 hours.

4. If adding the cheese, turn the cooker to warm. About 45 minutes before you'll be serving the casserole, sprinkle the Cheddar cheese over the cooked mixture in the slow cooker. After 30 minutes, uncover the casserole and let stand for 15 minutes before serving.

Serves 8

Ingredients:
Nonstick spray
1 (1-pound) loaf bread
12 large eggs
1 cup milk or heavy cream
¼ teaspoon salt
1 pound bacon
*1 medium onion, peeled and
    diced*
*2 cups frozen hash brown
    potatoes, thawed*
*Optional: ½-cup Cheddar
    cheese, grated*

Breakfast Buffet Tomato Topper

Ingredients:

2 tablespoons extra-virgin
    olive oil

2 large shallots, peeled and
    diced

1 (28-ounce) can crushed
    tomatoes with basil,
    undrained

¾ cup robust red wine

1 tablespoon orange zest,
    finely grated

1 tablespoon fresh Italian
    parsley, minced

1 tablespoon fresh basil,
    chopped

Salt and freshly ground black
    pepper, to taste

8 ounces fresh whole-milk
    mozzarella cheese

*You can substitute Teleme goat cheese for the mozzarella.
Zinfandel is a good choice for the wine.*

1. Add the oil and shallots to a microwave-safe bowl; cover and micro-wave on high for 1 minute; stir and repeat in 30-second increments until the shallots are soft and transparent. (You do not want them to brown.) Add to the slow cooker along with the tomatoes and wine. Cover and cook on high for 1 hour or until the mixture begins to bubble around the edges. If your slow cooker has a simmer setting, use that at this point. Otherwise, continue to cook uncovered, stirring occasion-ally, until the sauce is thickened.

2. Stir in the orange zest, parsley, basil, salt, and pepper. Reduce heat to low. Cut the cheese into small cubes and add it to the slow cooker, mak-ing sure it's completely covered with the tomato mixture. Cover and cook on low for 1 hour or until the cheese is melted. Stir well.

3. If serving as a sauce, have a ladle available alongside the slow cooker. If serving as a fondue, provide fondue forks and appropriately sized pieces of crusty baguettes.

Serving Breakfast Buffet Tomato Topper

For open-face brunch BLTs, top toast slices with grated lettuce and bacon; ladle the tomato topper over the top. Or you can ladle the sauce over toasted English muffin halves topped with scrambled, fried, or poached eggs. Serve crisp bacon slices, ham, Canadian bacon, or sausage links on the side or under the egg on top of the muffin.

Chapter 7
Chicken

Chicken Broth

Yield: About 4 cups

Ingredients:
3 pounds bone-in chicken
 pieces
1 large onion, peeled and
 quartered
2 large carrots, scrubbed
2 stalks of celery
Salt and freshly ground black
 pepper, to taste
4½ cups water

You can substitute a 3-pound chicken cut into pieces for this recipe. When you remove the meat from the bones, save the dark meat for use in a casserole and the white meat for chicken salad. (Return the chicken breast to the strained broth and let it cool overnight in the refrigerator before you chop it for the salad; the chicken breast will be more moist and succulent if you do.)

1. Add the chicken pieces and onion to the slow cooker.

2. Slice the carrot and cut the celery into pieces that will fit in the slow cooker and add them. Add the salt, pepper, and water. Cover and cook on low for 6 to 8 hours. (Cooking time will depend on the size of the chicken pieces.) Allow to cool to room temperature.

3. Strain, discarding the cooked vegetables. Remove any meat from the chicken bones and save for another use. Refrigerate the (cooled) broth overnight. Remove and discard the hardened fat. The resulting concentrated broth can be kept for 1 or 2 days in the refrigerator or frozen for up to 3 months.

Schmaltz
The chicken fat that will rise to the top of the broth and harden overnight in the refrigerator is known as schmaltz. You can save that fat and use it instead of butter for sautéing vegetables.

Chicken Paprikash

If you prefer not to cook with wine, replace it with an equal amount of chicken broth. You can also substitute an equal amount of drained plain yogurt for the sour cream.

1. Add the butter, oil, and onion to a microwave-safe bowl; cover and microwave on high for 1 minute. Stir, recover, and microwave on high for another minute or until the onions are transparent. Stir in the garlic; cover and microwave on high for 30 seconds. Add to the slow cooker.

2. Cut the chicken thighs into bite-sized pieces. Add the chicken to the slow cooker, and stir fry for 5 minutes. Stir in the salt, pepper, paprika, broth, and wine; cover and cook on low for 8 hours.

3. Stir in the sour cream; cover and continue to cook long enough to bring the sour cream sauce to temperature, or for about 30 minutes. Serve over cooked noodles or spaetzle. Sprinkle each serving with additional paprika if desired. Serve immediately.

Thickening or Thinning
If the resulting sauce for the chicken paprikash is too thin, add more sour cream. If it's too thick, slowly whisk in some milk.

Serves 8

Ingredients:
1 tablespoon butter
1 tablespoon extra-virgin olive oil
1 large yellow onion, peeled and diced
2 cloves of garlic, peeled and minced
3 pounds boneless skinless chicken thighs
Salt and freshly ground pepper, to taste
2 tablespoons Hungarian paprika
½ cup chicken broth
¼ cup dry white wine
1 (16-ounce) container sour cream
Cooked egg noodles or spaetzle
Optional: Additional paprika

Chicken in Lemon Sauce

Serves 4

Ingredients:

1 (1-pound) bag frozen cut
   green beans, thawed
1 small onion, peeled and cut
   into thin wedges
4 boneless, skinless chicken
   breast halves
4 medium potatoes, peeled
   and cut in quarters
2 cloves of garlic, peeled and
   minced
¼ teaspoon freshly ground
   black pepper
1 cup chicken broth
4 ounces cream cheese, cut
   into cubes
1 teaspoon freshly grated
   lemon peel
Optional: Lemon peel strips

*This recipe is for a one-pot meal. By completing a simple step at the end of
the cooking time, you have meat, potatoes, vegetables, and sauce all
ready to serve and eat. It doesn't get much easier than that.*

1. Place green beans and onion in the slow cooker. Arrange the chicken
    and potatoes over the vegetables. Sprinkle with the garlic and pepper.
    Pour broth over all. Cover and cook on low for 5 or more hours or until
    chicken is cooked through and moist.

2. Evenly divide the chicken, potatoes, and vegetables between 4 serving
    plates or onto a serving platter; cover to keep warm.

3. To make the sauce, add the cream cheese cubes and grated lemon
    peel to the broth in the slow cooker. Stir until cheese melts into the
    sauce. Pour the sauce over the chicken, potatoes, and vegetables. Gar-
    nish with lemon peel strips if desired.

Chicken and Gravy

Serves 4

Ingredients:

1 (10¾-ounce) can cream of
   chicken soup
1 (10½-ounce) can cream of
   mushroom soup
Freshly ground black pepper,
   to taste
4 (6-ounce) skinless, boneless
   chicken breasts
4 medium potatoes, peeled
   and quartered

*Serve this dish along with a tossed salad and steamed
vegetable and you have a complete meal.*

Add the soups and pepper to the slow cooker. Stir to combine. Add the
chicken breasts, pushing them down into the soup mixture. Add the
potatoes in a layer on top. Cover and cook on low for 4 to 6 hours.

Scalloped Chicken

*If you have leftover cooked chicken on hand, you can use it
in this recipe instead of the canned chicken.*

Treat the slow cooker with nonstick spray. Add the potatoes and sprinkle the seasoning mix over the top of them. Spread the chicken over the top of the potatoes. Pour in the water. Cover and cook on low for 5 hours.

Serves 4

Ingredients:
Nonstick spray
1 (5-ounce) box scalloped
   potatoes
1 (8-ounce) can white meat
   chicken
3¾ cups water

Teriyaki Chicken

Serve Teriyaki Chicken over cooked rice.

Cut the chicken breasts into strips or bite-sized pieces. Add to the slow cooker along with the vegetables, broth, and sauce. Stir to mix. Cover and cook on low for 6 hours.

Serves 6

Ingredients:
2 pounds boneless, skinless
   chicken breasts
1 (16-ounce) frozen stir-
   fry mixed vegetables,
   thawed
¼ cup chicken broth
1 cup teriyaki sauce

Chicken Stroganoff

Serves 6

Ingredients:
Nonstick spray
1 (10½-ounce) can cream of
    mushroom soup
1 (4-ounce) can sliced
    mushrooms, drained
1 tablespoon Worcestershire
    sauce
2½ pounds skinless, boneless
    chicken breasts
1 (16-ounce) carton sour
    cream
Cooked, buttered egg noodles

You can make this recipe for 8 servings by increasing the amount of chicken breasts to 3 pounds. There will be enough stroganoff sauce to accommodate more servings.

1. Treat crock of the slow cooker with nonstick spray. Add the soup, mushrooms, and Worcestershire sauce; stir to mix.

2. Cut the chicken breasts into bite-sized pieces; add to the cooker and stir into the sauce. Cover and cook on low for 8 hours.

3. Stir in the sour cream; cover and continue to cook long enough to bring the sour cream sauce to temperature, or for about 30 minutes. Serve over cooked, buttered egg noodles or, if you prefer, over toast or biscuits.

Italian Chicken

Serves 4

Ingredients:
1 (3-pound) chicken, cut into
    pieces
1 teaspoon Italian seasoning
2 tablespoons all-purpose
    flour
½ teaspoon salt
⅛ teaspoon pepper
2 tablespoons Parmesan
    cheese, grated
½ teaspoon paprika
Nonstick spray
1 medium zucchini, sliced
½ cup chicken broth
1 (4-ounce) can sliced
    mushrooms, drained

Serve Italian Chicken with a tossed salad and garlic bread. For a lower-fat meal, remove the skin from the chicken and omit the flour.

1. Add the chicken pieces, Italian seasoning, flour, salt, pepper, cheese, and paprika to a gallon plastic bag; seal and shake the bag to coat the chicken pieces.

2. Treat the crock of the slow cooker with nonstick spray. Arrange the zucchini slices over the bottom of the crock. Pour broth over the zucchini. Arrange chicken on top. Cover and cook on low for 8 hours or until the chicken is cooked through. Increase the heat to high, add the mushrooms, cover, and cook on high for another 15 minutes.

Orange Chicken

You can use light or dark brown sugar, depending on your preference. (Dark brown sugar will impart more molasses flavor to the dish.) Serve this dish over cooked rice or stir-fry vegetables, or with both.

1. Treat the crock of the slow cooker with nonstick spray. Cut the chicken breasts into bite-sized pieces. Add the chicken and the onion to the slow cooker.

2. In a bowl or measuring cup, mix together the orange juice, marmalade, brown sugar, vinegar, Worcestershire sauce, and mustard. Pour into the slow cooker. Stir to combine the sauce with the chicken and onions. Cover and cook on low for 8 hours.

Serves 8

Ingredients:
Nonstick spray
3 pounds boneless, skinless chicken breasts
1 small onion, peeled and diced
½ cup orange juice
1 tablespoon orange marmalade
1 tablespoon brown sugar
1 tablespoon apple cider vinegar
1 tablespoon Worcestershire sauce
1 teaspoon Dijon mustard

Curried Chicken in Coconut Milk

Chicken base is available from Minor's (www.soupbase.com) or Redi-Base (www.redibase.com), or you can use chicken bouillon concentrate.

Add the onion, garlic, curry powder, coconut milk, and broth base to the slow cooker. Stir to mix. Add the chicken thighs. Cover and cook on low for 6 hours. Use a slotted spoon to remove the thighs to a serving bowl. Whisk to combine the sauce and pour over the chicken. Serve immediately over rice.

Serves 4

Ingredients:
1 small onion, peeled and diced
2 cloves of garlic, peeled and minced
1½ tablespoons curry powder
1 cup coconut milk
¾ teaspoon chicken broth base
8 chicken thighs, skin removed
Cooked rice

Tarragon Chicken

This rich French dish can stand on its own when served with just a tossed salad and some crusty bread.

Ingredients:
½ cup plus 2 tablespoons all-purpose flour
½ teaspoon salt
8 chicken thighs, skin removed
2 tablespoons butter
2 tablespoons vegetable or olive oil
1 medium yellow onion, peeled and diced
1 cup dry white wine
1 cup chicken broth
½ teaspoon dried tarragon
1 cup heavy cream

1. Add ½ cup of the flour, the salt, and the chicken thighs to a gallon plastic bag; close and shake to coat the chicken. Add the butter and oil to a large sauté pan and bring it to temperature over medium-high heat. Add the chicken thighs; brown the chicken by cooking it on one side for 5 minutes, and then turning the pieces and frying them for another 5 minutes. Drain the chicken on papers towels and then place in the slow cooker. Cover the slow cooker. Set temperature to low.

2. Add the onion to the sauté pan; sauté until the onion is transparent. Stir in 2 tablespoons of flour, cooking the flour until the onion just begins to brown. Slowly pour the wine into the pan, stirring to scrape the browned bits off of the bottom of the pan and into the sauce. Add the broth. Cook and stir for 15 minutes or until the sauce is thickened enough to coat the back of a spoon. Stir the tarragon into the sauce, and then pour the sauce over the chicken in the slow cooker. Cover and cook for 4–8 hours.

3. Pour the cream into the slow cooker; cover and cook for an additional 15 minutes or until the cream is heated through. Test for seasoning and add additional salt and tarragon if needed. Serve immediately.

Tarragon Chicken Cooking Times
After 4 hours, the chicken will be cooked through. If you want to leave the chicken cooking all day, after 8 hours the meat will fall away from the bone. You can then remove the bones before you stir in the cream.

Chicken Cacciatore

If you prefer, you can remove the skin from a 3-pound chicken and cut it into 8 serving pieces and substitute that for the chicken thighs.

1. Add ½ cup of the flour, the salt, and the chicken thighs to a gallon plastic bag; close and shake to coat the chicken. Add the oil to a large sauté pan and bring it to temperature over medium-high heat. Add the chicken thighs; brown the chicken by cooking it on one side for 5 minutes, and then turning the pieces and frying them for another 5 minutes. Drain the chicken on papers towels and then place in the slow cooker. Cover the slow cooker. Set temperature to low.

2. Add the onion to the sauté pan; sauté until the onion just begins to brown. Stir in the garlic and sauté for 30 seconds. Coarsely chop the sun-dried tomatoes and add them to the pan. Slowly pour the wine into the pan, stirring to scrape the browned bits off of the bottom of the pan. Stir in the sage, rosemary, pepper flakes, and black pepper, and then pour the sauce over the chicken in the slow cooker. Cover and cook for 4–8 hours, depending on the sizes of the chicken pieces.

Serves 4

Ingredients:
¾ cup all-purpose flour
½ teaspoon salt
8 chicken thighs, skin removed
3 tablespoons vegetable or olive oil
1 medium yellow onion, peeled and diced
4 cloves of garlic, peeled and minced
3 tablespoons oil-packed sun-dried tomatoes
1 cup dry white wine
⅛ teaspoon dried sage
¼ teaspoon dried rosemary
Pinch dried red pepper flakes
Freshly ground black pepper, to taste

Almond Chicken

Serves 4

Ingredients:

1 (14-ounce) can chicken
    broth
4 strips bacon, cooked
2 pounds boneless, skinless
    chicken breasts
¼ cup dried minced onion
1 (4-ounce) can sliced
    mushrooms, drained
2 tablespoons soy sauce
1½ cups celery, sliced
    diagonally
Cooked rice
1 cup toasted slivered
    almonds

The dried minced onion (sometimes sold as dried onion flakes) will absorb some of the chicken broth during the cooking process and naturally thicken the sauce. For a subtler flavor, use freeze-dried shallots available from The Spice House (www.thespicehouse.com) instead.

Add the chicken broth to the slow cooker. Cut the bacon and chicken into bite-sized pieces; add to the slow cooker along with the dried minced onion, mushrooms, soy sauce, and celery. Stir to combine. Cover and cook on low for 6 hours. Serve over cooked rice and topped with the toasted slivered almonds.

Toasting Almonds

You can toast slivered almonds by adding them to a dry skillet over medium heat. Stir frequently until the almonds begin to brown. Alternatively, you can bake them at 400°F for about 5 minutes, stirring them occasionally. Whichever method you use, watch the almonds carefully because they quickly go from toasted to burnt.

Chicken and Artichokes

This is another dish that can be served with just a tossed salad and some crusty bread to make it a complete meal.

Add all ingredients to the slow cooker; stir to mix. Cover and cook on low for 6 hours. If necessary, uncover and allow to cook for ½ hour or more to thicken the sauce.

Artichoke Hearts

You can use thawed frozen artichoke hearts in place of canned ones. Or, if all you have on hand are marinated artichoke hearts, drain them and add them to the recipe; simply omit the thyme and garlic if you do.

Serves 4

Ingredients:
8 boneless, skinless chicken thighs
½ cup chicken broth
1 tablespoon fresh lemon juice
2 teaspoons dried thyme
1 clove of garlic, peeled and minced
¼ teaspoon freshly ground black pepper
1 (13-ounce) can artichoke hearts, drained

Easy Chicken and Dressing

Serve this dish with a tossed salad or steamed vegetable.

Serves 4

Ingredients:
Nonstick spray
1 (15¾-ounce) can cream of
    chicken soup
⅓ cup milk
4 (8-ounce) boneless, skinless
    chicken breasts
1 (6-ounce) package chicken-
    flavored stuffing mix
1⅔ cups water

1. Treat the crock of the slow cooker with nonstick spray. Add the soup and milk; stir to combine. Put the chicken in the slow cooker, pressing it down into the soup.

2. Mix together the stuffing mix and water in a bowl; spoon over the top of the chicken. Cover and cook on low for 8 hours.

Chicken in Plum Sauce

You can use commercial plum sauce or the one in Chapter 5 for this rich, sweet entrée. Serve it over rice along with steamed broccoli.

Serves 4

Ingredients:
Nonstick spray
1¼ cup plum sauce
2 tablespoons butter, melted
2 tablespoons orange juice
    concentrate, thawed
1 teaspoon Chinese five-spice
    powder
8 chicken thighs, skin
    removed
Optional: Toasted sesame oil
Optional: Soy sauce

1. Treat the crock of the slow cooker with nonstick spray. Add the plum sauce, butter, orange juice concentrate, and five-spice powder to the slow cooker; stir to combine.

2. Add the chicken thighs. Cover and cook on low for 6–8 hours. Top each serving with toasted sesame oil and soy sauce to taste if desired.

Chapter 8
Turkey

Turkey Broth

Yields about 4 cups

Ingredients:
3 pounds bone-in turkey
    wings
1 large onion, peeled and
    quartered
2 large carrots, scrubbed
2 stalks of celery
Salt and freshly ground black
    pepper, to taste
4½ cups water

This method makes a concentrated turkey broth. The amount of concentration will depend on how much meat is on the turkey wings and the amount of time you simmer them in the water. As a general rule, for regular turkey broth you can usually mix ½ cup of this broth with ½ cup water.

1. Add the turkey and onion to the slow cooker. Slice the carrot and cut the celery into pieces that will fit in the slow cooker and add them. Add the salt, pepper, and water. Cover and cook on low for 6 to 8 hours. (Cooking time will depend on the size of the turkey wings.) Allow to cool to room temperature.

2. Strain, discarding the cooked vegetables. Remove any meat from the bones and save for another use; discard the skin. Refrigerate the (cooled) broth overnight. Remove and discard the hardened fat. The resulting concentrated broth can be kept for 1 or 2 days in the refrigerator or frozen for up to 3 months.

Saving Time Later
Lightly coat pieces of turkey skin in all-purpose flour. Fry the skin in oil or butter in a nonstick skillet for about 6 minutes or until it's crispy. Add to the slow cooker along with the other ingredients for the broth. Use the resulting broth when you want to impart the added flavor achieved from browning turkey pieces, but want to skip that step before adding the turkey to the slow cooker.

Mock Bratwurst in Beer

Bavarian seasoning is a mix of a blend of Bavarian-style crushed brown mustard seeds, French rosemary, garlic, Dalmatian sage, French thyme, and bay leaves. The Spice House (www.thespicehouse.com) has a salt-free Bavarian Seasoning Blend that is appropriate for this recipe.

Add the ingredients to the slow cooker in the order given. Note that the liquid amount needed will depend on how wet the sauerkraut is when you add it. The liquid should come up halfway and cover the turkey breast, with the sauerkraut and potatoes being above the liquid line. Add more beer if necessary. Slow-cook on low for 8 hours. Taste for seasoning and adjust if necessary. Serve hot.

Bavarian Seasoning Substitution
You can substitute a tablespoon of stone-ground mustard along with ¼ teaspoon each of rosemary, garlic powder, sage, and thyme. Add a bay leaf (that will need to be removed before you serve the meal). Just before serving, taste for seasoning and adjust if necessary.

Serves 8

Ingredients:
2 stalks celery, finely chopped
1 (1-pound) bag baby carrots
1 large onion, peeled and sliced
2 cloves garlic, peeled and minced
4 slices of bacon, cut into small pieces
1 (3-pound) boneless turkey breast
1 (2-pound) bag sauerkraut, rinsed and drained
8 medium red potatoes, washed and pierced
1 (12-ounce) can beer
1 tablespoon Bavarian seasoning
Salt and freshly ground pepper, to taste

Turkey in Onion-Mushroom Gravy

Serves 8

Ingredients:
Nonstick spray
½ cup water
1 (3-pound) boneless turkey breast
1 envelope dry onion soup mix
1 small onion, peeled and thinly sliced
8 ounces fresh mushrooms, cleaned and sliced
8 medium red potatoes, peeled
1 tablespoon butter, softened
1 tablespoon all-purpose flour
1 cup heavy cream
Salt and freshly ground pepper, to taste

Add a tossed salad and steamed vegetable to make this dish a complete meal.

1. Treat the crock of the slow cooker with nonstick spray. Add the water. Place the turkey in the slow cooker and sprinkle the soup mix over the top of it. Add the onion, mushrooms, and potatoes. Cover and cook on low for 8 hours or until the turkey reaches an internal temperature of 170°F.

2. Move the turkey breast and potatoes to a serving platter; cover and keep warm.

3. Cover, increase the slow cooker to high, and cook for 15 minutes or until the liquid in the crock is bubbling around the edges. Mix the butter and flour together; dollop into the cooker. Whisk to work into the liquid, stirring and cooking for 5 minutes or until the flour taste is cooked out of the sauce and the mixture begins to thicken. Whisk in the cream and continue to cook for 15 minutes or until the cream comes to temperature and the gravy coats the back of a spoon. Taste for seasoning and add salt and pepper, to taste.

4. Slice the turkey and ladle the gravy over the slices, and serve the extra on the side.

Turkey Stroganoff
Omit the potatoes and cook the Turkey in Onion-Mushroom Gravy recipe as directed through Step 2. Stir 1 cup of sour cream into the liquid in the slow cooker, continuing to cook and stir until the mixture comes to temperature. Serve over cooked egg noodles and the sliced turkey.

Honey-Glazed Turkey

If the turkey legs are large, you can remove the meat from the bone before serving and increase the number of servings to six or eight.

1. Treat the crock of the slow cooker with nonstick spray. Turn the heat setting to high. Add the jam, honey, lemon juice, barbecue sauce, and soy sauce. Once the mixture has heated enough to melt the jam and honey into the mixture, stir in the paprika, salt, pepper, rosemary, and thyme. Add the turkey legs, spooning the sauce over them. Cover, reduce the heat setting to low, and cook for 8 hours. Uncover, increase heat setting to high, and cook for ½ hour to reduce the pan juices.

2. Remove the turkey legs to a serving platter; cover and keep warm. Add the cornstarch and water in a small bowl; stir to mix, and then thin with a little of the pan juices. Stir the resulting cornstarch slurry into the slow cooker. Cook and stir for 5 minutes or until thickened enough to coat the back of a spoon. Pour the glaze over the turkey legs and serve.

Turkey Sandwiches

Complete Step 1 of the Honey-Glazed Turkey recipe. Remove the turkey legs and allow to cool enough to remove the meat from the bones while you make the cornstarch slurry. Once the glaze is thickened, stir in the turkey meat. Serve on rolls or toasted whole-grain country bread.

Serves 4

Ingredients:
Nonstick spray
¼ cup apricot jam
2 tablespoons honey
1 tablespoon fresh lemon juice
1 tablespoon barbecue sauce
1 tablespoon soy sauce
1 teaspoon paprika
1 teaspoon salt
¼ teaspoon freshly ground black pepper
½ teaspoon dried rosemary
½ teaspoon dried thyme
4 turkey legs, skin removed
1 teaspoon cornstarch
1 teaspoon cold water

Spiced Apple Cider Turkey

This recipe makes candied sweet potatoes while it cooks the turkey in the sweetened cider sauce.

Serves 8

Ingredients:
Nonstick spray
1 (3-pound) boneless turkey breast
Salt and freshly ground black pepper, to taste
2 apples
4 large sweet potatoes
½ cup apple cider or apple juice
½ teaspoon ground cinnamon
¼ teaspoon ground cloves
¼ teaspoon ground allspice
2 tablespoons brown sugar

1. Treat the crock of the slow cooker with nonstick spray. Add turkey breast and season it with salt and pepper.

2. Peel, core, and slice the apples; arrange the slices over and around the turkey.

3. Peel the sweet potatoes and cut each in half; add to the slow cooker.

4. Add the cider or juice, cinnamon, cloves, allspice, and brown sugar to a bowl or measuring cup; stir to combine and pour over the ingredients in the slow cooker.

5. Cover and cook on low for 8 hours or until the internal temperature of the turkey is 170°F.

Turkey and Gravy

Season with your choice of Mrs. Dash Garlic Herb, Onion & Herb, Original, or Table Blend seasoning. For more servings, increase the size of the turkey breast; if necessary, increase the cooking time so it reaches an internal temperature of 170°F.

1. Add the broth to the slow cooker. Cut each celery stalk in half. Scrub and cut the carrot into four pieces. Add the celery, carrot, and onion to the slow cooker. Nestle the turkey breast on top of the vegetables, and sprinkle the seasoning blend over it. Cover and cook on low for 8 hours.

2. Remove the turkey breast to a serving platter; cover and keep warm.

3. Strain the pan juices through a cheesecloth-lined colander set over a large nonstick skillet, squeezing the vegetables in the cheesecloth to release the juices.

4. Transfer ¼ cup of the broth to a bowl and mix it together with the Madeira and instant flour; stir until the flour is dissolved. Bring the broth to a boil over medium-high heat. Whisk the flour mixture into the broth, stirring constantly until the gravy is thickened and coats the back of a spoon. Taste for seasoning, and add salt and pepper if needed. Slice the turkey and pour the gravy over the top of the slices, or serve the gravy on the side.

Or, if you prefer . . .

If you don't have instant flour on hand, you can instead strain the turkey broth into a bowl or large measuring cup. Melt ¼ cup butter in a large nonstick skillet and whisk ¼ cup all-purpose flour into the butter. Slowly whisk the broth into the resulting butter-flour roux; bring to a boil, stirring constantly, and cook until thickened.

Serves 8

Ingredients:

1¾ cups turkey or chicken broth
2 stalks celery
1 large carrot
1 medium onion, peeled and quartered
1 (3-pound) boneless turkey breast
1 teaspoon Mrs. Dash Seasoning Blend
¼ cup (Wondra) instant flour
Optional: 2 tablespoons Madeira
Salt and freshly ground black pepper, to taste

Turkey Mole

Serves 8

Ingredients:
2 tablespoons olive oil
1 small onion, peeled and
  diced
2 cloves of garlic, peeled and
  minced
1 tablespoon tomato paste
1 (8-ounce) can diced
  tomatoes
1 dried ancho chili
1½ tablespoons Mexican
  chocolate or semisweet
  chocolate chips
1 teaspoon sesame seeds
2 teaspoons slivered almonds
1 cup turkey or chicken broth
4 turkey legs, skin removed
Salt and freshly ground black
  pepper, to taste
Optional: Cinnamon, to taste

For extra heat, add a few of the ancho chili seeds to the cooker. For even more heat, add a dried pasilla negro chili, too. Use this dish as filling in heated corn or flour tortillas, or serve it with rice and refried beans.

1. Add the oil and onion to the slow cooker; cover and cook on high for 30 minutes or until the onion just begins to brown. Stir in the garlic and tomato paste; cover and cook for 15 more minutes.

2. Stir the diced tomatoes into the onion mixture. Remove the stem and seeds from the dried chili; snip it into small pieces and add it to the cooker along with the chocolate chips, sesame seeds, almonds, and broth. Stir to combine. Add the turkey; cover and cook on low for 8 hours.

3. Remove the turkey legs; allow to cool enough to remove the meat from the bones.

4. Use an immersion blender to purée the mole sauce in the slow cooker. Taste for seasoning and add salt, pepper, and cinnamon if desired. Stir the turkey into the sauce.

Sauce on the Side
The Turkey Mole recipe makes about 2 cups of sauce. You can stir the turkey into 1 cup of that sauce and reserve the remaining sauce to serve on the side.

Holiday Turkey Breast

Do not use jellied cranberry sauce in this recipe. Taste the whole cranberry sauce before adding it to the slow cooker. If it's sweet enough for your taste, then substitute water for the apple juice.

1. Treat the crock of the slow cooker with nonstick spray. Add the soup mix, cranberry sauce, and juice to the slow cooker; stir to combine.

2. Add turkey breast and spoon the cranberry sauce mixture over the turkey. Cover and cook on low for 8 hours or until the internal temperature of the turkey is 170°F.

Serves 8

Ingredients:
Nonstick spray
1 envelope onion and herb soup mix
1 (16-ounce) can whole cranberry sauce
¼ cup apple juice
1 (3-pound) boneless turkey breast

Turkey in Onion Sauce

This is an African-inspired dish. Serve it over cooked rice.

1. Add the onions, garlic, lemon juice, salt, and cayenne pepper to the slow cooker; stir to combine. Nestle the turkey legs into the onion mixture. Cover and cook on low for 8 hours.

2. Remove the turkey legs and allow to cool enough to remove the meat from the bone. Leave the cover off of the slow cooker and allow the onion mixture to continue to cook until the liquid has totally evaporated. (You can raise the setting to high to speed things up if you wish. Just be sure to stir the mixture occasionally to prevent the onions from burning.) Stir the turkey into the onion mixture. Taste for seasoning and add pepper if desired. For more heat, add additional cayenne pepper, too.

Serves 8

Ingredients:
5 large onions, peeled and thinly sliced
4 cloves of garlic, peeled and minced
¼ cup fresh lemon juice
1 teaspoon salt
¼ teaspoon cayenne pepper
4 turkey thighs, skin removed
Freshly ground black pepper, to taste

Barbecue Turkey

Dark meat turkey stays moist, even after long slow-cooking times. Left to cook long enough, it becomes tender enough to use to make "pulled" turkey sandwiches that are especially good if you add coleslaw or shredded lettuce, bacon, and tomato. An alternative is to serve Barbecue Turkey over cooked rice or noodles.

Serves 4

Ingredients:
½ cup ketchup
2 tablespoons brown sugar
1 tablespoon quick-cooking tapioca
1 tablespoon apple cider vinegar
1 teaspoon Worcestershire sauce
1 teaspoon soy or steak sauce
¼ teaspoon ground cinnamon
⅛ teaspoon ground cloves
Optional: Dried red pepper flakes, to taste
2 turkey thighs, skin removed

1. Add the ketchup, brown sugar, tapioca, vinegar, Worcestershire sauce, soy or steak sauce (or both), cinnamon, cloves, and red pepper flakes, if using, to the slow cooker; stir to combine.

2. Place the turkey thighs in the slow cooker, meaty side down. Cover and cook on low for 8 or more hours or until the turkey is tender and pulls away from the bone. Remove the turkey; allow to cool enough to remove the meat from the bones. Skim any fat off of the top of the barbecue sauce in the slow cooker. Stir the turkey into the sauce and continue to cook long enough for it to come back to temperature.

Fruited Turkey Roast

A pinch of dried red pepper flakes acts as a flavor enhancer. Add more if you prefer sweet and spicy sauce. You can add more kick to the sauce by substituting spicy mustard for the stone-ground.

1. Treat the crock of the slow cooker with nonstick spray. Add the turkey. Pour the diced onion, cranberries, and diced peaches around the turkey. Add the broth, brown sugar, mustard, and red pepper flakes, if using, to a bowl; stir to mix, adding the orange zest if using. Pour into the slow cooker. Cover and cook on low for 8 hours or until the internal temperature of the roast reaches 170°F.

2. Remove the turkey to a serving platter. (If the turkey roast is held together with a net, you can remove it at this time. Some find it easier to carve with the net in place. Regardless, allow the turkey to "rest" for at least 10 minutes before you slice it.) Cover and keep warm.

3. Use an immersion blender to purée the pan liquids. Taste for seasoning and adjust if necessary. Transfer to a gravy boat and serve alongside the roast.

Serves 8

Ingredients:
Nonstick spray
1 (3-pound) turkey roast
1 medium onion, peeled and diced
1 cup cranberries
2 peaches, peeled, seeded, and diced
¼ cup turkey or chicken broth
¼ cup brown sugar
3 tablespoons stone-ground mustard
Optional: Dried red pepper flakes, to taste
Optional: Zest of 1 orange
Optional: Salt and freshly ground black pepper, to taste

Turkey Sausage and Beans Medley

Serves 8

Ingredients:

1 pound cooked smoked turkey sausage

1 (15-ounce) can black beans, rinsed and drained

1 (15-ounce) can butter beans, rinsed and drained

1 (15-ounce) can Great Northern beans, rinsed and drained

1 (15-ounce) can red kidney beans, rinsed and drained

1 (8-ounce) can tomato sauce

½ cup ketchup

1 medium red bell pepper, seeded and diced

1 large sweet onion, peeled and diced

¼ cup brown sugar

1 tablespoon Worcestershire sauce

1 teaspoon Dijon or dry mustard

Optional: Hot sauce or dried red pepper flakes, to taste

You can serve this dish as a main course along with a salad and some crusty bread or as a baked beans alternative. Either way, it's even better if you add some diced bacon to the slow cooker when you add the other ingredients, or crumble crisp bacon and sprinkle chopped green onions over the top of each serving.

Dice the smoked turkey sausage and add to the slow cooker along with the other ingredients. Cover and cook on low for 8 hours.

Asian-Spiced Turkey Breast

*A 3-pound turkey breast or roast will yield about 8 (4-ounce) servings.
If you prefer larger portions, adjust the servings or increase the size
of the roast. If you do the latter, you may need to increase
the cooking time to ensure the meat gets done.*

Add the marmalade, ginger, garlic, spice powder, salt, pepper, and orange juice to the slow cooker. Stir to mix. Place the turkey breast or roast into the cooker. Spoon some of the sauce over the meat. Cover and cook on low for 8 hours or until the internal temperature of the meat is 170°F.

Serves 8

Ingredients:

½ cup orange marmalade

1 tablespoon fresh ginger, peeled and grated

1 clove of garlic, peeled and minced

½ teaspoon Chinese five-spice powder

Salt and freshly ground black pepper, to taste

¼ cup orange juice

1 (3-pound) turkey breast or roast

Honey-Mustard Turkey

*You can substitute maple syrup for the honey. Another alternative is to substitute
Dijon mustard instead of stone-ground and white wine vinegar for the cider.*

Treat the crock of the slow cooker with nonstick spray. Place the thighs in the slow cooker, meaty side down. Layer the potatoes over the thighs. Add the mustard, honey, vinegar, and tapioca to a bowl; mix well, then pour into the slow cooker. Cover and cook on low for 8 hours. When serving, drizzle extra-virgin olive oil over the potatoes if desired.

Serves 4

Ingredients:

Nonstick spray

2 turkey thighs, skin removed

4 red potatoes, peeled and quartered

¼ cup stone-ground mustard

⅓ cup honey

1 tablespoon apple cider vinegar

1 tablespoon quick-cooking tapioca

Optional: Extra-virgin olive oil

Turkey in Red Wine Sauce

Serves 4

Ingredients:

4 strips bacon
2 medium carrots, diced
½ stalk celery, finely diced
1 medium onion, peeled and
    diced
8 ounces fresh mushrooms,
    cleaned and sliced
2 cloves of garlic, peeled and
    minced
2 turkey thighs, skin removed
Salt and freshly ground black
    pepper, to taste
2 teaspoons dried parsley
½ teaspoon dried thyme
1 bay leaf
½ cup dry red wine
½ cup double-strength
    chicken or turkey broth
1 (10-ounce) package frozen
    artichoke hearts, thawed
Optional: 2 tablespoons
    butter, softened
Optional: 2 tablespoons all-
    purpose flour

A hearty wine like Zinfandel works well in this Coq au Vine-inspired dish. If you prefer, you can make the dish with 8 chicken thighs instead of with turkey.

1. Add the bacon, carrots, and celery to a microwave-safe bowl. Cover and microwave on high for 1 minute; stir, recover, and microwave on high for another minute. Stir in the onion; cover and microwave on high for 2 minutes. Stir in the mushrooms; stirring occasionally, microwave uncovered on high for 3–5 minutes or until the mushrooms have given off their liquid. Stir in the garlic, and then transfer to the slow cooker.

2. Place the turkey thighs meaty side down in the slow cooker. Sprinkle with the salt, pepper, parsley, and thyme. Add the bay leaf. Pour in the wine and chicken broth. Cover and cook on low for 7 hours. Remove the turkey thighs and take the meat off the bone. Return the meat to the slow cooker. Add the artichokes; cover and cook on low for 1 hour.

3. To thicken the sauce by cooking down the pan juices, transfer the artichokes to a serving dish; cover and keep warm. Skim any fat from the surface of the pan liquids; cook, stirring occasionally, uncovered on high for 15–30 minutes or until the liquid has reduced by half. Taste for seasoning, adjust if necessary, and then pour the sauce over the turkey and vegetables.

4. To thicken the sauce using the optional butter and flour, use a slotted spoon to transfer the meat, mushrooms, and artichokes to a serving bowl; cover and keep warm. Cover and increase the heat to high. Mix the butter and flour together in a small bowl along with about ½ cup of the pan liquids. Once the liquids in the slow cooker are bubbling around the edges, remove the cover and whisk in the butter-flour mixture. Cook, stirring constantly, for 10 minutes or until the flour taste is cooked out of the sauce and it coats the back of a spoon. Taste for seasoning, adjust if necessary, and then pour the sauce over the turkey and vegetables.

Chapter 9
Beef

Beef Broth

Yield: About 4 cups

Ingredients:

1 (2-pound) bone-in chuck
   roast
1 pound beef bones
1 large onion, peeled and
   quartered
2 large carrots, scrubbed
2 stalks of celery
Salt and freshly ground black
   pepper, to taste
4½ cups water

Unlike chicken or turkey broth, beef broth requires a larger ratio of meat to the amount of bones used to make it. This method makes a concentrated broth. As a general rule, for regular beef broth you can usually mix ½ cup of this broth with ½ cup water.

1. Add the chuck roast, beef bones, and onion to the slow cooker. Slice the carrot and cut the celery into pieces that will fit in the slow cooker and add them. Add the salt, pepper, and water. Cover and cook on low for 8 hours.

2. Use a slotted spoon to remove the roast and beef bones. Reserve the roast and the meat removed from the bones for another use; discard the bones.

3. Once the broth has cooled enough to make it easier to handle, strain it; discard the cooked vegetables. Refrigerate the (cooled) broth overnight. Remove and discard the hardened fat. The resulting concentrated broth can be kept for 1 or 2 days in the refrigerator or frozen for up to 3 months.

Boiling Broth

You don't want to let broth come to a boil during the initial cooking process because fat that will render from the meat will incorporate into the broth and make it cloudy. However, after you have strained the broth and removed the fat, you can keep it in the refrigerator longer if you bring it to a boil every other day; cool it and return it to the refrigerator until needed.

Brown Stock

When you add ¼ cup of this concentrated broth to a slow-cooked beef dish, you'll get the same, succulent flavor as if you first seared the meat in a hot skillet before adding it to the slow cooker. The broth also gives a delicious flavor boost to slow-cooked tomato sauce or tomato gravy.

1. Preheat the oven to 450°F. Cut the carrots and celery into large pieces. Put them along with the meat, bones, and onions into a roasting pan. Season with salt and pepper. Put the pan in the middle part of the oven and, turning the meat and vegetables occasionally, roast for 45 minutes or until evenly browned.

2. Transfer the roasted meat, bones, and vegetable to the slow cooker. Add the water to the roasting pan; scrape any browned bits clinging to the pan and then pour the water into the slow cooker. Cover and cook on low for 8 hours. (It may be necessary to skim accumulated fat and scum from the top of the pan juices; check the broth after 4 and 6 hours to see if that's needed.)

3. Use a slotted spoon to remove the roast and beef bones. Reserve the roast and the meat removed from the bones for another use; discard the bones.

4. Once the broth has cooled enough to handle, strain it; discard the cooked vegetables. Refrigerate the (cooled) broth overnight. Remove and discard the hardened fat. The resulting concentrated broth can be kept for 1 or 2 days in the refrigerator, or frozen for up to 3 months.

Yield: About 4 cups

Ingredients:
2 large carrots, scrubbed
2 stalks of celery
1½ pounds bone-in chuck roast
1½ pounds cracked beef bones
1 large onion, peeled and quartered
Salt and freshly ground black pepper, to taste
4½ cups water

Beef and Cabbage

Serves 4

Ingredients:
1 pound cooked beef
1 small head of cabbage, chopped
1 medium onion, diced
2 carrots, peeled and thinly sliced
2 stalks celery, sliced in ½-inch pieces
1 clove garlic, peeled and minced
2 cups beef broth
1 (14½-ounce) can diced tomatoes
¼ teaspoon sugar
Salt, to taste
⅛ teaspoon freshly ground black pepper

The longer cooking time helps the flavors develop. But because the meat is already cooked, this meal is done when the cabbage is tender, or in about 4 hours on low. Serve over cooked brown rice or mashed potatoes.

1. Cut the cooked beef into bite-sized pieces and add it to the slow cooker along with the cabbage, onion, carrots, and celery; stir to mix.

2. Add the garlic, broth, tomatoes, sugar, salt, and pepper to a bowl; mix well and pour over the beef. Set the slow cooker on high and cook for 1 hour or until the cabbage has begun to wilt.

3. Reduce heat to low and cook for 4 hours. Adjust seasonings if necessary.

Easy Beef Stroganoff

Serves 4

Ingredients:
1 pound cooked beef
1 small onion, peeled and thinly sliced
1 (4-ounce) can sliced mushrooms, drained
1 (10¾-ounce) can cream of mushroom soup
1 tablespoon balsamic vinegar
1 teaspoon sugar
¼ teaspoon garlic powder
1 (4-ounce) package cream cheese
½ cup sour cream

Adding some balsamic vinegar and sugar to this recipe mimics the flavor of using beef cooked in wine. The combination of cream cheese and sour cream gives this dish a much richer flavor, but you can use all sour cream if you prefer.

1. Dice or shred the cooked beef and add to the slow cooker along with the onion. Add the mushrooms, soup, vinegar, sugar, and garlic powder to a bowl; stir to mix and then pour into the slow cooker. Cover and cook on low for 4 hours.

2. Cut the cream cheese into small cubes; stir into the beef mixture in the slow cooker. Cover and cook on low for ½ hour or until the cheese is melted. Stir in the sour cream; cover and cook on low until the sour cream comes to temperature. Serve over hot cooked egg noodles.

New England Boiled Dinner

Cutting the meat into serving-sized pieces before you add it to the slow cooker will make the meat cook up more tender, but you can keep it in one piece if you prefer to carve it at the table.

1. Cut the beef into eight serving pieces and add it along with the soup, horseradish, bay leaf, and garlic to the slow cooker. Add the carrots, rutabagas, potatoes, and cabbage wedges. Cover and cook on low for 8 hours.

2. Remove meat and vegetables to a serving platter; cover and keep warm.

3. Increase the slow cooker setting to high; cover and cook until the pan juices begin to bubble around the edges. Mix the butter and flour in a bowl together with ½ cup of the pan juices; strain out any lumps and whisk the mixture into the simmering liquid in the slow cooker. Cook and stir for 15 minutes or the flour flavor is cooked out and the resulting gravy is thickened enough to coat the back of a spoon. Taste for seasoning and add salt and pepper if desired. Stir in the sour cream if using. Serve alongside or over the meat and vegetables.

Horseradish Gravy

If you prefer a more intense horseradish flavor with cooked beef, increase the amount to 1 tablespoon. Taste the pan juices before you thicken it with the butter and flour mixture, and add more horseradish at that time if desired. Of course, you can have some horseradish or some horseradish mayonnaise available as a condiment for those who want more.

Serves 8

Ingredients:
1 (3-pound) boneless beef round rump roast
2 (10¾-ounce) cans onion soup
1 teaspoon prepared horseradish
1 bay leaf
1 clove of garlic, peeled and minced
6 large carrots, peeled and cut into 1-inch pieces
3 rutabagas, peeled and quartered
4 large potatoes, peeled and quartered
1 (2-pound) head of cabbage, cut into 8 wedges
2 tablespoons butter
2 tablespoons all-purpose flour
Salt and freshly ground black pepper, to taste
Optional: 1 cup sour cream

Pastrami

New York-style pastrami is peppercorn-crusted smoked corned beef that is sometimes steamed before serving. Smoked paprika will impart a subtle smoky flavor. For a more intense smoked flavor, use liquid smoke, too.

Serves 12

Ingredients:
1 (4-pound) corned beef brisket
2 large onions, peeled and sliced
2 cloves of garlic, peeled and minced
2 tablespoons pickling spices
1½ cups water
1 tablespoon black peppercorns, crushed
¾ teaspoon freshly grated nutmeg
¾ teaspoon ground allspice
2 teaspoons smoked paprika
Optional: ¼ teaspoon liquid smoke

1. Trim any fat from the corned beef brisket. Add the brisket, onions, garlic, pickling spice, and water to the slow cooker. Cover and cook for 8 hours. Turn off the cooker and allow the meat to cool enough to handle it.

2. Preheat the oven to 350°F.

3. Add the crushed (or cracked) peppercorns, nutmeg, allspice, paprika, and liquid smoke (if using) to a small bowl; mix well. Rub the peppercorn mixture over all sides of the corned beef. Place on a roasting pan; roast on the middle shelf for 45 minutes. Let the meat rest for 10 minutes, then carve by slicing it against the grain or on the diagonal.

Deli-Style Pastrami Sandwich
Pile thin slices of pastrami on a slice of deli rye slathered with mustard. Top with another slice of rye bread. Serve with a big, crisp kosher dill pickle.

Yankee Pot Roast

*New England cooking is traditionally plain and straightforward. If
your family prefers a heartier flavor, add 1 teaspoon of
Mrs. Dash Garlic Herb Seasoning Blend.*

Serves 8

Ingredients:
*¼ pound salt pork or bacon,
    cut into cubes*
2 stalks celery, diced
*1 (4-pound) chuck or English
    roast*
*Salt and freshly ground black
    pepper, to taste*
*2 large onions, peeled and
    quartered*
*1 (1-pound) bag of baby
    carrots*
2 turnips, peeled and diced
8 medium potatoes, peeled
2 cups beef broth
4 tablespoons butter
*4 tablespoons all-purpose
    flour*

1. Add the salt pork or bacon and the celery to the bottom of the slow cooker. Place the roast on top of the pork; salt and pepper to taste. Add the onion, carrots, turnips, and potatoes. Pour in the beef broth. Cover and cook on low for 8 hours.

2. Use a slotted spoon to move the meat and vegetables to a serving platter; cover and keep warm.

3. Mix the butter and flour together with ½ cup of the broth. Increase the slow cooker heat setting to high; cover and cook until the mixture begins to bubble around the edges. Whisk the flour mixture into the broth; cook, stirring constantly, for 10 minutes, or until the flour flavor is cooked out of the gravy and it's thickened enough to coat the back of a spoon. Taste the gravy for seasoning and stir in more salt and pepper if needed. Serve over or alongside the meat and vegetables.

Mocking the Maillard Reaction

Contrary to myth, searing meat before it's braised doesn't seal in the juices, but it does—through a process known as the Maillard reaction—enhance the flavor of the meat through a caramelization process. Using beef broth (or, even better, a combination of brown stock and water) mimics that flavor and lets you skip the browning step.

Onion Pot Roast

Serves 8

Ingredients:
1 (3-pound) boneless chuck
  roast
1 (1-pound) bag of baby
  carrots
2 stalks of celery, diced
1 green bell pepper, seeded
  and diced
1 large yellow onion, peeled
  and sliced
1 envelope onion soup mix
½ teaspoon black pepper
1 cup water
1 cup tomato juice
2 cloves of garlic, peeled and
  minced
1 tablespoon Worcestershire
  sauce
1 tablespoon steak sauce

Turn this into two 4-servings meals by making roast beef sandwiches the next day. The meat will be tender and moist if you refrigerate leftovers in the pan juices.

1. Cut the roast into serving-sized portions. Add the carrots, celery, green bell pepper, and onion to the slow cooker. Place the roast pieces on top of the vegetables and sprinkle with soup mix and black pepper.

2. Add the water, tomato juice, garlic, Worcestershire sauce, and steak sauce to a bowl or measuring cup; mix well and then pour into the slow cooker. Cover and cook on low for 8 hours.

French Dip Sandwiches
Reheat leftover pan juices from the Onion Pot Roast and serve it as a sauce in which to dip roast beef sandwiches. Be sure to have horseradish and mayonnaise available for those who want to add it to their sandwiches.

Lone Star State Chili

Word has it that Texans prefer their chili without beans, but you can add a can or two of rinsed and drained kidney beans if you prefer it that way. Doing so will increase the number of servings to 10 or 12. Serve this dish with baked corn tortilla chips and a tossed salad with a sour cream dressing.

Add all of the ingredients to the slow cooker in the order given, and stir to combine. The liquid in your slow cooker should completely cover the meat and vegetables. If additional liquid is needed add more crushed tomatoes, broth, or some water. Cover and cook on low for 8 hours. Taste for seasoning, and add more chili powder if desired.

Hot Pepper Precautions

Wear gloves or sandwich bags over your hands when you clean and dice hot peppers. It's important to avoid having the peppers come into contact with any of your skin, or especially your eyes. As an added precaution, wash your hands (and under your fingernails) thoroughly with hot soapy water after you remove the gloves or sandwich bags.

Serves 8

Ingredients:
¼ pound bacon, diced
1 stalk celery, finely chopped
1 large carrot, peeled and finely chopped
1 (3-pound) chuck roast, cut into small cubes
2 large yellow onions, peeled and diced
6 cloves garlic, peeled and minced
6 jalapeño peppers, seeded and diced
Salt and freshly ground pepper, to taste
4 tablespoons chili powder
1 teaspoon Mexican oregano
1 teaspoon ground cumin
1 teaspoon brown sugar
1 (28-ounce) can diced tomatoes
1 cup beef broth

Beef in Beer

Serves 6

Ingredients:

2 tablespoons butter

2 large onions, peeled and
sliced

2 cloves of garlic, peeled and
minced

1 (3-pound) boneless chuck
roast

¼ cup water

½ double-strength beef broth

½ cup lager beer

1 tablespoon light brown
sugar

1 tablespoon Dijon mustard

1 tablespoon apple cider
vinegar

*You can thicken the pan juices with a cornstarch slurry if you wish.
Serve alongside potatoes and a steamed vegetable. For a change
of pace, serve pretzels instead of having bread at the table
and provide beer for those who want it.*

1. Melt the butter in a large nonstick skillet over medium-high heat. Add the onions and sauté for 5 minutes or until the onions are lightly browned; stir in the garlic and sauté for 30 seconds. Pour the onions and garlic into the slow cooker.

2. Trim the roast of any fat and cut into six serving-sized pieces. Put the skillet back over the heat; add the meat to the skillet and fry for 2 minutes on each side. Move the meat to the slow cooker.

3. Put the skillet back over the heat. Add the water, stirring well to bring up any browned meat clinging to the pan. Stir in the broth, beer, brown sugar, mustard, and vinegar. Mix well, and then pour over the meat in the slow cooker. Cover and cook on low for 8 hours. Ladle onions and broth over each serving of meat.

Mushroom Steak and Vegetables

Serve this dish over mashed potatoes along with your choice of microwave steam-in-bag vegetables or a tossed salad.

Serves 8

Ingredients:
2 pounds boneless beef round
   steak, cut ¾ inch thick
2 medium onions, peeled and
   sliced
3 cups sliced fresh
   mushrooms
1 (12-ounce) jar beef gravy
1 (1-ounce) envelope dry
   mushroom gravy mix

1. Trim fat from the steak; cut it into eight serving-size pieces. Spread the onions over the bottom of the crock. Add the meat on top of the onions and the mushrooms to the top of the meat.

2. Combine beef gravy and mushroom gravy mix. Pour the gravy mixture into the slow cooker; cover and cook on low for 8 hours.

Barbecue Western Ribs

At the end of the 8-hour cooking time, the meat will be tender and falling off of the bones. You can stretch this recipe to 8 servings if you serve barbecue beef sandwiches instead of 4 servings of beef. Add potato chips and coleslaw for a delicious, casual meal.

Serves 4

Ingredients:
1 cup barbecue sauce
½ cup orange marmalade
½ cup water
3 pounds beef Western ribs

1. Add the barbecue sauce, marmalade, and water to the slow cooker. Stir to mix.

2. Add the ribs, ladling some of the sauce over the ribs. Cover and cook on low for 8 hours. To thicken the sauce, if desired, use a slotted spoon to remove the meat and bones; cover and keep warm. Skim any fat from the sauce in the cooker; increase the heat setting to high and cook uncovered for 15 minutes or until the sauce is reduced and coats the back of a spoon.

Sirloin Dinner

Serves 8

Ingredients:
1 (4-pound) beef sirloin tip roast
2 tablespoons extra-virgin olive oil
1 teaspoon kosher or sea salt
½ teaspoon freshly ground pepper
1 teaspoon garlic powder
1 teaspoon onion powder
1 teaspoon ground cumin
1 teaspoon dried thyme leaves, crushed
½ teaspoon sweet paprika
2 turnips, peeled and cut into 2-inch pieces
2 parsnips, peeled and cut into 2-inch pieces
4 large red potatoes, peeled and quartered
1 (1-pound) bag baby carrots
8 cloves garlic, peeled and cut in half lengthwise
2 large onions, peeled and sliced
½ cup dry red wine
1 cup beef broth
Salt and freshly ground black pepper, to taste

Add a tossed salad and some warm dinner rolls and this recipe makes a complete meal.

1. To ensure the roast cooks evenly, tie it into an even form using butcher's twine. Rub the oil onto the meat.

2. Mix the salt, pepper, garlic powder, onion powder, cumin, thyme, and paprika together. Pat the seasoning mixture on all sides of the roast. Place the roast in the slow cooker.

3. Arrange the turnips, parsnips, potatoes, and carrots around the roast. Evenly disperse the garlic around the vegetables. Arrange the onion slices over the vegetables. Pour the wine and broth into the slow cooker. Season with salt and pepper, to taste. Cover and cook on low for 8 hours.

4. Use a slotted spoon to remove the roast and vegetables to a serving platter; cover and keep warm. Let the roast rest for at least 10 minutes before carving. To serve, thinly slice the roast across the grain. Serve drizzled with some of the pan juices.

Rare Sirloin Roast
If you prefer a rare roast, use a probe thermometer set to your preferred doneness setting. (130°F for rare.) You'll need to be close by so that you hear the thermometer alarm when it goes off. Remove the roast to a platter; cover and keep warm. Cover and continue to cook the vegetables if necessary.

Swiss Steak

Minute steaks are usually tenderized pieces of round steak. You can instead buy 2½ pounds of round steak, trim it of fat, cut it into 6 portions, and pound each portion thin between two pieces of plastic wrap. Serve Swiss Steak over mashed potatoes.

Serves 6

Ingredients:
½ cup all-purpose flour
1 teaspoon salt
¼ teaspoon freshly ground
    black pepper
6 (6-ounce) beef minute
    steaks
2 tablespoons vegetable oil
2 teaspoons butter
½ stalk celery, finely diced
1 large yellow onion, peeled
    and diced
1 cup beef broth
1 cup water
1 (1-pound) bag baby carrots
Optional: Worcestershire or
    steak sauce, to taste

1. Add the flour, salt, pepper, and minute steaks to a gallon plastic bag; seal and shake to coat the meat.

2. Add the oil and butter to a large skillet and bring it to temperature over medium-high heat. Add the meat and brown it for 5 minutes on each side. Transfer the meat to the slow cooker.

3. Add the celery to the skillet and sauté while you add the onion to the plastic bag; seal and shake to coat the onion in flour. Add the flour-coated onions to the skillet and, stirring constantly, sauté for 10 minutes or until the onions are lightly browned. Add the beef broth to the skillet and stir to scrape up any browned bits clinging to the pan. Add the water and continue to cook until the liquid is thickened enough to lightly coat the back of a spoon. Pour into the slow cooker. Add the carrots. Cover and cook on low for 8 hours.

4. Transfer the meat and carrots to a serving platter. Taste the gravy for seasoning, and add Worcestershire or steak sauce to taste if desired. Serve alongside or over the meat and carrots.

Swiss Steak and Pasta
If instead of mashed potatoes, you'd prefer the serve the Swiss Steak over cooked pasta, stir 2 tablespoons of tomato paste into the onions before you make the gravy in Step 3. Or, you can substitute 1 cup of diced tomatoes for the water.

Horseradish Roast Beef and Potatoes

Horseradish gives this beef dish an extra flavor dimension.

Ingredients:

⅓ cup prepared horseradish

2 tablespoons extra-virgin olive oil

1 teaspoon freshly ground black pepper

1 teaspoon dried thyme, crushed

½ teaspoon salt

1 (3-pound) boneless beef chuck roast

2 celery stalks, cut in half

¼ cup dry white wine or beef broth

1¼ cups beef broth

2 pounds (about 12–16) small red potatoes

Optional: Water

1 (1-pound) package baby carrots

Optional: 2 tablespoons all-purpose flour

Optional: 2 tablespoons butter

1. In a small bowl, mix together the horseradish, oil, pepper, thyme, and salt. Trim the fat from the roast and cut it into 2-inch cubes. Rub the horseradish mixture into meat. Add the seasoned roast, celery, white wine, and broth to a 4-quart slow cooker. Cover and cook for 1–2 hours on high or until the celery is limp. Discard the celery. Add water or more broth, if necessary, to bring the liquid level up to just the top of the meat.

2. Wash the potatoes. Add the potatoes and carrots to the cooker. Cover and cook on low for 6 hours, or until meat is tender and the vegetables are cooked through. Serve warm.

3. Optional: If you wish to thicken the pan juices, remove the meat and vegetables to a serving platter. Cover and keep warm. Turn the slow cooker to the high setting; cover and cook until the juices bubble around the edges. Mix the flour together with the butter and ½ cup of the pan juices; whisk into the slow cooker. Cook, stirring constantly, for 15 minutes or until the flour taste is cooked out of the gravy and it is thickened enough to coat the back of a spoon.

Improvised Beef Stew

If you have leftovers, you can make a hearty beef stew by cutting the beef, potatoes, and carrots into bite-sized pieces and stirring them into the thickened pan juices. Add a tablespoon or two of ketchup or some hot sauce for an extra punch of flavor if desired. Reheat and serve with hard rolls, or over biscuits.

Pot Roast in Fruit-Infused Gravy

You can substitute 8 medium red potatoes, washed and halved or quartered, for the parsnips. To truly infuse the fruit flavors into the gravy, use an immersion blender to purée the fruit before you begin making the gravy in Step 3.

1. In a small bowl, stir together garlic, sage, salt, black pepper, and cayenne. Spread the garlic mixture over both sides of the meat. Add the oil to a large skillet and bring it to temperature over medium-high heat; add the roast and brown it on both sides. Add the browned roast to the slow cooker. Pour the broth over roast. Add the onion, prunes, apples, parsnips, and baby carrots. Cover and cook on low for 8 hours.

2. With a slotted spoon transfer the meat and vegetables to a serving platter; cover and keep warm.

3. Skim the fat off the juices that remain in the pan. Add water if necessary to bring the pan juices to 1½ cups. Increase the heat setting to high; cover and cook until the liquid bubbles around the edges. In a bowl, mix the butter, flour, and ½ cup of the pan juices together, and then whisk into the slow cooker. Cook, stirring constantly, for 15 minutes or until the flour taste is cooked out of the gravy and it's thickened enough to coat the back of a spoon. Taste for seasoning and add salt and pepper if necessary. Stir in the balsamic vinegar. Serve the gravy over the roast, vegetables, and fruit.

Adding a German Influence
Stir several finely crushed ginger snaps into the pan juices before you add the flour mixture. Once it's thickened, substitute red wine or apple cider vinegar for the balsamic vinegar.

Serves 8

Ingredients:
2 cloves garlic, peeled minced
1 teaspoon dried sage, crushed
½ teaspoon salt
½ teaspoon freshly ground black pepper
⅛ teaspoon cayenne pepper
1 (3-pound) boneless beef chuck roast
2 tablespoons vegetable oil
1 cup beef broth
1 large onion, peeled and diced
1 cup pitted prunes (dried plums), cut in half
2 large apples, peeled, cored and cut into thick slices
1 pound parsnips, peeled and cut into ½-inch pieces
1 (1-pound) bag of baby carrots
¼ cup butter
¼ cup all-purpose flour
1 tablespoon balsamic vinegar

Beef Bourguignon

*For a complete fine-dining experience, serve Beef Bourguignon
over buttered noodles with a salad.*

Serves 8

Ingredients:

8 slices of bacon, diced

1 large yellow onion, peeled
and diced

3 cloves of garlic, peeled and
minced

1 (3-pound) boneless English
or chuck roast

16 ounces fresh mushrooms,
cleaned and sliced

2 tablespoons tomato paste

2 cups beef broth or water

4 cups burgundy

½ teaspoon thyme

1 bay leaf

Salt and freshly ground black
pepper, to taste

1 large yellow onion, peeled
and thinly sliced

Optional: ½ cup butter,
softened

Optional: ½ cup all-purpose
flour

1. In a large nonstick skillet fry the bacon over medium heat until it renders its fat. Use a slotted spoon to remove the bacon and reserve it for another use. Add the onion to the skillet and sauté for 5 minutes or until it is transparent. Stir in the garlic, sauté for 30 seconds, and then transfer the onion mixture to the slow cooker. Cover the cooker.

2. Trim the roast of any fat and cut it into bite-sized pieces; add the beef pieces to the skillet and brown the meat over medium-high heat for 5 minutes. Transfer the meat to the slow cooker. Cover the cooker. Add half of the sliced mushrooms to the skillet; stir-fry for 5 minutes or until the mushroom liquids have evaporated; transfer to the slow cooker and replace the cover.

3. Add the tomato paste to the skillet and sauté for 3 minutes or until the tomato paste just begins to brown. Stir in the broth or water, scraping the bottom of the pan to remove any browned bits and work them into the sauce. Remove the pan from the heat and stir in the burgundy, thyme, bay leaf, salt, and pepper; stir to combine. Pour into the slow cooker. Add the remaining mushrooms and sliced onion to slow cooker. Cover and cook on low for 8 hours.

4. Optional: To thicken the sauce, use a slotted spoon to transfer the meat, cooked onions and mushrooms to a serving platter; cover and keep warm. In a small bowl, mix the butter together with the flour to form a paste; whisk in some of the pan liquid a little at a time to thin the paste. Strain out any lumps. Increase the heat of the cooker to high. When the pan liquids begin to bubble around the edges, whisk in the flour mixture. Cook, stirring constantly, for 15 minutes or until the sauce has thickened enough to coat the back of a spoon. Pour over the meat, mushrooms, and onions on the serving platter.

Apple-Mustard Beef Brisket

Serve Apple-Mustard Beef Brisket with a crusty bread and a tossed salad with honey-mustard dressing. If you wish, you can add some peeled and quartered root vegetables (carrots, parsnips, or turnips) to the cooker, too.

Add all ingredients to the slow cooker in the order given. If using, peel, core, and slice the apples and put them in a layer on top of the meat. Cover and cook on low for 8 hours or until meat is tender.

Delayed Satisfaction

Brisket will become even more moist and tender if you allow it to cool in the broth, so this makes a good dish to make the day before. To reheat it, bake it for 45 minutes at 325°F. Baste it with some additional sauce and put it under the broiler for a few minutes to allow the meat to develop a glaze.

Serves 8

Ingredients:
1 (3-pound) beef brisket
1 large yellow onion, peeled
    and quartered
2 large cloves of garlic, peeled
    and minced
4 large cloves of garlic, peeled
    and left whole
1 (10-ounce) jar apple jelly
3 tablespoons Dijon mustard
Salt and freshly ground
    pepper, to taste
¾ teaspoon curry powder
⅓ cup dry white wine
1 cup apple juice
1 cup water
Optional: 2 apples

Beef Barbecue

Ingredients:
1 (3-pound) beef English roast
1 cup water
½ cup red wine
½ cup ketchup
1 tablespoon red wine
  vinegar
2 teaspoons Worcestershire
  sauce
2 teaspoons mustard powder
2 tablespoons dried minced
  onion
1 teaspoon dried minced
  garlic
1 teaspoon cracked black
  pepper
1 tablespoon brown sugar
1 teaspoon chili powder
½ teaspoon ground
  cinnamon
¼ teaspoon ground cloves
¼ teaspoon ground ginger
Pinch ground allspice
Pinch dried pepper flakes,
  crushed

*An English roast tends to pull apart easier, which makes it perfect
for beef barbecue sandwiches. You can speed up the cooking
process by cutting the roast into smaller pieces.*

1. Add the roast to the slow cooker. Mix all remaining ingredients together and pour over the beef. Cover and cook on low for 8 hours.

2. Use a slotted spoon to remove the beef from the slow cooker; pull it apart, discarding any fat or gristle. Taste the meat and sauce and adjust seasonings if necessary.

3. To thicken the sauce, increase the heat of the cooker to high, skim any fat off the surface of the sauce (or blot it with a paper towel), and let cook uncovered while you pull apart the beef.

Barbecue Spaghetti
Serve beef barbecue over your favorite cooked pasta. Top with some grated Cheddar cheese and diced sweet or green onion.

Chapter 10
Pork

Pork Broth

Yields about 4 cups

Ingredients:

1 (3-pound) bone-in pork
    butt roast
1 large onion, peeled and
    quartered
12 baby carrots
2 stalks celery, cut in half
4½ cups water

Pork broth is seldom called for in recipes, but it can add layers of flavor when mixed with chicken and ham broth in bean or vegetable soups.

1. Add all ingredients to the slow cooker. Cover and cook on low for 6 hours or until the pork is tender and pulls away from the bone.

2. Strain; discard the celery and onion. Reserve the pork roast and carrots for another use. Once cooled, cover and refrigerate the broth overnight. Remove and discard the hardened fat. The broth can be kept for 1 or 2 days in the refrigerator, or frozen up to 3 months.

Pork Roast Dinner

To make concentrated broth and a pork roast dinner at the same time, increase the amount of carrots, decrease the water to 2½ cups, and add 4 peeled medium potatoes or sweet potatoes (cut in half) on top. Cook according to the instructions above. (White potatoes will cloud the broth, but the starch from them will naturally thicken it a little.)

Pork Roast Dinner

Using soda adds a sweet background note to the taste of the cooked pork. If you prefer, you can substitute 1½ cups of water for the Coca-Cola or Dr. Pepper.

Place the pork roast in the slow cooker. Sprinkle the soup mix over the pork. Pour in the soda. Add the onion, carrots, and potatoes. Cover and cook on low for 6 hours or until the internal temperature of the roast reaches 160°F.

Serves 4

Ingredients:
1 (3-pound) pork sirloin or butt roast
1 envelope dry onion soup mix
1 (12-ounce) can Coca-Cola or Dr. Pepper
1 medium sweet onion, peeled and slice
1 (1-pound) bag baby carrots
4 medium potatoes, peeled

Ham Broth

In the same way that adding a ham bone to the cooking liquid for ham and bean soup improves the soup's flavor, ¼ cup of ham broth for every ¾ cup of chicken broth can give a boost to potato soup, too.

1. Add all ingredients to the slow cooker. Cover and cook on low for 6 hours or until the ham pulls away from the bone.

2. Strain; discard the celery and onion. Reserve any ham removed from the bones and the carrots for another use. Once cooled, cover and refrigerate the broth overnight. Remove and discard any hardened fat. The broth can be kept for 1 or 2 days in the refrigerator or frozen up to 3 months.

Yields about 4 cups

Ingredients:
1 (3-pound) bone-in ham or 3 pounds of ham bones
1 large onion, peeled and quartered
12 baby carrots
2 stalks celery, cut in half
4½ cups water

Apple Cider Pork Loin

Serves 8

Ingredients:
1 (4-pound) pork loin
¼ cup Dijon mustard
1 teaspoon dried thyme
¼ cup light brown sugar
1 cup apple cider
4 cups unsweetened
   applesauce
Optional: 1 medium onion,
   peeled and sliced

Pork loin can dry out in the slow cooker. The pork will be juicier if you let it cool completely in the pan juices before you remove it and slice it. Return the slices to the pan juices when you reheat it. Serve the loin with the cider sauce ladled over the slices.

1. Trim any fat from the pork loin.

2. Add the mustard, thyme, and brown sugar to a bowl; mix it to make a paste and then rub it into the pork loin.

3. Add the cider and then the loin to the slow cooker. Pour the applesauce over the loin. If using, add the onion slices in a layer on top of the applesauce. Cover and cook on low for 6 hours or until the internal temperature of the loin is 160°F. If serving immediately, remove the pork loin, cover it to keep warm, and allow it to rest for 10 minutes before you slice it into servings. Skim any fat from the surface of the cider-applesauce sauce from the slow cooker and then ladle it over the slices.

Sauced-Up Applesauce
To add an extra kick to the pan juices from the Apple Cider Pork Loin recipe, stir in 3 tablespoons of prepared horseradish and 2 teaspoons of fresh lemon juice.

Apricot Pork Sirloin Roast

A pork sirloin roast is low in fat, yet it cooks up tender and moist. If you prefer gravy instead of sauce, simply mix the reduced pan juices with some heavy cream.

1. Add the prunes and apricots to the slow cooker. Pour the boiling water over the dried fruit; cover and let set for 15 minutes.

2. Add the chicken broth, wine or apple juice, pork sirloin roast, and sweet potatoes. Salt and pepper to taste. Cover and cook on low for 5–6 hours or until the internal temperature of the roast is 160°F.

3. Remove the meat and sweet potatoes from the cooker; cover and keep warm.

4. Turn the cooker to high. Use an immersion blender to purée the fruit. In a small bowl, mix the cornstarch into the cold water. Once the liquid in the slow cooker begins to bubble around the edges, slowly whisk in the cornstarch liquid. Reduce the heat to low and simmer the sauce for several minutes, stirring occasionally, until thickened. Place the pork roast on a serving platter and carve into eight slices. Arrange the sweet potatoes around the pork. Ladle the sauce over the meat. Serve immediately.

Serves 8

Ingredients:
15 pitted prunes (dried plums)
12 dried apricots, pitted
½ cup boiling water
1 cup chicken broth
1 cup dry white wine or apple juice
1 (3½-pound) pork sirloin roast, trimmed of fat and silver skin
4 large sweet potatoes, peeled and quartered
Salt and freshly ground pepper, to taste
1 tablespoon cornstarch
2 tablespoons cold water

Ham and Sweet Potatoes

Serve this dish with a tossed salad, some applesauce, a steamed vegetable, and some warm dinner rolls or buttered rye bread toast.

Ingredients:

1 (20-ounce) can pineapple tidbits

1 (2-pound) boneless ham steak

3 large sweet potatoes, peeled and diced

1 large sweet onion, peeled and diced

½ cup orange marmalade

2 cloves of garlic, peeled and minced

¼ teaspoon freshly ground black pepper

½ teaspoon dried parsley

Optional: 1 tablespoon brown sugar

1. Drain the pineapple, reserving 2 tablespoons of the juice.

2. Trim the ham of any fat and cut it into bite-sized pieces. Add the pineapple, 2 tablespoons pineapple juice, and ham to the slow cooker along with the sweet potatoes, onion, marmalade, garlic, black pepper, parsley, and brown sugar if using. Stir to combine. Cover and cook on low for 6 hours.

Bratwurst in Beer

You can serve the bratwurst and sauerkraut over mashed potatoes or on warmed bakery hot dog buns slathered with stone-ground mustard. The beer you use is your choice, or you can substitute apple juice or cider if you prefer.

Ingredients:

8 precooked bratwurst sausages

2 large sweet onions, peeled and sliced

1 (2-pound) bag of sauerkraut, rinsed and drained

1 (12-ounce) bottle of beer

1. Add the sausages and onions to the slow cooker. Cover and cook on high for 30 minutes or until the sausage begins to render its fat and the onions are limp.

2. Add the sauerkraut and beer to the slow cooker. Cover and cook on low for 3 hours.

3. Optional cooking step: For added flavor, you can brown the bratwurst on the grill or under the broiler before serving.

Pork Steaks in Apple and Prune Sauce

*Serve this dish over some mashed potatoes (available premade
in most supermarket refrigerator or freezer cases) and
alongside some steam-in-the-bag green beans.*

Serves 6

Ingredients:
12 pitted prunes (dried plums)
*3 pounds boneless pork
    steaks, trimmed of fat*
*2 Granny Smith apples,
    peeled, cored, and sliced*
*¾ cup dry white wine or
    apple juice*
¾ cup heavy cream
*Salt and freshly ground
    pepper, to taste*
1 tablespoon red currant jelly
Optional: 1 tablespoon butter

1. Add the prunes, pork steak, apple slices, wine or apple juice, and cream to a 4-quart or larger slow cooker. Salt and pepper to taste. Cover and cook on low for 6 hours.

2. Now you have a choice: You can either remove the meat and fruit to a serving platter and keep warm or you can remove the meat, skim the fat from the liquid in the slow cooker, and use an immersion blender to blend the fruit into the creamy broth.

3. Cook uncovered on high for 30 minutes or until the pan juices begin to bubble around the edges. Reduce the setting to low or simmer, and cook for 15 more minutes or until the mixture is reduced by half and thickened. Whisk in the red currant jelly. Taste for seasoning and add more salt and pepper if needed. Whisk in the butter a teaspoon at a time if you want a richer, glossier sauce. Ladle the sauce over the meat or pour it into a heated gravy boat.

Roast Pork with Cinnamon Cranberries and Sweet Potatoes

Serves 6

Ingredients:

1 (3-pound) pork butt roast

Salt and freshly ground pepper, to taste

1 (16-ounce) can sweetened whole cranberries

1 medium onion, peeled and diced

¼ cup orange marmalade

½ cup orange juice

¼ teaspoon ground cinnamon

¼ teaspoon ground cloves

3 large sweet potatoes, peeled and quartered

Optional: 1 tablespoon cornstarch

Optional: 2 tablespoons cold water

You can substitute peach marmalade (Chapter 5) for the orange marmalade and orange juice called for in this recipe. Doing so will add a subtle taste of peaches and pineapple to the dish, too.

1. Place the pork, fat side up, in the slow cooker. Salt and pepper to taste. Combine the cranberries, onion, marmalade, orange juice, cinnamon, and cloves in a large measuring cup; stir to mix and then pour over the pork roast. Arrange the sweet potatoes around the meat. Cover and cook on low for 6 hours or until the pork is tender and pulls apart easily.

2. To serve with a thickened sauce, transfer the meat and sweet potatoes to a serving platter. Cover and keep warm. Skim any fat off of the pan juices. (You'll want about 2 cups of juice remaining in the cooker.) Cover and cook on the high setting for 30 minutes, or until the pan liquids begin to bubble around the edges. In a coffee cup, combine the cornstarch with the water. Whisk into the liquid in the slow cooker. Reduce temperature setting to low and continue to cook and stir for an additional 2 minutes or the cornstarch flavor has cooked out of the sauce and it is thickened and bubbly.

Mexican Pork Roast

Serve this pork over rice and with Fat-Free Refried Beans (page 214) on the side, or in burritos (see sidebar below).

Serves 4

Ingredients:
1 tablespoon olive oil
1 large sweet onion, peeled and sliced
1 medium carrot, peeled and finely diced
1 jalapeño pepper, seeded and minced
1 clove of garlic, peeled and minced
Salt, to taste
¼ teaspoon dried Mexican oregano
¼ teaspoon ground coriander
¼ teaspoon freshly ground black pepper
1 (3-pound) pork shoulder or butt roast
1 cup chicken broth

1. Add the olive oil, onion, carrot, and jalapeño to the slow cooker. Stir to coat the vegetables in the oil. Cover and cook on high for 30 minutes or until the onions are softened. Stir in the garlic.

2. Add the salt, oregano, coriander, and black pepper to a bowl; stir to mix. Rub the spice mixture into the pork roast. Add the pork roast and broth to the slow cooker. Cover and cook on low for 6 hours or until the pork is tender and pulls apart easily.

3. Use a slotted spoon to remove the pork and vegetables to a serving platter. Cover and let rest for 10 minutes.

4. Increase the temperature of the slow cooker to high. Cook and reduce the pan juices by half.

5. Use two forks to shred the pork and mix it in with the cooked onion and jalapeño. Ladle the reduced pan juices over the pork.

Mexican Pork Roast Burritos

Warm 4 large flour tortillas. Spread refried beans on each tortilla. Divide the pork between the tortillas and top with salsa and, if desired, grated cheese, shredded lettuce, and sour cream. Roll and serve.

Asian Pork Ribs

Serves 6

Ingredients:
4 pounds country pork ribs
1¾ cups ketchup
¼ cup hoisin sauce
2 tablespoons honey
2 tablespoons white wine or rice vinegar
2 tablespoons soy sauce
¼ teaspoon five-spice powder
1 large sweet onion, peeled and diced
2 teaspoons fresh ginger, minced
1 clove of garlic, peeled and minced
2 teaspoons toasted sesame oil
Pinch dried red pepper flakes
Optional: 1 teaspoon cornstarch
Optional: 1 tablespoon cold water

If hoisin sauce isn't available, you can use all ketchup instead. If you prefer a hotter kick to the barbecue sauce, add more dried red pepper flakes or hot sauce to taste.

1. Cut the ribs into individual rib portions. Optional cooking step: Position the broiler rack about 6 inches from the source of the heat and preheat the broiler. Broil the ribs for 5 minutes on each side or until browned.

2. Add the ketchup, hoisin sauce, honey, vinegar, soy sauce, five-spice powder, onion, ginger, garlic, sesame oil, and dried red pepper flakes to the slow cooker; stir to mix. Transfer the ribs to the slow cooker, coating the ribs with the sauce as you do so. Cover and cook on low for 8 hours or until the ribs are tender.

3. Optional: If you want thicker sauce available to serve over the ribs, transfer the ribs to a platter and keep warm. Skim any surface fat from the sauce in the slow cooker. Cook, stirring occasionally, uncovered on high until the sauce is reduced to about 1 cup. Mix the cornstarch together with the cold water in a small bowl. Whisk into the sauce, and cook, gently stirring constantly, for 5 minutes or until the cornstarch taste is cooked out of the sauce and it is thickened enough to coat the back of a spoon. Either serve the sauce on the side or pour it over the ribs.

Country Pork Ribs

The heat in this sauce comes from the cinnamon, ginger, and allspice.
If you prefer a more hot and sweet sauce, add ⅛ teaspoon or
more of cayenne pepper or dried red pepper flakes.

Serves 4

Ingredients:
3 pounds country pork ribs
1 medium sweet onion,
     peeled and diced
½ cup maple syrup
2 tablespoons light brown
     sugar
2 tablespoons soy sauce
½ teaspoon ground
     cinnamon
½ teaspoon ground ginger
½ teaspoon ground allspice
3 cloves of garlic, peeled and
     minced
¼ teaspoon freshly ground
     black pepper
Optional: Cayenne pepper or
     dried red pepper flakes,
     to taste

1. Cut the ribs into individual ribs. Add the ribs and onion to the slow cooker.

2. Add the maple syrup, brown sugar, soy sauce, cinnamon, ginger, allspice, garlic, black pepper, and cayenne pepper or red pepper flakes, if using, to a bowl; stir to mix. Pour the maple syrup mixture into the slow cooker.

3. Cover and cook on low for 8 hours or until the meat is tender enough to pull away from the bone.

A Finger Foods Meal
Forego the silverware and serve Country Pork Ribs along with potato chips and an assortment of crudités (raw fresh vegetables like green onions, celery stalks, carrot sticks, bell pepper slices, etc.) and dip. Provide plenty of napkins!

Pacific Pork Cassoulet

Serves 4

Ingredients:

1 pound boneless pork
 shoulder

2 slices bacon

1 large onion, peeled and
 diced

2 cloves of garlic, peeled and
 minced

1 cup chicken broth

1 (15-ounce) can diced
 tomatoes

1 (15-ounce) can cannelloni
 beans, rinsed and
 drained

1 (1-pound) bag baby carrots

2 stalks celery, thinly sliced

Salt and freshly ground black
 pepper, to taste

Optional: 1½ teaspoons Mrs.
 Dash Onion and Herb
 Blend

---

*If you need more than 4 servings, a 4-quart slow cooker is large enough to
hold all of the ingredients if you double the recipe.*

1. Trim the pork of any fat, and cut it into bite-sized pieces. Cut the bacon into 1-inch pieces. Add the bacon to a nonstick skillet; cook over medium-high heat for 2 minutes or until it begins to render its fat. Add the pork and sauté for 5 minutes or until the pork is browned on all sides. Transfer the meat to the slow cooker.

2. Add the onion to the skillet; sauté for 3 minutes or until the onion is transparent. Add the garlic and sauté for 30 seconds. Transfer the onion and garlic to the slow cooker.

3. Add the remaining ingredients to the slow cooker. Cover and cook on low for 6 hours or until the pork is tender.

Skip the Browning

If you have Brown Stock (Chapter 9) on hand, you can substitute ¼ cup of the chicken broth for an equal amount of the Brown Stock. This will impart the browned meat flavor to the Cassoulet. Likewise, if you have pork broth made from pork that had been browned prior to slow cooking it, you can substitute ¼ cup of that instead.

Chapter 11
Ground Meat

Turkey Meatloaf

Serves 6

Ingredients:
2 pounds ground turkey
1 large yellow onion, peeled
  and diced
2 stalks of celery, finely diced
1 green bell pepper, seeded
  and diced
2 cloves of garlic, peeled and
  minced
2 large eggs
1 cup fresh bread crumbs or
  cracker crumbs
Salt and freshly ground black
  pepper, to taste
Optional: 6 slices bacon
½ cup ketchup
1 tablespoon brown sugar
Optional: Chili powder, to
  taste

Instead of making the meatloaf entirely from ground turkey, you can use a combination of ground beef, ground pork, and ground turkey.

1. Add the ground turkey, onion, celery, bell pepper, garlic, eggs, bread crumbs, salt, and pepper to a large bowl; mix well with your hands. Form into a loaf to fit the size (round or oval) of your slow cooker.

2. Line the slow cooker with two pieces of heavy-duty aluminum foil long enough to reach up both sides of the slow cooker and over the edge, crossing one piece over the other. Place a piece of nonstick foil the size of the bottom of the slow cooker crock inside the crossed pieces of foil to form a platform for the meatloaf. (This is to make it easier to lift the meatloaf out of the slow cooker.)

3. Place three pieces of bacon over the top of the nonstick foil. Put the meat loaf over the top of the bacon. Spread the ketchup over the top of the meatloaf. Sprinkle the brown sugar and chili powder, if using, over the top of the ketchup. Place the remaining three slices of bacon over the top of the seasoned ketchup. Cover and cook on low for 7 hours or until the internal temperature of the meatloaf registers 165°F.

4. Lift the meatloaf out of the slow cooker and place it on a cooling rack. Allow it to rest for 20 minutes before transferring it to a serving platter and slicing it.

Slow Cooker Liner
Instead of placing two pieces of heavy-duty aluminum foil across each other and over the sides of the slow cooker, you can instead line it with a Reynolds Slow Cooker Liner (www.reynoldspkg.com) and then place the nonstick foil piece inside the liner.

Barbecue Meatloaf

This recipe assumes you're using commercial barbecue sauce, which is usually thicker than homemade sauce. The brown sugar sprinkled over the top of the meatloaf helps caramelize the sauce.

1. Add the ground beef, ground pork, eggs, onion, salt, pepper, oatmeal, parsley, and 1 cup of the barbecue sauce to a large bowl; mix well with your hands. Form into a loaf to fit the size (round or oval) of your slow cooker.

2. Line the slow cooker with two pieces of heavy-duty aluminum foil long enough to reach up both sides of the slow cooker and over the edge, crossing one piece over the other. Place a piece of nonstick foil the size of the bottom of the slow cooker crock inside the crossed pieces of foil or slow cooker liner to form a platform for the meatloaf. (This is to make it easier to lift the meatloaf out of the slow cooker.)

3. Put the meatloaf over the top of the nonstick foil. Spread the remaining ½ cup of barbecue sauce over the top of the meatloaf. Sprinkle the brown sugar and Mrs. Dash Extra Spicy Seasoning Blend, if using, over the top of the ketchup. Cover and cook on low for 8 hours or until the internal temperature of the meatloaf registers 165°F.

4. Lift the meatloaf out of the slow cooker and place it on a cooling rack. Allow it to rest for 20 minutes before transferring it to a serving platter and slicing it.

Serves 8

Ingredients:
2 pounds lean ground beef
½ pound lean ground pork
2 large eggs
1 large yellow onion, peeled and diced
Salt and freshly ground pepper, to taste
1½ cups quick-cooking oatmeal
1 teaspoon dried parsley
1½ cups barbecue sauce
1 tablespoon brown sugar
Optional: Mrs. Dash Extra Spicy Seasoning Blend, to taste

Zesty Meatloaf

Serves 8

Ingredients:

2 pounds lean ground beef

1 large egg

1 (10½-ounce) can condensed French onion soup

Salt and freshly ground pepper, to taste

2 cups herb-seasoned stuffing mix or crushed seasoned croutons

1 (15-ounce) can tomato sauce

2 tablespoons Worcestershire sauce

⅓ cup brown sugar, packed

2 tablespoons red wine or balsamic vinegar

Optional: Mrs. Dash Extra Spicy Seasoning Blend, to taste

As an alternative, you can form the meatloaf mixture into about fifty cocktail-size meatballs, bake at 350°F for 18 minutes, and then add them with the sauce (in Step 2) to the slow cooker; cover and cook on low for 3 hours.

1. Add the ground beef, egg, onion soup, salt, pepper, and stuffing mix or crushed croutons to a large bowl; mix well with your hands. Form into a loaf to fit the size (round or oval) of your slow cooker.

2. Put the meatloaf in the slow cooker. Add the tomato sauce, Worcestershire sauce, brown sugar, vinegar, and Mrs. Dash Extra Spicy Seasoning Blend, if using, to a bowl and stir to mix. Pour over the meatloaf. Cover and cook on low for 7 hours or until the internal temperature of the meatloaf registers 165°F. Slice and serve with the sauce from the slow cooker.

Taco Chili

Serves 8

Ingredients:

3 pounds lean ground beef

1 (1.2-ounce) package taco seasoning mix

2 (15-ounce) cans chunky Mexican-style tomatoes

1 (15-ounce) can red kidney beans

1 (15-ounce) can whole kernel corn

Note that you don't drain any of the canned ingredients used in this recipe. You include the entire contents of each can.

1. Brown the ground beef in a large nonstick skillet over medium heat, breaking apart the meat as you do so. Remove and discard any fat rendered from the meat before transferring it to the slow cooker.

2. Stir in the taco seasoning mix, tomatoes, kidney beans, and corn. Cover and cook on low for 4 to 6 hours.

Pineapple Sausage Meatballs

If you slow-cook meatballs in sauce for longer than 3 hours, you run the risk that they'll break apart and become a part of the sauce. Serve this dish over cooked rice.

1. Add the drained crushed pineapple, dried onion, ketchup, 1 cup of the barbecue sauce, brown sugar, chili powder, and Mrs. Dash Extra Spicy Seasoning Blend, if using, to the slow cooker. Cover and cook on low while you make the meatballs.

2. Preheat the oven to 425°F. Add the remaining cup of barbecue sauce, ground beef, ground pork, egg, diced onion, salt and pepper, oatmeal, and parsley to a large bowl; use hands to mix. Form into twenty-four meatballs. Place on a baking sheet; bake for 10 minutes or until browned on the outside but still rare on the inside.

3. Add the browned meatballs to the sauce. Cover and cook on low for 3 hours.

Serves 8

Ingredients:
1 (20-ounce) can crushed pineapple packed in juice, drained
¼ cup dried minced onion
1 cup ketchup
2 cups barbecue sauce
1 tablespoon brown sugar
1 teaspoon chili powder
Optional: Mrs. Dash Extra Spicy Seasoning Blend, to taste
1 pound lean ground beef
1 pound lean ground pork
2 large eggs
1 large yellow onion, peeled and diced
Salt and freshly ground pepper, to taste
1½ cups quick-cooking oatmeal
1 teaspoon dried parsley

Meatballs in Chipotle Sauce

Ingredients:
1 tablespoon vegetable oil
1 large onion, thinly sliced
1½ teaspoon garlic powder
1 tablespoon chili powder
¼ teaspoon dried Mexican
    oregano
2 canned chipotle chili
    peppers in adobo sauce
1 (28-ounce) can crushed
    tomatoes
1 cup chicken broth
Salt and freshly ground black
    pepper, to taste
1½ pounds lean ground beef
½ pound ground pork
1 large egg
1 small white onion, peeled
    and diced
1 tablespoon chili powder
1½ teaspoons garlic powder
10 soda crackers, crumbled

Serve these meatballs with some of the sauce over cooked rice. Top with guacamole and sour cream, if desired, or serve along with an avocado salad.

1. Add the vegetable oil and sliced onions to the slow cooker; stir to coat the onions in the oil. Cover and cook on high for 30 minutes or until the onions are transparent. Stir in the garlic powder, chili powder, and oregano. Cover and cook on high for 15 minutes. Stir in the chipotles in adobo sauce, tomatoes, broth, salt, and pepper. Cover and cook on high while you prepare the meatballs.

2. Preheat the oven to 425°F. Add the ground beef, ground pork, egg, diced onion, chili powder, garlic powder, and crumbled crackers to a large bowl; use hands to mix. Form into eighteen meatballs. Place on a baking sheet; bake for 10 minutes or until browned on the outside but still rare on the inside.

3. Use an immersion blender to purée the sauce in the slow cooker. Add the browned meatballs to the sauce. Cover and cook on low for 3 hours.

For Hotter Sauce
You can add extra heat to the sauce by adding more than 2 of the canned chipotles or some Mrs. Dash Extra Spicy Seasoning Blend.

Cola-Cravin' Ground Beef

Browning ground beef before it's added to the slow cooker lets you improve its flavor by rendering and removing the fat out of the meat and replacing it with extra-virgin olive oil. Serve this sauce over macaroni or rigatoni; it's perfect for those who prefer to top pasta dishes with grated Cheddar cheese.

1. Brown the ground beef in a large nonstick skillet over medium heat, breaking apart the meat as you do so. Remove and discard any fat rendered from the meat.

2. Stir in the oil and onion; sauté for 5 minutes or until the onion is transparent. Stir in the garlic. Transfer the meat mixture to the slow cooker. Add the cola and pasta sauce. Stir to combine. Cover and cook on low for 4 hours or longer.

Serves 8

Ingredients:
3 pounds lean ground beef
2 tablespoons extra-virgin olive oil
1 large sweet onion, peeled and diced
2 cloves of garlic, peeled and minced
1 cup Coca-Cola
1 (26-ounce) jar pasta sauce

Sloppy Joes

The longer you slow-cook Sloppy Joe's, the more the flavors develop. Serve on hamburger or other soft sandwich rolls.

1. Brown the ground beef in a large nonstick skillet over medium heat, breaking apart the meat as you do so. Remove and discard any fat rendered from the meat.

2. Stir in the oil and onion; sauté for 5 minutes or until the onion is transparent. Transfer the cooked ground beef and onions to the slow cooker.

3. Stir in the remaining ingredients. Cover and cook on low for 4 hours or longer.

Serves 12

Ingredients:
3 pounds lean ground beef
2 tablespoons extra-virgin olive oil
1 large onion, peeled and diced
1 (15-ounce) can diced tomatoes
1 cup ketchup
¼ cup brown sugar
1 tablespoon apple cider vinegar
1 tablespoon balsamic vinegar
2 tablespoons Worcestershire sauce
1 tablespoon garlic powder
2 teaspoons chili powder
¼ teaspoon cinnamon
⅛ teaspoon ground cloves
Salt and freshly ground black pepper, to taste

Tamale Pie

Serves 8

Ingredients:

2 pounds lean ground beef

1 large white onion, peeled and diced

3 tablespoons chili powder

Nonstick spray

1½ cups cornmeal

2½ cups whole milk

4 large eggs

Salt, freshly ground black pepper, and ground cumin, to taste

2 (16-ounce) cans stewed tomatoes

2 (14-ounce) cans pitted black olives, drained

4 cups frozen whole kernel corn, thawed

2 cups (8 ounces) Cheddar cheese, grated

1 cup (4 ounces) Monterey jack cheese, grated

For a flavor boost, drizzle some extra-virgin olive oil over each serving.

1. Brown the ground beef together with the onion in a large nonstick skillet over medium heat, breaking apart the meat as you do so. Remove and discard any fat rendered from the meat. Stir in the chili powder; sauté for 2 minutes.

2. Treat the crock of the slow cooker with nonstick spray. Transfer the ground beef mixture to the slow cooker.

3. Add the cornmeal, milk, eggs, salt, pepper, and cumin to a large bowl and whisk until smooth. Coarsely chop the tomatoes and drained black olives. Stir the tomatoes, black olives, and corn into the cornmeal mixture. Pour into the slow cooker. Stir to mix together with the ground beef. Cover and cook on high for 5 hours or until the mixture is set in the center.

4. Sprinkle the cheeses over the top of the tamale pie. Cover and cook on high for 10 minutes or until the cheese is melted. Spoon directly from the slow cooker to serve.

Hot Tamale Pie
Add heat to the Tamale Pie by including seeded and diced jalapeño or other hot peppers to taste when you fry the ground beef and onions in Step 1.

Frito Pie

You can easily increase the number of servings in this recipe by adding another can of pinto beans or serving it over a large helping of Fritos. Choose mild, medium, or sharp Cheddar according to your preference.

1. Brown the ground beef in a large nonstick skillet over medium heat, breaking apart the meat as you do so. Remove and discard any fat rendered from the meat.

2. Stir in the oil and onion, garlic powder, chili powder, cumin, salt, and pepper; sauté for 5 minutes or until the onion is transparent. Transfer the ground beef mixture to the slow cooker.

3. Stir in the tomatoes and pinto beans. Cover and cook on low for 5 to 8 hours. (When you taste the chili for seasoning, keep in mind that it'll be served over salty corn chips.)

4. To serve, place a (1-ounce or more) handful of Fritos on each plate. Ladle the chili over the Fritos. Top with grated cheese and diced green onion if desired.

Restaurant-Style Taco Pie

For each serving, tear open (on the side, not the top) an individual serving–sized (1-ounce) bag of Fritos and place it flat on a serving plate. Ladle the chili into the bag and over the corn chips.

Serves 12

Ingredients:

3 cups lean ground beef

2 tablespoons extra-virgin olive oil

1 large white onion, peeled and diced

2½ teaspoons garlic powder

3 tablespoons chili powder

4 teaspoons ground cumin

Salt and freshly ground black pepper, to taste

2 (28-ounce) cans diced tomatoes

1 (15-ounce) can pinto beans, rinsed and drained

1 (12-ounce) bag Fritos original corn chips

4 cups (1 pound) Cheddar cheese, grated

Optional: Green onions, diced

Italian Meatballs

There are no eggs and only a small amount of bread crumbs in these meatballs so they'll stand up to the long cooking time without falling apart. You can serve these meatballs and the sauce over cooked rice or pasta, or in meatball sandwiches.

Serves 8

Ingredients:

4 tablespoons extra-virgin or light olive oil
1 large sweet onion, peeled and diced
4 cloves of garlic, peeled and minced
2 (28-ounce) cans plum tomatoes, drained and chopped
1 (6-ounce) can tomato paste
1 cup chicken broth
Salt and freshly ground black pepper, to taste
½ teaspoon sugar
Pinch dried red pepper flakes
1 pound lean ground beef
½ pound ground veal
½ pound lean ground pork
⅓ cup fresh bread crumbs
¼ cup freshly grated Parmesan-Reggiano or Romano cheese
6 tablespoons fresh Italian parsley, minced

1. Add the oil and onion to the slow cooker; stir to coat the onions in the oil. Cover and cook on high for 30 minutes or until the onion is transparent. Stir in 2 cloves of the minced garlic, tomatoes, tomato paste, broth, salt, pepper, sugar, and dried red pepper flakes. Cover and cook on high while you make the meatballs.

2. Add the remaining 2 cloves of minced garlic, beef, veal, pork, bread crumbs, cheese, parsley, and salt and pepper, to taste, to a bowl; use your hands to mix. Shape into sixteen equal-sized meatballs. Add the meatballs to the slow cooker. Reduce the temperature of the slow cooker to low; cover and cook for 7 hours or until the internal temperature of the meatballs is 160°F.

Dealing with the Fat
Some fat will be rendered from the Italian meatballs during the slow-cooking process. It will rise to the surface, so skim it from the sauce and discard. Carefully ladle the meatballs from the slow cooker before you whisk the sauce to evenly distribute the onions and other ingredients, or use an immersion blender if you prefer a smoother sauce.

Stuffed Onions

Serve with a salad and a steamed vegetable.

1. Cutting across the onions (not from bottom to top), cut the onions in half. Scoop out the onion cores.

2. Chop the onion cores and add to the ground beef or lamb, allspice, dill, 2 tablespoons of the lemon juice, parsley, salt, pepper, and egg; mix well.

3. Fill the onion halves with the meat mixture. (The meat will overflow the onions and form a mound on top.) Sprinkle the flour over the top of the meat.

4. Add the oil to a deep 3½-quart nonstick skillet or electric skillet and bring it to temperature over medium heat. Add the onions to the pan, meat side down, and sauté for 10 minutes or until browned.

5. Arrange the onions in the slow cooker so that the meat side is up. Mix the other tablespoon of lemon juice into the broth; pour the broth around the onions. Cover and cook on high for 4 hours or low for 8 hours or until the onion is soft and the meat is cooked through.

Serves 4

Ingredients:
4 medium onions, peeled
1 pound ground beef or lamb
¼ teaspoon ground allspice
¼ teaspoon dried dill
3 tablespoons fresh lemon juice
2 teaspoons dried parsley
Salt and freshly ground black pepper, to taste
1 large egg
1–2 tablespoons all-purpose flour
2 tablespoons extra-virgin olive oil
1 cup chicken broth

Chapter 12
Fish and Seafood

Fish Stock

Chefs use fish heads to make Fish Stock. Most home cooks simply use whitefish. You can add a French flair to fish stock by substituting 1 cup of dry white wine or ¾ cup of dry vermouth for an equal amount of water.

Yields about 4 cups

Ingredients:
2 pounds bone-in whitefish (flounder, halibut, etc.)
1 large onion, peeled and thinly sliced
1 tablespoon fresh lemon juice
4 cups water
¼ teaspoon sea salt

1. Add the fish, onion, lemon juice, water, and salt to the slow cooker. Cover and cook on low for 4 to 8 hours.

2. Strain through a fine sieve or fine wire-mesh strainer. Reserve the cooked fish for another use if desired. Discard the bones and onions. Refrigerate in a covered container and use within 2 days, or freeze for up to 3 months.

Warm Fish Fillet and Potato Salad

If you use meaty bone-in fish pieces to make Fish Stock, you can shred and cube the fish removed from those bones and add that fish over the top of some warm, boiled sliced red potatoes, diced red onion, and minced parsley. Dress with commercial red wine vinaigrette or one made using fresh lemon juice, Dijon mustard, salt, pepper, and extra-virgin olive oil.

Seafood Stock

This recipe calls for using the shells only because the amount of time it takes to slow-cook the stock would result in seafood that would be too tough to eat.

Yields about 4 cups

Ingredients:
2 pounds shrimp, crab, or
    lobster shells
1 large onion, peeled and
    thinly sliced
1 tablespoon fresh lemon
    juice
4 cups water
¼ teaspoon sea salt

1. Add the seafood shells, onion, lemon juice, water, and salt to the slow cooker. Cover and cook on low for 4 to 8 hours.

2. Strain through a fine sieve or fine wire-mesh strainer. Discard the shells and onions. Refrigerate in a covered container and use within 2 days or freeze for up to 3 months.

Fish or Seafood Stock in a Hurry

For each cup of seafood or fish stock called for in a recipe, you can substitute ¼ cup of bottled clam juice and ¾ cup of water. Just keep in mind that the clam juice is very salty, so adjust any recipe in which you use it accordingly.

Poached Salmon

Serves 4

Ingredients:
1 tablespoon butter
4 thin slices sweet onion
1½ cups water
1 tablespoon lemon juice
1 sprig fresh dill
4 (6-ounce) salmon fillets
Sea salt, to taste
Optional: 1 lemon, quartered
Optional: Dill Sauce (recipe
     below)

To add more flavor to the poached salmon, you can replace ½ cup of the water with an equal amount of dry white wine. Another option is to add some fresh parsley stems (without the leaves) to the poaching liquid.

1. Use the butter to grease the bottom and halfway up the side of the slow cooker. Arrange the onion slices over the bottom of the slow cooker, pressing them into the butter so that they stay in place. Pour in the water. Cover and cook on high for 30 minutes.

2. Place a salmon fillet over each onion slice. Cover and cook on high for 30 minutes or until the salmon is opaque. Transfer the (well-drained) fillets to individual serving plates or to a serving platter. Salt to taste. Garnish with lemon wedges and serve with Dill Sauce (see below) if desired.

Dill Sauce
Peel and grate 1 English cucumber; add the grated cucumber to a bowl, lightly salt it, and set it aside for 1 hour. Drain any liquid off the cucumber and then squeeze it dry with paper towels. Stir in 1½ cups sour cream, ½ cup mayonnaise, 1 tablespoon fresh lemon juice, 1 small minced clove of garlic, sea salt to taste, and ⅔ cup fresh, finely chopped dill. Cover with plastic wrap, chill for an hour, and then serve alongside the Poached Salmon.

Crab Supreme

You can serve Crab Supreme directly from the slow cooker as a dip. Or you can use it as a warm sandwich filling by slathering it on slices of French bread. Serve the sandwiches along with a tossed greens and cucumber salad or coleslaw mix dressed with Lemon Dill Dressing (recipe below).

Yields 8 cups

Ingredients:
1 quart (full-fat) mayonnaise
2 cups (full-fat) sour cream
¼ cup dry sherry or chicken broth
3 tablespoons fresh lemon juice
¼ cup fresh Italian parsley, minced
2 pounds fresh crabmeat
Salt and freshly ground white pepper, to taste
Hot sauce, to taste

1. Add the mayonnaise, sour cream, sherry or broth, and lemon juice to the slow cooker. Whisk to mix. Cover and cook on low for 2 hours.

2. Stir in the parsley. Pick over the crabmeat to remove any shells and cartilage, and then stir it into the mayonnaise mixture in the slow cooker. Cover and cook on low for 30 minutes or until the crab is heated through. Taste for seasoning and add salt, white pepper, and hot sauce if desired.

Lemon Dill Dressing
To make 1½ cups of dressing, in a bowl whisk together 1 cup mayonnaise, ¼ cup buttermilk, 2 tablespoons chopped fresh dill, 1 tablespoon minced fresh Italian parsley, 1 tablespoon grated lemon zest, 2 teaspoons fresh lemon juice, 1 small minced clove of garlic, and salt and freshly ground pepper to taste. Cover bowl and refrigerate until chilled. (The dressing will thicken as it chills.)

Fish "Bake"

Ingredients:

2 tablespoons olive oil

4 flounder or cod fillets

1 clove of garlic, peeled and minced

1 small onion, peeled and thinly sliced

1 green bell pepper, seeded and diced

1 (14½-ounce) can stewed tomatoes

½ teaspoon dried basil

½ teaspoon dried oregano

1 teaspoon dried parsley

Salt and freshly ground black pepper, to taste

2 tablespoons freshly grated Parmesan-Reggiano cheese

The stewed tomatoes helps prevent the fish from overcooking and makes a sauce perfect for serving the fish over cooked couscous, pasta, rice, or steamed cabbage, or alongside polenta.

1. Add the oil to the slow cooker. Use the oil to coat the bottom of and the sides of the crock.

2. Rinse the fish fillets and pat dry with paper towels. Add in a single layer over the oil.

3. Evenly distribute the garlic, onion, and green bell pepper over the fish. Pour the stewed tomatoes over the fish. Evenly sprinkle the basil, oregano, parsley, salt, pepper, and cheese over the tomatoes.

4. Cover and cook on low for 6 hours or until the fish is opaque and flakes apart.

Salmon Loaf

If you're using saltine crackers, add dill pickles to Salmon Loaf. If you prefer butter-style crackers, use sweet pickles. Serve it as you would meatloaf, topped with Creamy Dill Sauce (see recipe below) instead of gravy.

Serves 4

Ingredients:
2 cans (7½-ounce) red sockeye salmon, drained, skin removed
¼ cup crackers, finely crushed
1 small onion, peeled and minced
1 large egg
2 tablespoons mayonnaise
1 tablespoon fresh lemon juice
1 tablespoon fresh parsley, minced
1 tablespoon fresh dill, chopped
½ teaspoon freshly ground black pepper
Optional: 2 tablespoons pickles, finely minced

1. Add the salmon, crackers, onion, egg, mayonnaise, lemon juice, parsley, dill, pepper, and pickles, if using, to a bowl. Gently mix with a fork until evenly combined.

2. Place two long pieces of heavy-duty aluminum foil across each other in the crock of the slow cooker. Press into the crock and top with a piece of nonstick foil shaped to hold the salmon loaf. Use your hands to shape the salmon loaf and place it on top of the nonstick foil.

3. Cover the slow cooker, tucking the ends of the heavy-duty foil under lid. Cook on low for 6 to 8 hours or on high for 3 to 4 hours or until the salmon loaf is cooked through and set. Turn off the slow cooker, remove the lid, and let the salmon loaf stand for 15 minutes. Use the heavy-duty foil as handles to lift the loaf out of the slow cooker. Transfer the loaf to a serving plate. Slice and serve with Creamy Dill Sauce if desired.

Creamy Dill Sauce

Melt 1 tablespoon of butter in a nonstick skillet over medium heat. Whisk in 1 tablespoon flour, ¼ teaspoon sea salt, and ¼ teaspoon freshly ground black pepper. Slowly whisk in 1 cup milk and 2 tablespoons minced fresh dill. Stirring constantly, bring to a boil and boil for 1 minute; lower heat and simmer and stir until the mixture is thick enough to coat the back of a spoon. Serve over the Salmon Loaf.

Cioppino

Serve Cioppino with warm sourdough bread or ladled over cooked spaghetti. You can substitute any nonoily fish (such as red snapper fillets with the skin removed) for the cod.

Serves 6

Ingredients:

2 tablespoons olive oil
1 large sweet onion, peeled and diced
2 stalks celery, finely diced
2 cloves of garlic, peeled and minced
3 cups bottled clam juice or fish stock
2 cups water
1 (28-ounce) can diced or peeled Italian tomatoes
1 cup Zinfandel or other dry red wine
2 teaspoons dried parsley
1 teaspoon dried basil
1 teaspoon dried thyme
Dried red pepper flakes, to taste
1 teaspoon sugar
1 bay leaf
1 pound cod, cut into 1-inch pieces
½ pound raw shrimp, peeled and deveined
½ pound scallops
Sea salt and freshly ground black pepper, to taste

1. Add the oil, onion, and celery to the slow cooker. Stir to mix the vegetables together with the oil. Cover and cook on high for 30 minutes or until the onions are transparent.

2. Add the clam juice or fish stock, water, tomatoes, wine, parsley, basil, thyme, red pepper flakes, sugar, and bay leaf. Stir to combine. Cover, reduce the slow cooker setting to low, and cook for 5 hours.

3. If you used whole peeled tomatoes, use a spoon to break them apart. Gently stir in the cod, shrimp, and scallops. Increase the slow cooker setting to high. Cover and cook for 30 minutes or until the seafood is cooked through. Ladle into soup bowls and serve immediately.

Almond-Stuffed Flounder

Making this dish in the slow cooker lets you layer the fish and stuffing rather than stuffing and rolling the fillets. You can substitute sole for the flounder. Serve with warm dinner rolls, a tossed salad, and cooked wild rice.

1. Treat the crock of the slow cooker with nonstick spray. Rinse the fish and pat dry with paper towels. Lay 2 fillets flat in the slow cooker. Sprinkle the grated cheese, almonds, and chives (if using) over the fillets. Place the remaining fillets on top. Sprinkle paprika over the fish fillets. Pour the wine around the fish.

2. Add the butter and carrots to a microwave-safe bowl or measuring cup. Cover and microwave on high for 1 minute; stir and microwave on high for 1 more minute. Stir in the flour, tarragon, salt, and pepper. Whisk in the milk. Cover and microwave on high for 1 minute. Stir in the cream. Pour the sauce over the fish.

3. Cover and cook on low for 2 hours or until the fish is cooked through, the cheese is melted, and the sauce is thickened. Sprinkle with additional paprika before serving if desired. Turn off the slow cooker and let rest for 15 minutes. To serve, use a knife to cut through all layers into four wedges. Spoon each wedge onto a plate (so that there is fish and filling in each serving).

Serves 4

Ingredients:
Nonstick spray
4 (4-ounce) fresh or frozen
    flounder fillets
1 cup (4 ounces) Swiss cheese,
    grated
½ cup slivered almonds
Optional: 1 tablespoon freeze-
    dried chives
Sweet paprika, to taste
Optional: ¼ cup dry white
    wine
1 tablespoon butter
½ cup carrot, grated
1 tablespoon all-purpose
    flour
¼ teaspoon dried tarragon
Sea salt, to taste
White pepper, to taste
½ cup milk
½ cup heavy cream

Etouffée

Serve Etouffé over cooked rice.

Serves 6

Ingredients:

2 tablespoons vegetable oil

1 large onion, peeled and diced

6 scallions

2 stalks celery, finely diced

1 green bell pepper, seeded and diced

1 jalapeño, seeded and diced

2 cloves of garlic, peeled and minced

3 tablespoons tomato paste

3 (15-ounce) cans diced tomatoes

Salt, to taste

½ teaspoon dried basil

½ teaspoon dried oregano

½ teaspoon dried thyme

¼ teaspoon cayenne pepper

1 pound raw shrimp, peeled and deveined

1 pound scallops, quartered

2 teaspoons cornstarch

1 tablespoon cold water

Hot sauce, to taste

1. Add the oil and onion to the slow cooker. Clean the scallions and chop the white parts and about 1 inch of the greens. Add to the slow cooker along with the celery, green bell pepper, and jalapeño. Stir to coat the vegetables in the oil. Cover and cook on high for 30 minutes or until the vegetables are soft.

2. Stir in the garlic and tomato paste. Cover and cook on high for 15 minutes.

3. Stir in the tomatoes, salt, basil, oregano, thyme, and cayenne pepper. Reduce the heat setting of the slow cooker to low; cover and cook for 6 hours.

4. Stir in the shrimp and scallops. Increase the heat setting of the slow cooker to high, cover, and cook for 15 minutes.

5. Add the cornstarch and water to a small bowl. Stir to mix. Remove any lumps if necessary. Uncover the slow cooker and stir in the cornstarch mixture. Cook and stir for 5 minutes, or until the mixture is thickened and the cornstarch flavor is cooked out. Stir in hot sauce, to taste.

Jambalaya

This is a one-pot main dish that you can serve along with a tossed salad and garlic toast, crackers, or corn bread. Have hot sauce at the table for those who wish to add it.

1. Add the oil, kielbasa, onion, red bell pepper, and celery to the slow cooker. Stir to coat the vegetables in the oil. Cover and, stirring halfway through, cook on high for 45 minutes, or until the onion is transparent. Stir in the garlic and rice.

2. Cut the chicken into bite-sized pieces and stir in with the other ingredients in the slow cooker. Cover and cook on high for 15 minutes.

3. Add the tomatoes, clam juice or fish stock, water or chicken broth, Worcestershire sauce, thyme, oregano, sugar, dried red pepper flakes, and black pepper. Stir to mix. Reduce the heat setting of the slow cooker to low, cover, and cook for 6 hours or until the rice is tender.

4. Increase the temperature of the slow cooker to high. Stir in the shrimp and scallops. Cover and cook for 15 minutes or until the shrimp and scallops are cooked through. Taste for seasoning and add salt if needed.

Serves 8

Ingredients:
2 tablespoons olive oil
8 ounces kielbasa sausage, diced
1 large onion, peeled and diced
1 large red bell pepper, seeded and diced
2 stalks celery, finely diced
2 cloves of garlic, peeled and minced
1 cup converted long-grain rice
8 ounces boneless, skinless chicken thighs
1 (15-ounce) can diced tomatoes
1 cup bottled clam juice or fish stock
1 cup water or chicken broth
1 tablespoon Worcestershire sauce
½ teaspoon dried thyme
½ teaspoon dried oregano
½ teaspoon sugar
Dried red pepper flakes, to taste
¼ teaspoon freshly ground black pepper
8 ounces raw shrimp, peeled and deveined
8 ounces scallops, cut in half
Sea salt, to taste

Halibut in White Wine Sauce

Serves 4

Ingredients:
Nonstick spray
2 (12-ounce) packages frozen
    halibut fillets, thawed
¼ cup butter
2 tablespoons all-purpose
    flour
1 tablespoon sugar
¼ teaspoon sea salt
⅓ cup dry white wine
⅔ cup milk
Optional: Fresh dill
Optional: Lemon wedges

You can omit the wine in the sauce and replace it with milk. Then, when you taste the sauce for seasoning before you pour it over the fish, whisk in a little white wine or champagne vinegar and mayonnaise.

1. Treat the inside of the slow cooker with nonstick spray. Rinse the halibut and pat dry with paper towels. Place them in the slow cooker.

2. Melt the butter in a small saucepan. Stir in the flour, sugar, and salt. When well blended, whisk in the wine and milk. Cook and stir for 5 minutes (allowing the sauce to boil for at least 1 minute), or until thickened. Taste for seasoning and add additional salt if needed.

3. Pour the sauce over the fish. Cover and cook on high for 3 hours or until the fish is opaque and flakes easily with a fork. Garnish with fresh dill and lemon wedges if desired.

Shrimp in Creole Sauce

Serve Shrimp in Creole Sauce over cooked white or brown long-grain rice.

Serves 8

Ingredients:
3 tablespoons olive or
   vegetable oil
1 large yellow onion, peeled
   and diced
3 stalks celery, diced
1 large red bell pepper,
   seeded and diced
1 tablespoon butter
¼ cup all-purpose flour
1 (6-ounce) can tomato paste
2 (28-ounce) cans diced
   tomatoes
½ teaspoon dried thyme
1 bay leaf
⅛ teaspoon dried red pepper
   flakes
½ teaspoon light brown
   sugar
1 cup chicken broth
2 pounds raw shrimp, peeled
   and deveined
Sea salt and freshly ground
   black pepper, to taste
Optional: Hot sauce

1. Add 2 tablespoons of the oil and the onion, celery, and red bell pepper to the slow cooker. Stir to coat the vegetables in oil. Cover and cook on high for 30 minutes, or until the onion is transparent.

2. Add the remaining tablespoon of oil and the butter to a skillet over medium heat. When the butter is melted into the oil, stir in the flour. Stirring constantly, cook for 5 minutes or until the flour mixture turns a light golden brown.

3. Stir the browned flour mixture and the tomato paste into the slow cooker. Reduce the heat setting to low and add the tomatoes, thyme, bay leaf, dried red pepper flakes, brown sugar, and broth. Stir to combine. Cover and cook on low for 6 to 8 hours.

4. Remove and discard the bay leaf. Increase the heat setting to high. Stir in the shrimp, cover, and cook for 15 minutes or until the shrimp are pink and cooked through. Taste for seasoning; add salt and pepper, if needed, and hot sauce if desired. Serve immediately.

Poached Swordfish with Lemon-Parsley Sauce

Serves 4

Ingredients:
1 tablespoon butter
4 thin slices sweet onion
2 cups water
4 (6-ounce) swordfish steaks
Sea salt, to taste
1 lemon
2 tablespoons extra-virgin
    olive oil
2 teaspoons fresh lemon juice
¼ teaspoon Dijon mustard
Optional: Freshly ground
    white or black pepper, to
    taste
1 tablespoon fresh flat leaf
    parsley, minced

Swordfish steaks are usually cut thicker than most fish fillets, plus they're a firmer fish so it takes longer to poach them. You can speed up the poaching process a little if you remove the steaks from the refrigerator and put them in room-temperature water during the 30 minutes of Step 1.

1. Use the butter to grease the bottom and halfway up the side of the slow cooker. Arrange the onion slices over the bottom of the slow cooker, pressing them into the butter so that they stay in place. Pour in the water. Cover and cook on high for 30 minutes.

2. Place a swordfish steak over each onion slice. Salt to taste. Thinly slice the lemon; discard the seeds and place the slices over the fish. Cover and cook on high for 45 minutes or until the fish is opaque. Transfer the (well-drained) fish to individual serving plates or to a serving platter.

3. Add the oil, lemon juice, mustard, and white or black pepper, if using, to a bowl; whisk to combine. Immediately before serving the swordfish, fold in the parsley. Evenly divide the sauce between the swordfish steaks.

Swordfish Salad
Triple the amount of lemon-parsley sauce and toss ⅔ of it together with 8 cups of salad greens. Arrange 2 cups of greens on each serving plate. Place a hot or chilled swordfish steak over each plate of the dressed greens. Spoon the additional sauce over the fish.

Chapter 13
Vegetarian Dishes

Vegetable Stock

Yields 4 cups

Ingredients:
2 large onions, peeled and
    halved
2 medium carrots, cleaned
    and cut into large pieces
3 stalks of celery, cut in half
1 whole bulb of garlic
10 peppercorns
1 bay leaf
4½ cups water

Vegetable stock, which is also sometimes referred to as vegetable broth, is called for in many vegetarian recipes. A vegetarian diet excludes all forms of meat, poultry, and fish, but does include some animal-produced fare such as dairy products and eggs. Because it doesn't include any meat, it's especially important that a vegetarian diet include a wide variety of foods, including fruits, vegetables, plenty of leafy greens, whole-grain products, nuts, seeds, and high-protein legumes.

1. Add the onions, carrots, and celery to the slow cooker. Break the bulb of garlic into individual cloves; peel the garlic and add to the slow cooker. Add the peppercorns, bay leaf, and water. Add additional water if necessary to completely cover the vegetables. Cover and cook on low for 4–8 hours.

2. Strain the stock through a fine-mesh strainer or through cheesecloth placed in a colander. Store in a covered container in the refrigerator, or freeze until needed.

Vegetable Stock Variations
Garlic is the base flavor of this light vegetable stock. For a darker, rich sauce, oven-roast the vegetables until the onions are caramelized before adding them to the slow cooker. For a tomato-based flavor, substitute 2 cups of tomato juice for an equal amount of the water, or add 4 large, quartered tomatoes and reduce the water by ½ cup. Adding potatoes or using potato water (water used to cook potatoes) will result in a somewhat thickened stock.

Meatless Moussaka

If you get your eggplant at the supermarket and suspect that it's been waxed, peel it before dicing it and adding it to the slow cooker.

1. Add the lentils, potatoes, water, celery, onion, garlic, salt, cinnamon, nutmeg, pepper, basil, oregano, and parsley to the slow cooker; stir. Top with eggplant and carrots. Cover and cook on low for 6 hours or until the lentils are cooked through.

2. Stir in undrained tomatoes. Mix cream cheese and eggs together; dollop over lentil mixture. Cover and cook on low for an additional ½ hour.

Serves 8

Ingredients:
¾ cup dry brown or yellow lentils, rinsed and drained
2 large potatoes, peeled and diced
1 cup water
1 stalk celery, diced fine
1 medium sweet onion, peeled and diced
3 cloves of garlic, peeled and minced
½ teaspoon salt
¼ teaspoon ground cinnamon
Pinch freshly ground nutmeg
¼ teaspoon freshly ground black pepper
¼ teaspoon dried basil
¼ teaspoon dried oregano
¼ teaspoon dried parsley
1 medium eggplant, diced
12 baby carrots, each cut into 3 pieces
1 (14½-ounce) can diced tomatoes
1 (8-ounce) package cream cheese, softened
2 large eggs

Vegetable Casserole

Serves 8

Ingredients:

1 medium eggplant, diced

2 medium zucchini, sliced

1 teaspoon salt

¾ cup extra-virgin olive oil

3 cloves of garlic, peeled and
minced

1 tablespoon Dijon mustard

1½ teaspoon dried marjoram

½ teaspoon red pepper flakes

2 medium potatoes, peeled
and diced

2 medium carrots, peeled and
sliced

2 celery stalks, diced

2 medium onions, peeled and
sliced

½ small head cabbage, cored
and thinly sliced

1 (15-ounce) can peeled
tomatoes, drained and
chopped

This vegetable casserole, which is an adaptation of the Romanian vegetable stew known as ghivisu, can be served as a vegetarian main course or as a side dish with chicken or grilled sausage.

1. Add the eggplant and zucchini to a colander. Salt the vegetables, and let stand for an hour. Rinse well under cold running water. A handful at a time, squeeze the vegetables to release the moisture, and then pat dry with paper towels.

2. Add the oil, garlic, mustard, marjoram, red pepper flakes, and salt to taste to a bowl or measuring cup; whisk to mix.

3. In the following order, layer the vegetables in the slow cooker, drizzling each layer with some of the oil mixture: eggplant and zucchini, carrots, celery, onion, cabbage, and tomatoes. Cover and cook on low for 8 hours or until all vegetables are tender. Stir well before serving.

Meatless Mincemeat

Serve this mincemeat as a chutney or use as a filling in a mincemeat pie that's succulent enough to be a special occasion meal's main dish.

Yields about 2 quarts

Ingredients:
2 cups fresh apple cider
2 cups light brown sugar,
    lightly packed
½ cup (1 stick) butter, cubed
1 medium orange
1 cup raisins
1 cup dried currants
8 ounces dried figs
6 ounces dried apricots
2 medium cooking apples
2 Bosc pears
⅓ cup and ¼ cup brandy,
    divided
⅓ cup dark rum
1 teaspoon salt
1 teaspoon ground cinnamon
1 teaspoon ground cloves
1 teaspoon ground allspice
1 teaspoon ground nutmeg

1. Add the cider, brown sugar, and butter to the slow cooker; cover and, stirring occasionally, cook on high while you prepare the fruit for the recipe.

2. Cut the orange into quarters, remove the seeds and add to a food processor along with the raisins, currants, figs, and apricots; pulse to coarsely chop. Stir into the other ingredients already in the slow cooker.

3. Peel, core, and seed the apples and pears. Add to the food processor and pulse until finely grated; alternatively, you can feed through the food processor using the grater attachment. Add to the slow cooker along with ⅓ cup of the brandy, rum, salt, cinnamon, cloves, allspice, and nutmeg. Cover and cook on high for 1 hour or until mixture reaches a simmer.

4. Uncover, and stirring occasionally, continue to cook for 2–3 hours or until the mixture is reduced to about 2 quarts. Ladle the mincemeat into two sterilized 1-quart canning jars. Top the mincemeat in each jar with 2 tablespoons of brandy. Screw on the two-piece lids; allow to cool to room temperature. Refrigerate for at least 1 week, or for up to 6 months.

Mincemeat without Alcohol
To make mincemeat without alcohol, replace ⅓ cup of the brandy and the rum with cider. Reduce the amount of brown sugar to 1½ cups. Then, after you've ladled the mincemeat into the jars, spoon 2 tablespoons of honey into each jar instead of the brandy.

Moroccan Root Vegetables

Serves 8

Ingredients:

1 pound parsnips, peeled and
    diced
1 pound turnips, peeled and
    diced
2 medium onions, chopped
1 pound carrots, peeled and
    diced
6 dried apricots, chopped
4 pitted prunes, chopped
1 teaspoon ground turmeric
1 teaspoon ground cumin
½ teaspoon ground ginger
½ teaspoon ground
    cinnamon
¼ teaspoon ground cayenne
    pepper
1 tablespoon dried parsley
1 tablespoon dried cilantro
1 (14-ounce) can vegetable
    broth

*Moroccan Root Vegetables is good served with couscous and
Cucumber-Yogurt Salad (see recipe below).*

Add the parsnips, turnips, onions, carrots, apricots, prunes, turmeric, cumin, ginger, cinnamon, cayenne pepper, parsley, and cilantro to the slow cooker. Pour in the vegetable broth. Cover, and cook on low for 9 hours or until the vegetables are cooked through.

Cucumber-Yogurt Salad

In a serving bowl, mix together 3 cups of drained plain yogurt (or a mixture of drained yogurt and sour cream for a salad that's less tart) and 2 or 3 peeled, seeded, and thinly sliced cucumbers. Add 12 fresh chopped mint leaves, 2 peeled and minced cloves of garlic, and some salt to a small bowl, and crush them together. Stir the mint mixture into the salad. Add more salt if needed. Chill until ready to serve.

Wild Rice Casserole

Using instant rice mixes in this recipe takes away the worry about whether or not the rice will get done.

Add the onions, celery, rice mix, water, condensed cream of mushroom soup, butter, American cheese, and mushrooms to the slow cooker; stir to mix. Cover and cook on low 8 hours or until all of the water has been absorbed by the rice. Stir the mixture; test for seasoning and add salt and pepper if desired.

Serves 8

Ingredients:

2 medium onions, peeled and chopped

3 stalks of celery, thinly sliced

2 (6-ounce) packages dry instant long-grain and wild rice mix

2½ cups water

1 (10.75-ounce) can condensed cream of mushroom soup

1 stick (½ cup) butter, melted

½ pound processed American cheese, shredded

½ cup fresh mushrooms, cleaned and sliced

Salt and freshly ground black pepper, to taste

Vegetable-Cheese Soup

Instead of serving this soup with crackers, ladle it over biscuits or corn bread.

1. Add the corn, potatoes, carrots, onion, celery seeds, pepper, broth, and lentils to the slow cooker. Stir to combine. Cover and cook on low 8 hours.

2. Stir in the cheese; cover and cook an additional 30 minutes or until the cheese is melted and creates a sauce for the vegetables.

Serves 8

Ingredients:

1 (15-ounce) can creamed corn

4 large potatoes, peeled and diced

1 cup baby carrots, chopped

1 small onion, peeled and diced

1 teaspoon celery seed

½ teaspoon freshly ground black pepper

2 (14.5-ounce) cans vegetable broth

1 (15-ounce) can cooked lentils

1 (16-ounce) jar processed cheese sauce

Spicy Black Bean Chili

Serves 4

Ingredients:

1 tablespoon extra-virgin olive oil

1 large yellow onion, peeled and diced

1 medium red bell pepper, seeded and diced

2 cloves of garlic, peeled and minced

2 tablespoons chili powder, or to taste

1 (28-ounce) can crushed tomatoes

2 (15.5-ounce) cans black beans, drained and rinsed

1 cup water

1 (4-ounce) can diced green chilies

Salt and freshly ground black pepper, to taste

Serve this rich chili over noodles or rice cooked with a pinch of turmeric. It's good topped with some diced avocado, chopped green onion, and sour cream.

1. Add the oil, onion, and bell pepper to a microwave-safe bowl; cover and microwave on high for 1 minute or until the onions are transparent and the bell pepper is soft. Add the garlic and chili powder to the bowl, stir, and microwave on high for 30 seconds.

2. Add the onion mixture to the slow cooker along with the tomatoes, beans, water, and chilies. Cover and cook on low for 8 hours or until the chili is thick. Taste for seasoning, and add salt and pepper to taste.

Curried Cauliflower and Potatoes

Serves 8

Ingredients:

½ cup wheat berries

2¼ cups water

6 medium potatoes, peeled and quartered

1 small cauliflower, cut into florets

Pinch asafetida

¾ teaspoon ground turmeric

½ teaspoon chili powder

1½ teaspoons ground cumin

¾ teaspoon salt

Pinch sugar

2 tomatoes, chopped

½ teaspoon garam masala

If you only need 6 servings, you can omit the wheat berries. Reduce the amount of water by a cup and go a bit lighter on the seasoning if you do.

1. Add the wheat berries to the slow cooker. Bring 1 cup of the water to a boil and pour it over the wheat berries. Cover and cook on high for 1 hour.

2. Add the remaining ingredients, reduce the heat setting to low, cover and cook for 6 hours or until the potatoes are cooked through.

Lentil Soup

In this Lentil Soup recipe, you can substitute cooked collards, chard, or other dark greens for the kale. The greens are cooked separately (see sidebar) because cooking the raw greens directly in the soup can impart a bitter flavor.

1. Add the oil, celery, and carrot to a microwave-safe bowl; cover and microwave on high for 2 minutes. Stir in the onion; cover and microwave on high for 1 minute or until the onion is transparent. Add the garlic; cover and microwave on high for 30 seconds.

2. Add to the slow cooker along with the lentils, stock or water, and tamari sauce. Cover and cook on low for 8 hours. Stir the cooked greens into the soup, and season with salt and pepper, to taste.

Cooking the Greens
Remove the tough stems from the kale leaves, and then tightly roll them like a cigar; cut them crosswise into thin ribbons. Cook the kale in a pot of boiling salted water until tender. Drain and stir into the soup immediately before serving.

Serves 6

Ingredients:
1 tablespoon extra-virgin olive oil
1 celery stalk, diced
1 large carrot, peeled and diced
1 large yellow onion, peeled and diced
2 cloves of garlic, peeled and minced
1¼ cups dried brown lentils, rinsed and drained
6 cups vegetable stock or water
1 tablespoon tamari sauce
Salt and freshly ground black pepper, to taste
5 large cooked kale leaves, tough stems removed

Vegetarian Gravy

This recipe makes a cream gravy. For a rich, dark gravy, stir 1 tablespoon of tomato paste into the onions before you add the mushrooms.

Yields about 4 cups

Ingredients:
2 tablespoons extra-virgin olive oil
1 large sweet onion, peeled and diced
Optional: 1 stalk celery, finely diced
Optional: 1 carrot, finely diced
8 ounces fresh mushrooms, cleaned and sliced
1 clove of garlic, peeled and minced
2 cups vegetable broth
¼ cup butter, softened
¼ cup all-purpose flour
½–1 cup heavy cream

1. Add the oil and onion and, if using, the celery and carrot to the slow cooker. Stir to combine. Cover and cook on high for 1 hour or until the onion is transparent.

2. Stir the mushrooms and garlic into the onion mixture in the slow cooker. Add the vegetable broth. Cover and cook on low for 2 hours.

3. Uncover the slow cooker and increase the heat setting to high. In a small bowl, mix the butter together with the flour. When the broth in the slow cooker begins to bubble around the edges, drop the butter-flour mixture into the cooker a teaspoon at a time. Whisk to blend the butter-flour mixture into the broth. Continue to cook on high, stirring occasionally, for 5 minutes or until the broth is thickened. Taste to make sure the flour taste has cooked out; if not, continue to cook and stir for another few minutes.

4. Whisk in the cream; the amount you add will depend on how thick or thin you want the gravy. Stir until the cream comes to temperature. Serve immediately.

Vegetarian Gravy Base
If, for example, you only need about 1 cup of gravy for your meal, before completing Step 4 you can ladle out 3 cups of the thickened mushroom-broth mixture into three 1-cup, freezer-appropriate containers. (Allow to cool to room temperature and then cover and freeze for later.) Add cream to taste to the gravy base remaining in the slow cooker.

Cashews and Lentils Loaf

This recipe is for the vegetarian equivalent of a meatloaf. Serve it alongside a steamed vegetable. It's good topped with the Vegetarian Gravy (page 152).

1. Toast the cumin seeds in a dry pan over medium heat until they start to brown and release their aroma. Either in a spice grinder or using a mortar and a pestle, grind to a powder and set it aside.

2. Add the oil and celery to a large microwave-safe bowl; cover and microwave on high for 1 minute. Add the onion, carrots, red bell pepper, and chili pepper, if using, to the bowl; stir, cover, and then microwave on high in 1-minute increments, until the onions are transparent and the bell pepper is soft. (Uncover and stir between each 1-minute microwave cooking session.) Stir in salt and cracked pepper. Add the lentils, cheese, and cashews to the bowl and stir into the cooked vegetables. Add the eggs and mix well.

3. Put the cooking rack into the crock of the slow cooker. Create a loaf pan out of two layers of heavy-duty aluminum foil. Line with a piece of nonstick aluminum foil or spray with nonstick spray. Shape the loaf in the pan created out of foil and place it on the cooking rack. Pour enough boiling water into the slow cooker to reach just under the top of the rack. Cover and cook on high for 4 to 5 hours or until the loaf has set. Remove from the slow cooker and allow loaf to rest for 15 minutes before slicing and serving.

Loaf Pan Handles
Create handles to make it easier to lift the loaf out of the slow cooker by crossing doubled strips of foil long enough to span the cooking rack and both sides of the cooker under the foil packet holding the nut loaf. When the nut loaf is done, you can cross the strips over the top of the nut loaf, and grabbing them with one hand use a wide spatula to reach under the loaf to lift it out of the slow cooker.

Serves 6

Ingredients:
1 tablespoon cumin seed
1 tablespoon vegetable oil
2 stalks celery, diced
1 large onion, peeled and diced
2 cups carrots, shredded
2 cloves of garlic, peeled and minced
1 red bell pepper, seeded and diced
Optional: 1 chili pepper, seeded and diced
Sea salt, to taste
½ teaspoon cracked or freshly ground black pepper
2 cups cooked lentils
3 cups Cheddar cheese, shredded
1 cup cashews, coarsely chopped
3 large eggs, beaten
Optional: Nonstick spray
Boiling water

Peanuts and Potatoes Loaf

This meatloaf substitute is good served topped with marinara sauce or mushroom-tomato sauce.

Serves 6

Ingredients:

6 medium potatoes
1 cup roasted unsalted peanuts, chopped
¼ cup green onion, finely chopped
¼ cup fresh parsley, finely chopped
2 sun-dried tomatoes, reconstituted and finely chopped
½ teaspoon sea salt
½ teaspoon chili powder
Freshly ground black pepper, to taste
2 large eggs, beaten
½ cup chili sauce
4 ounces cream cheese, softened
¼ cup plus 2 tablespoons freshly grated Parmesan-Reggiano cheese
Optional: Nonstick spray
Boiling water

1. Peel, dice, and cook the potatoes until tender. Add the cooked potatoes to a large bowl along with the peanuts, green onions, parsley, sun-dried tomatoes, salt, chili powder, pepper, eggs, chili sauce, cream cheese (cut into cubes), and ¼ cup of the Parmesan cheese. Mix well.

2. Put the cooking rack into the crock of the slow cooker. Create a loaf pan out of two layers of heavy-duty aluminum foil that are long enough to bring up and over the top of the loaf. Line with a piece of nonstick aluminum foil or spray with nonstick spray. Shape the loaf in the pan created out of foil and sprinkle the additional 2 tablespoons of Parmesan cheese over the top of the loaf. Bring the foil edges up and over the top of the loaf, and crimp it to close it. Place the foil-enclosed loaf on the cooking rack. Pour enough boiling water into the slow cooker to reach just under the top of the rack. Cover and cook on low for 8 hours or high for 4 hours.

Nut Loaf

This meatloaf substitute is good served with the Vegetarian Gravy (page 152).

1. Add the onions, mushrooms, green bell pepper, and butter to a large microwave-safe bowl; cover and microwave on high for 1 minute. Stir, recover, and microwave on high for 1 more minute or until the onions are transparent and the green bell pepper is tender. Stir in the carrots, celery, eggs, walnuts, sunflower kernels, salt, basil, oregano, pepper, and bread crumbs.

2. Put the cooking rack into the crock of the slow cooker. Create a loaf pan out of two layers of heavy-duty aluminum foil. Line with a piece of nonstick aluminum foil or spray with nonstick spray. Shape the loaf in the pan created out of foil and place it on the cooking rack. Pour enough boiling water into the slow cooker to reach just under the top of the rack. Cover and cook on high for 4 to 5 hours or until the loaf has set. Remove from the slow cooker and allow loaf to rest for 15 minutes before slicing and serving.

Temperature Check
A nut loaf (or other baked goods containing eggs) is usually done when the internal temperature reaches 160°F. You can check the temperature by inserting an instant-read meat thermometer into the center of the loaf. Or, use a programmable food thermometer that has a probe attached with a cord; set it for 160°F and an alarm will go off when the food reaches that temperature.

Serves 8

Ingredients:
2 large onions, peeled and finely diced
8 ounces fresh mushrooms, cleaned and chopped
1 small green bell pepper, seeded and finely diced
2 tablespoons butter
3 cups carrots, grated
1½ cups celery, finely diced
5 large eggs, beaten
½ cup walnuts, chopped
¼ cup unsalted sunflower kernels
½ teaspoon sea salt
½ teaspoon dried basil
½ teaspoon dried oregano
¼ teaspoon freshly ground black pepper
3 cups soft whole wheat bread crumbs
Optional: Nonstick spray
Boiling water

Quinoa Pilaf

Serves 4

Ingredients:

1 cup quinoa

1 cup celery, diced

½ cup red bell pepper, seeded
and diced

2 tablespoons extra-virgin
olive oil

Pinch asafetida or 1 clove of
garlic, peeled and minced

½ cup raw cashews

1 bay leaf

½ teaspoon dried thyme

¼ teaspoon turmeric

½ teaspoon ground coriander

½ teaspoon ground cumin

¼ teaspoon ground ginger

½ teaspoon salt

1¾ cup boiling water

¼ cup fresh parsley or cilantro,
minced

Freshly ground black pepper,
to taste

Asafetida, which is also sometimes spelled as asoefetida, is an herb with a foul smell raw, but it imparts a flavor similar to leeks when it's cooked. If you're uncertain about using it, or any of the other suggested seasonings, cook the quinoa as instructed and then do a test sample using a sprinkling of the herbs and spices on a small portion that you cook for 30 seconds in the microwave.

1. Soak quinoa in water for 5 minutes; rinse twice, then drain.

2. Add the celery, bell pepper, and oil to a microwave-safe bowl; cover and microwave on high for 1 minute or until the celery is tender. Stir in the asafetida or garlic, cashews, and bay leaf. Cover and microwave on high for 2 minutes, or until cashews begin to take on a golden color. Let rest covered for 5 minutes.

3. Add the contents of the microwave-safe bowl to the slow cooker along with the quinoa, thyme, turmeric, coriander, cumin, ginger, and salt. Stir to combine. Pour in the boiling water, cover, and cook on low for 2 hours, or until all of the water is absorbed. Discard the bay leaf. Stir in the chopped parsley or cilantro, pepper, and serve.

What Is Quinoa?

Although it's usually thought of as a grain, quinoa (pronounced keen-wah) is technically an herb. Its high oil content makes uncooked quinoa perishable, so it should be stored in the refrigerator; it will keep refrigerated for up to a month, or it can be frozen. Quinoa is high in protein and can be used in place of bulgur, couscous, or rice.

Stuffed Bell Peppers

For this stuffed peppers recipe, you can use red, green, orange, or yellow bell peppers and hot or mild salsa, according to your preference.

1. Cut the tops off of the bell peppers. Remove and discard the stems. Scrape out the seeds and membranes in the peppers and discard.

2. Add the rice, beans, salsa, scallions, salt, and pepper to a bowl and mix well. Evenly fill the pepper cavities with the rice mixture, packing it lightly. Replace the pepper tops. Arrange the peppers upright in the slow cooker.

3. In the bowl, mix the tomatoes together with the cumin, oregano, sugar, and some additional salt and pepper. Pour over the peppers in the slow cooker. Cover and cook on low for 4 hours or until the peppers are tender but still hold their shape.

Serves 4

Ingredients:
4 large bell peppers
2½ cups cooked white or brown rice
1 (15.5-ounce) can red kidney beans, drained and rinsed
1 cup tomato salsa
3 scallions, chopped
Salt and freshly ground black pepper, to taste
1 (14½-ounce) can crushed tomatoes
½ teaspoon ground cumin
¼ teaspoon dried oregano
½ teaspoon sugar
Salt and freshly ground black pepper

Vegetarian Lasagna

Ingredients:

1 (26-ounce) jar marinara
   sauce
1 (14.5-ounce) can diced
   tomatoes
Nonstick spray
1 (8-ounce) package no-boil
   lasagna noodles
1 (15-ounce) container part-
   skim ricotta cheese
1 (8-ounce) package
   shredded Italian cheese
   blend or 8 ounces
   shredded mozzarella
   cheese
1 (10-ounce) package
   frozen chopped spinach,
   thawed and squeezed dry
1 cup frozen ground (veggie)
   burger crumbles, thawed

*Frozen Ground Burger Crumbles are a soy-based meat substitute
available from BOCA (www.bocaburger.com).*

1. Mix the marinara sauce and tomatoes with their juice together in a bowl.

2. Spray the inside of the crock in the slow cooker with nonstick spray. Spoon 1 cup of the sauce-tomato mixture into slow cooker. Arrange ¼ of the noodles over sauce, overlapping the noodles and breaking them into pieces so they are sized to cover as much sauce as possible. Spoon about ¾ cup sauce over the noodles, and then top that with ½ cup ricotta and ½ cup shredded cheese. Spread half of the spinach over cheese. Repeat layering two more times beginning with noodles, but in middle layer, replace the spinach with the thawed ground burger crumbles. Place remaining noodles over spinach, then top with remaining sauce and shredded cheese.

3. Cover and cook on low for 3 hours or until the noodles are cooked and the cheese is melted.

New Mexican Pot Pie

Serve this dish with an avocado salad. Have chopped jalapeño and green onions available for those who want to add it.

Serves 4

Ingredients:
2 tablespoons light olive oil, divided
1 small onion, peeled and diced
1 medium carrot, chopped
1 bell pepper, seeded and diced
2 cloves of garlic, peeled and minced
1 cup frozen corn, thawed
2 (15.5-ounce) cans of pinto beans, rinsed and drained
1 jalapeño, seeded and minced
¾ cup vegetable stock
1 tablespoon tamari or other soy sauce
2 tablespoons fresh cilantro, chopped
Salt and freshly ground black pepper, to taste
½ cup cornmeal
½ cup all-purpose flour
2 teaspoons baking powder
½ teaspoon baking soda
½ cup milk or soymilk

1. Add 1 tablespoon of the oil to the slow cooker. Stir in the onion and carrot. Cover and cook on high for 30 minutes or until the onions are transparent and the carrots are softened. Stir in the bell pepper, garlic, corn, pinto beans, jalapeño, vegetable stock, tamari or soy sauce, cilantro, salt, and pepper. Cover and cook on low for 5 hours. Taste for seasoning and add more salt and pepper if needed.

2. To make the top crust for the pot pie, add the cornmeal, flour, baking powder, and baking soda to a bowl, and mix well. Stir in the remaining tablespoon of oil and milk or soymilk, and mix until just combined. On a lightly floured surface, roll or pat the resulting dough into a shape about the same size as your cooker. Place the crust on top of the cooked bean mixture in the slow cooker, and cover and cook on high for 1 hour more or until crust is cooked through.

Or, if you prefer ...
Instead of making a top crust for the New Mexican Pot Pie, you can mix a corn muffin mix according to package directions and drop teaspoon-sized dollops of the batter on top of the bean mixture in the slow cooker. Or, you can reduce the amount of salt that you add to the bean mixture and serve it with corn chips or baked tortilla chips instead.

Reduced Fat Chili

You can alter the seasoning for this chili by using a specialty chili powder, like a chipotle pepper blend, or by adding some smoked paprika in addition to or instead of some of the chili powder.

1. Add the oil, green pepper, carrots, and onion to the slow cooker; stir to coat the vegetables in the oil. Cover and cook on high for 30 minutes or until the onion is transparent and the carrots are softened.

2. Stir in the garlic, beans, crushed tomatoes, tofu, water, corn, salt, chili powder, cumin, and cayenne pepper. Cover and cook on high for 1 hour or on low for 2 hours.

Minestrone

It's up to you whether or not you want to cut the carrots and green beans into smaller pieces. The cooking time will be sufficient to cook them either way, but chopping them into smaller pieces makes them match the size of the other vegetables in this minestrone. If you're using frozen green beans, however, remember to thaw them first.

Add all ingredients except the cheese to the slow cooker. Cover and cook on high for 2 hours or on low for 4 hours or until the macaroni is cooked el dente. Ladle the minestrone into bowls and sprinkle each serving with teaspoon of the cheese, or more to taste.

Or, if you prefer . . .
Minestrone is the perfect way to use leftover vegetables, so feel free to substitute peas, corn, or whatever else is on hand. Add some basil or Italian seasoning if that suits your tastes, or use vegetable broth instead of water for even more flavor. You can even Americanize the recipe by using kidney beans and make it even more healthful by using whole wheat macaroni.

Serves 4

Ingredients:
1 small onion, peeled and diced
3 cups water
2 medium zucchini, peeled and diced
1 cup baby carrots, chopped
1 cup green beans, chopped
1 (15-ounce) can cannelloni beans, rinsed and drained
¾ cup celery, diced
½ teaspoon dried basil
½ teaspoon dried oregano
Freshly ground black pepper, to taste
1 (14½-ounce) can diced tomatoes
1 clove of garlic, peeled and minced
¼ cup uncooked macaroni
4 teaspoons freshly grated Parmesan-Reggiano cheese

Chapter 14
International Flavors

Mu Shu-Style Pork

Rather than cooking the eggs in a skillet and then cutting them into noodles, this recipe uses the eggs to thicken the pan juices. Some of the eggs will scramble during the process, which will add texture to the filling similar to that found in egg drop soup.

Serves 8

Ingredients:
2 plums
1 clove of garlic, peeled and minced
2 tablespoons fresh ginger, grated
¼ cup soy sauce
2 tablespoons dry sherry or beer
2 teaspoons toasted sesame oil
⅛ teaspoon five-spice powder
1 tablespoon rice vinegar
3 tablespoons sugar
3 pounds boneless pork shoulder or sirloin
5 large eggs, beaten
2 cups bean sprouts
2 cups coleslaw mix
16 (6-inch) flour tortillas
Hoisin sauce
16 scallions, cleaned

1. Pit the plums and finely chop them; add to the slow cooker along with the garlic, ginger, soy sauce, sherry or beer, sesame oil, five-spice powder, vinegar, and sugar. Stir to mix. Cover and cook on low while you prepare the pork.

2. Trim the pork of any fat and cut it (against the grain) into several pieces. Add to the slow cooker, turning it to coat all sides of the meat with the sauce. Cover and cook on low for 8 hours or until the pork is fork-tender.

3. Remove the pork to a cutting board and use two forks to pull it apart. Cover and keep warm. Skim any fat from the sauce in the slow cooker. Whisk the beaten eggs into the sauce, and then stir in the bean sprouts and coleslaw mix. Cover and cook on low for 15 minutes or until the bean sprouts are heated through yet still crisp. Stir the pork into the sauce and vegetable mixture in the slow cooker.

4. If you need to soften the tortillas, you can put them in several stacks on a baking sheet, sprinkle a few drops of water between the stacks, cover them with foil, and bake at 350°F for 10 minutes.

5. Allow two filled tortillas per serving. To fill, spread a thin layer of hoisin sauce or a mixture of soy sauce and hoisin sauce over the inside of a tortilla. Top that with about ⅓ cup of the pork mixture. Either place a single scallion over the pork mixture or, if you prefer, first chop the scallions and sprinkle a layer of chopped scallions over the pork. Wrap and enjoy!

Indochinese Pork

Unsweetened coconut is available at most health food stores or from online sources like Nutty Guys (www.nuttyguys.com).

1. Add the oil to a large nonstick skillet and bring it to temperature over medium-high heat. Cut the pork into bite-sized pieces and add it along with the soy sauce to the skillet. Stir-fry the pork until it is browned on all sides. Add the onion, jalapeño, and garlic; sauté for 5 minutes or until the onion is soft and transparent.

2. Add the curry powder, salt, ginger, cumin, and cayenne to a bowl; stir to mix. Sprinkle the spice mixture over the meat mixture in the skillet. Stir-fry for 1 minute (being careful that the spices do not burn), and then transfer the pork mixture to the slow cooker. Cover and cook on low for 7 hours. Immediately before serving, stir in the coconut, peanuts, and yogurt.

Sweetened Coconut Fix
If the only coconut you have available is sweetened, you can use it in the Indonesian Pork recipe if you rinse it first (to lessen its sugar content). Put the coconut in a fine-mesh strainer and rinse well with hot water; pat the coconut dry with paper towels before using.

Serves 6

Ingredients:
1 tablespoon peanut oil
2½ pounds boneless pork shoulder
2 tablespoons soy sauce
1 medium onion, peeled and diced
1 jalapeño, seeded and minced
2 cloves of garlic, peeled and minced
2 teaspoons curry powder
¼ teaspoon salt
1 teaspoon ground ginger
½ teaspoon ground cumin
⅛ teaspoon cayenne pepper
1 cup shredded unsweetened coconut
½ cup unsalted peanuts
½ cup plain yogurt

Hungarian Goulash

Serves 6

Ingredients:

1 green bell pepper, seeded
and diced

4 large potatoes, peeled and
diced

3 strips bacon, cut into 1-inch
pieces

1 large yellow onion, peeled
and diced

1 tablespoon extra-virgin
olive oil

2 tablespoons sweet paprika

2½ pounds stewing beef or
round steak

1 clove of garlic, peeled and
minced

Pinch caraway seeds,
chopped

2 cups beef broth

1 (15-ounce) can diced
tomatoes

Salt and freshly ground black
pepper, to taste

2 tablespoons sour cream,
plus more for serving

*Hungarian goulash is often served with prepared spaetzle (German dumplings)
or hot buttered egg noodles and cucumber salad. Make the cucumber salad
in advance of preparing the goulash so that the cucumbers marinate
in the dressing while you make the stew.*

1. Add the bell pepper, potatoes, bacon, onion, and oil to the slow cooker;
   stir to mix. Cover and cook on high for 30 minutes or until the onion is
   transparent and the fat is rendering from the bacon. Stir in the paprika.
   Trim the beef of any fat and cut it into ½-inch cubes. Stir the beef into
   the vegetable mixture in the slow cooker along with the garlic and
   caraway seeds. Cover and, stirring occasionally, cook on high for 15
   minutes.

2. Reduce the heat of the slow cooker to low. Pour in the beef broth and
   tomatoes. Cover and cook on low for 8 hours or until the beef is tender
   and the potatoes are cooked through. Stir the 2 tablespoons of sour
   cream into the goulash. Taste for seasoning and add salt, pepper, and
   additional paprika if needed. Serve with additional sour cream on the
   side, and over prepared spaetzle or egg noodles if desired.

Supplemental Recipe: Cucumber Salad
*Thinly slice 2 cucumbers; put slices in a bowl and sprinkle with salt. Let
rest for 30 minutes. Drain off the excess moisture and add a small, thinly
sliced onion; 1 or 2 tablespoons white wine, or cider vinegar; ¼ cup
heavy or sour cream; 2 teaspoons sugar; ⅛ teaspoon sweet paprika; a
pinch of dried or fresh dill; and freshly ground black pepper, to taste. Mix
well, cover, and refrigerate until ready to serve.*

Moroccan Chicken and Vegetables

This is an adaptation of a chicken tagine recipe traditionally served in deep soup bowls over the top of cooked rice, noodles, or couscous.

1. Add the oil to a large nonstick skillet and bring to temperature over medium-high heat. Add the chicken pieces and brown on both sides. Remove from the pan and keep warm.

2. Add the onion, garlic, and eggplant to the slow cooker; cover and cook on high for 30 minutes or until the onion is transparent. Stir in the broth, cinnamon sticks, curry powder, cumin, turmeric, and black pepper. Add the chicken pieces along with the carrots, zucchini, turnip, red pepper, tomato, raisins, and half of the cilantro. Cover, reduce heat setting on slow cooker to low, and cook for 6 hours or until the chicken is cooked through. Taste for seasoning and add more salt and pepper if necessary. Garnish with the remaining cilantro.

Tomato Swap
If fresh tomatoes aren't available, you can exchange 1 (15-ounce) can of diced tomatoes for the 2 cups of fresh tomatoes. Reduce the amount of chicken broth to 2½ cups.

Serves 8

Ingredients:
- 3 tablespoons extra-virgin olive oil
- 4 chicken thighs, skin removed
- 2 chicken breasts, cut in half and skin removed
- 1 large yellow onion, peeled and diced
- 3 cloves of garlic, peeled and minced
- 1 large eggplant
- 3 cups chicken broth
- 2 (2-inch) long cinnamon sticks
- 1 teaspoon curry powder
- 1 teaspoon ground cumin
- ¼ teaspoon turmeric
- ¼ teaspoon freshly ground black pepper
- 2 large carrots, peeled and diced
- 1 large zucchini, diced
- 1 large white turnip, peeled and diced
- 1 small red pepper, seeded and diced
- 2 cups tomatoes, diced
- ½ cup golden raisins
- 2 tablespoons fresh cilantro, chopped

Bubble and Squeak

Adding some ham and bacon to this traditional British dish makes it a complete meal, even if you choose to serve it without a salad.

Serves 6

Ingredients:
6 strips bacon, cut into pieces
2 stalks celery, finely diced
3 large carrots, peeled and grated
1 medium yellow onion, peeled and diced
2 zucchini, grated and squeezed dry
3 large potatoes, peeled and diced
½ cup ham, chopped
3 cups coleslaw mix
Salt and freshly ground black pepper, to taste

1. In the order given, add (in layers) the bacon, celery, carrots, onion, zucchini, potatoes, and ham; cover and cook on high for 3 hours or until the potatoes are soft enough to mash down. Use the back of a large spoon or ladle to press the mixture down into the slow cooker to compress it.

2. Spread the coleslaw mix over the ham. Cover and continue to cook on high for 30 minutes or until the cabbage is tender. If necessary, leave the pan over the heat until any excess moisture from the cabbage and zucchini evaporates. To serve, invert onto a serving plate or ladle servings directly from the slow cooker.

Vietnamese Beef Noodle Soup

*This is a simplified, Americanized version of Pho, substituting brown
sugar for the yellow rock sugar found in Asian markets.*

Serves 10

Ingredients:
3 pound English-cut chuck
    roast
3 medium yellow onions
4-inch piece ginger (about 4
    ounces)
5 star anise
6 whole cloves
1 3-inch cinnamon stick
¼ teaspoon salt
2 cups beef broth
Water
1½–2 pounds small (⅛-inch
    wide) dried or fresh banh
    pho noodles ("rice sticks"
    or Thai chantaboon)
4 tablespoons fish sauce
1 tablespoon brown sugar
3 or 4 scallions, green part
    only, cut into thin rings
⅓ cup fresh cilantro, chopped
Freshly ground black pepper

1. Trim the roast of any fat; cut it into bite-sized pieces and add to the slow cooker. Peel 2 onions; cut into quarters. Cut the ginger into 1-inch pieces. Add the onion and ginger to the slow cooker along with the star anise, cloves, cinnamon stick, salt, broth, and enough water to cover the meat by about an inch. Cook on low for 6 hours or until the beef is pull-apart tender.

2. About a half hour before serving, peel the remaining onion; cut it into paper-thin slices and soak them in cold water. For dried rice noodles: Cover them with hot water and allow to soak for 15–20 minutes, or until softened and opaque white; drain in colander.

3. Remove the meat from the broth with a slotted spoon; shred the meat. Strain the broth through a fine strainer, discarding the spices and onion; return strained broth to the slow cooker along with the shredded meat. Set the slow cooker on the high setting to bring the meat and broth to a boil. Stir the fish sauce and brown sugar into the broth.

4. Blanch the noodles in stages by adding as many noodles to a strainer as you can submerge in the boiling broth without causing the slow cooker to boil over. The noodles will collapse and lose their stiffness in about 15–20 seconds. At that time, pull strainer from the broth, letting the excess broth clinging to them drain back into cooker. Empty noodles into bowls, allowing each serving to fill about ⅓ of the bowl, and then ladle hot broth and beef over the noodles. Garnish with onion slices, scallions, and chopped cilantro, and finish with freshly ground black pepper.

Irish Boiled Dinner

You can substitute additional beef broth for the lager if you'd prefer to cook without alcohol.

Serves 8

Ingredients:

2 tablespoons extra-virgin olive oil
1 tablespoon butter, melted
2 cups leeks, white part only, chopped and rinsed
1 large yellow onion, peeled and sliced
3 cloves of garlic, peeled and minced
1 (3½-pound) beef brisket
2 bay leaves
10 black peppercorns
½ cup fresh parsley, chopped
2 teaspoons salt
1 (1-pound) bag baby carrots
16 small red potatoes
2 medium turnips, peeled and quartered
1 (12-ounce) bottle beer, lager
1 cup beef broth
2 small heads cabbage, cored and cut into wedges
Salt and freshly ground black pepper, to taste

1. Add the oil and butter to the slow cooker along with the leeks and onion; stir to coat the vegetables in oil. Cover and cook on high for 30 minutes or until the leeks and onions are soft and transparent. Stir in the garlic.

2. Add the brisket to the slow cooker along with the bay leaves, peppercorns, parsley, salt, carrots, potatoes, turnips, beer, and broth; cover, reduce the temperature of the slow cooker to low, and cook for 7 hours. Add the cabbage wedges, pressing them down into the liquid; cover and cook for an additional 30 minutes to an hour or until all vegetables are cooked according to your preference. Taste for seasoning and add additional salt and pepper if needed.

Cuban Black Bean Soup

Like with almost any bean dish, you can add diced celery and carrot slices to this soup. In fact, adding some along with another cup of chicken broth will let you increase the servings to 8. You can wait until after it's cooked to decide if you think it needs additional cumin, paprika, or chili powder.

Serves 8

Ingredients:
1 green bell pepper, seeded and diced
1 large yellow onion, peeled and diced
½ pound bacon, chopped
3 cloves garlic, peeled and minced
2 teaspoons paprika
½ teaspoon ground cumin
¼ teaspoon chili powder
1 bay leaf
6 cups chicken broth
2 smoked ham hocks
2 (15-ounce) cans black beans, rinsed and drained
1 tablespoon red wine vinegar
Salt and freshly ground black pepper, to taste

1. Add the green pepper, onion, and bacon to the slow cooker. Cover and cook on high for 10 minutes; stir, then cover and cook on high for an additional 30 minutes or until the green pepper is tender and the onion is transparent. Stir in the garlic along with the paprika, cumin, and chili powder. Add the bay leaf, broth, ham hocks, and beans. Cover and cook on low for 6 hours.

2. Remove the ham hocks and take the meat off of the bones; return meat to the pot. Remove and discard the bay leaves. Stir in the vinegar, salt, and pepper. Taste for seasoning and adjust if desired.

Portuguese Kale Soup

Collard greens can be substituted for the kale, but doing so will change the flavor somewhat.

Serves 6

Ingredients:
1 pound kale
1 tablespoon extra-virgin olive oil
1 large yellow onion, peeled and thinly sliced
½ pound linguica or kielbasa, sliced
4 large potatoes, peeled and diced
4 cups chicken broth
2 (15-ounce) cans cannelloni beans, rinsed and drained
Salt and freshly ground black pepper, to taste

1. Trim the large ribs from the kale. Slice it into thin strips. Put the kale strips into a bowl of cold water and soak for an hour; drain well.

2. Add the oil, onions, and linguica or kielbasa to the slow cooker; stir to combine. Cover and cook on high for 30 minutes or until the onions are transparent. Add the potatoes, chicken broth, drained kale, and beans. Cover and cook on high for 3 hours or low for 6 hours or until the potatoes are cooked through. Taste for seasoning and add salt and pepper to taste.

Scotch Broth

Serves 4

Ingredients:
2 leeks, white part only
4 lamb shoulder chops
⅓ cup pearl barley
1 large carrot, peeled and diced
1 stalk of celery, thinly sliced
2 medium potatoes, peeled and diced
6 cups water
Salt and freshly ground black pepper, to taste
Optional: Fresh parsley, minced

Scotch Broth is not a broth in the traditional sense. Instead, it's the name for a barley soup.

Dice the white part of the leeks; rinse well and drain. Add the leeks to the slow cooker along with the lamb chops, barley, carrot, celery, potatoes, water, salt, and pepper. Cover and cook on low for 6 to 8 hours or until the meat is tender and the potatoes are cooked through. Transfer a lamb chop to each of four bowls and ladle the soup over the meat. Garnish with parsley if desired.

Irish Cheese Pudding

Serves 6

Ingredients:
Nonstick spray
7 cups 1-inch bread cubes
3 cups (12 ounces) sharp Cheddar cheese, grated
4 large eggs
2 cups chicken broth
1 cup beer
1 cup heavy cream
Pinch cayenne pepper
2 teaspoons Dijon mustard
Salt and freshly ground black pepper, to taste

Think of this dish as Welsh Rarebit with the bread baked into the cheese sauce instead of dipped into it.

1. Treat the crock of the slow cooker with nonstick spray. Add the bread cubes and 2½ cups of the grated cheese. Toss to mix.

2. Add the eggs to a bowl or measuring cup; whisk until frothy. Whisk in the broth, beer, cream, cayenne, mustard, salt, and pepper. Pour the egg mixture over the bread cubes in the slow cooker. Push the bread down into the liquid. Cover and cook on low for 3 hours or until the eggs are set. Sprinkle the remaining cheese over the top. Partially cover and cook for 20 minutes or until the cheese is melted. Serve immediately.

Or, if you prefer . . .
You can use all chicken broth or all beer in the Irish Cheese Pudding recipe. For a heartier flavor, use a lager or dark beer.

Moussaka

An alternative way to make this dish is to start with a third of the cooked meat in the bottom of the slow cooker, add a layer of potato or replace the potato with eggplant, top that with another third of the meat, add the eggplant layer, and top that with the remaining meat.

Serves 4

Ingredients:
1 tablespoon extra-virgin olive oil
1 large potato, peeled and thinly sliced
1 small eggplant, peeled and sliced
1 pound lean ground lamb or beef
1 large yellow onion, peeled and diced
4 cloves of garlic, peeled and minced
½ teaspoon cinnamon
¼ teaspoon ground cloves
¼ teaspoon freshly ground black pepper
⅛ teaspoon ground allspice
Cayenne pepper, to taste
Salt, to taste
½ cup dry red wine
1 (15-ounce) can crushed or diced tomatoes
3 cups low-fat milk
½ cup all-purpose flour
Freshly ground nutmeg, to taste
2 large eggs
1 cup (4 ounces) Gruyère or Swiss cheese, grated

1. Use the oil to grease the crock of the slow cooker. Arrange the potato slices over the bottom of the slow cooker, and arrange the eggplant slices on top of the potatoes.

2. Sauté the ground lamb or beef, onion, and garlic in a large nonstick skillet over medium-high heat for 8 minutes or until the meat is browned and the onions are tender. Skim off any fat rendered from the meat and discard. Stir in the ground cinnamon, cloves, black pepper, allspice, cayenne pepper, and salt, breaking apart the meat as you do so. Stir in the wine and tomatoes; reduce the heat and, stirring occasionally, simmer for 10 minutes or until much of the liquid has evaporated and the sauce has thickened.

3. Transfer the meat mixture to the slow cooker. Cover and cook on low for 3 hours or until the potatoes are cooked through.

4. Add ½ cup of the milk and the flour to a nonstick skillet over medium-high heat; whisk to make a paste and then slowly whisk in the remaining milk. Stirring constantly, cook for 10 minutes or until thickened enough to coat the back of a spoon. Remove from the heat and stir in the nutmeg. Whisk the eggs and some of the thickened milk together in a bowl, and then whisk the egg mixture into the thickened milk sauce. Stir in the cheese.

5. Pour the cheese and milk mixture into the slow cooker. Cover and cook on high for 2 hours or until the topping is firm. Turn off the slow cooker and let the moussaka rest for 30 minutes before serving.

Indian Chicken Vindaloo

Serves 4

Ingredients:
¼ cup ghee, melted
2 large yellow onions, peeled and diced
3 cloves of garlic, peeled and minced
2 tablespoons fresh ginger, grated
2 teaspoons ground cumin
2 teaspoons yellow mustard seeds, crushed
1 teaspoon ground cinnamon
½ teaspoon ground cloves
1 tablespoon turmeric
1½ teaspoons cayenne pepper, or to taste
1 tablespoon paprika
1 tablespoon tamarind paste
2 teaspoons fresh lemon juice
2 tablespoons white vinegar
1 teaspoon brown sugar
Salt, to taste
2 cups water
8 chicken thighs, skin removed

Indian Chicken Vindaloo is a rich, spicy stew you can serve over cooked rice or cook diced potatoes along with the chicken.

1. Add the ghee and onions to the slow cooker. Cover and cook on high for 30 minutes or until the onion is transparent.

2. Stir in the garlic, ginger, cumin, mustard seed, cinnamon, cloves, turmeric, cayenne, paprika, tamarind paste, lemon juice, vinegar, brown sugar, salt, and water. Add the chicken thighs. Cover and cook on low for 4 hours, or until the chicken is cooked through.

3. Use a slotted spoon to remove the thighs from the slow cooker. Uncover and allow the stew to continue to cook, which will thicken the sauce. Remove the chicken from the bones and use two forks to shred it. Return to the slow cooker and stir into the thickened sauce.

Cucumber Salad with Yogurt
Chicken Vindaloo is good with a simple cucumber salad. Thinly slice 2 cucumbers; dress the slices with 2 tablespoons of fresh lemon juice, ¼ cup extra-virgin olive oil, and salt and freshly ground black pepper to taste. Add a dollop of plain yogurt to each serving of the salad.

Greek Meatball Soup

This recipe is adapted from a Greek soup (Youvarlakia Avgolemono). The traditional version doesn't have the vegetables added to the broth, but it's those vegetables that make this soup a one-pot meal. Serve it with some feta cheese and crusty bread.

1. In a large bowl, mix the meat, onion, garlic, rice, parsley, dill or mint, oregano, salt, pepper, and 1 of the eggs. Shape into small meatballs and set aside.

2. Add 2 cups of broth or water to the slow cooker. Add the meatballs, onion, carrots, and celery, and then pour in enough broth or water to cover the meatballs and vegetables. Cover and cook on low for 6 hours.

3. In a small bowl or measuring cup, beat the two remaining eggs and then whisk in the corn flour. Gradually whisk in the lemon juice, and then ladle in about a cup of the hot broth from the slow cooker, doing so in a slow, steady stream, beating continuously until all of the hot liquid has been incorporated into the egg-corn flour mixture. Stir this mixture into the slow cooker, being careful not to break the meatballs. Continue to cook on low for an hour, or until mixture is thickened.

Serves 6

Ingredients:

1 pound lean ground beef
¼ pound ground pork
1 small onion, peeled and minced
1 clove of garlic, peeled and minced
6 tablespoons (uncooked) converted long-grain white rice
1 tablespoon dried parsley
2 teaspoons dried dill or mint
1 teaspoon dried oregano
Salt and freshly ground black pepper, to taste
3 large eggs
4–6 cups chicken or vegetable broth, or water
1 medium onion, peeled and chopped
1 cup baby carrots, each sliced into thirds
2 large potatoes, peeled and cut into cubes
1 stalk celery, finely chopped
2 tablespoons masa harina (corn flour)
⅓ cup fresh lemon juice

Iranian Beef Roast

Serves 8

Ingredients:
2 stalks celery, diced
1 (3-pound) boneless beef
    chuck roast
Salt and freshly ground black
    pepper, to taste
2 large onions, peeled and
    quartered
2 cloves garlic, peeled and
    minced
2 cups beef broth
¼ cup red wine vinegar
2 (15-ounce) cans diced
    tomatoes
1 tablespoon freeze-dried
    cilantro
¾ teaspoon freshly ground
    black pepper
¾ teaspoon ground cumin
½ teaspoon ground coriander
¼ teaspoon ground cloves
⅛ teaspoon ground
    cardamom
⅛ teaspoon ground nutmeg
⅛ teaspoon ground
    cinnamon
8 medium red potatoes
1 (16-ounce) bag frozen cut
    green beans, thawed
Optional: ¼ cup butter,
    softened
Optional: ¼ cup all-purpose
    flour

Instead of adding the potatoes to the slow cooker, you can stretch this recipe to more than 8 servings if you shred the beef, return it to the pan juices or gravy, and serve it over cooked rice or couscous.

1. Add the celery, roast, salt, pepper, onion, garlic, broth, vinegar, diced tomatoes, cilantro, black pepper, cumin, coriander, ground cloves, cardamom, nutmeg, and cinnamon to the slow cooker. Wash and cut a strip around each potato. Add to the slow cooker on top of the other ingredients. Cover and cook on low for 6 hours.

2. Add the green beans to the slow cooker. Cover and cook an additional 30 minutes on low or until the green beans are heated through.

3. Optional: If you wish to thicken the pan juices to make gravy, use a slotted spoon to transfer meat and vegetables to a serving platter; cover and keep warm. Strain the broth remaining in the pan and then return 1½ cup of the strained pan juices to the slow cooker. Increase the temperature on the slow cooker to high; cover and cook for 15 minutes or until the juices are bubbling around the edges. In a small bowl, use a fork to blend together the butter and flour. Whisk the butter-flour mixture into the boiling juices, a teaspoon at a time. Once you've added all of the mixture, continue to cook and stir for 10 minutes or until the flour taste is cooked out of the gravy and it is thickened enough to coat the back of a spoon. Taste for seasoning and add salt and pepper if desired.

Green Bean Salad
Instead of adding green beans to the slow cooker, you can instead steam them and serve them warm dressed with your favorite vinaigrette. Salt and pepper, to taste.

Pork Lo Mein

You may have to experiment with the timing, but you can steam thin dried egg noodles or angel-hair pasta by adding them along with the other ingredients in your slow cooker during the end of the cooking time, before you add the sugar snap peas and broccoli florets.

1. Trim the fat from the pork; cut pork into ¾-inch pieces. Add the pork, onions, carrots, teriyaki glaze, celery, water chestnuts, bamboo shoots, and ginger to the slow cooker. Cover and cook on low for 7 hours.

2. Add the sugar snap peas and broccoli. Cover and cook for 15 minutes or until pea pods are crisp-tender. Stir the cooked pasta into the other ingredients in the slow cooker. Serve immediately. Sprinkle cashews or almonds over each serving.

Serves 6

Ingredients:

1½ pounds boneless pork shoulder

2 medium onions, peeled and sliced

2 cups frozen sliced carrots, thawed

1 (12-ounce) jar teriyaki glaze

1 cup celery, thinly bias-sliced

1 (8-ounce) can sliced water chestnuts, drained

1 (5-ounce) can sliced bamboo shoots, drained

1 teaspoon fresh ginger, grated

1 (6-ounce) package frozen sugar snap peas, thawed

1 cup frozen broccoli florets, thawed

8 ounces angel-hair pasta, cooked

½ cup unsalted cashew halves or slivered almonds

Chapter 15
Soups

Herbed Chicken and Vegetable Soup

Serves 8

Ingredients:

7 large carrots

2 stalks celery, finely diced

1 large sweet onion, peeled and diced

8 ounces fresh mushrooms, cleaned and sliced

1 tablespoon extra-virgin olive oil

1 teaspoon butter, melted

1 clove of garlic, peeled and minced

4 cups chicken broth

6 medium potatoes, peeled and diced

1 tablespoon dried parsley

¼ teaspoon dried oregano

¼ teaspoon dried rosemary

1 bay leaf

2 strips orange zest

Salt and freshly ground black pepper, to taste

8 chicken thighs, skin removed

1 (10-ounce) package frozen green beans, thawed

1 (10-ounce) package frozen whole kernel corn, thawed

1 (10-ounce) package frozen baby peas, thawed

Optional: Fresh parsley

This soup is also delicious if you use a roux to thicken the broth and serve it pot pie-style: ladled over split buttermilk biscuits. If you need to let the soup cook all day so that it's done when you get home, it's okay to add the green beans, corn, and peas when you add the other ingredients.

1. Peel the carrots. Dice 6 of the carrots and grate 1. Add the grated carrot, celery, onion, mushrooms, oil, and butter to the slow cooker. Stir to coat the vegetables in the oil and butter. Cover and cook on high for 30 minutes or until the vegetables are soft.

2. Stir in the garlic. Add the broth, diced carrots, potatoes, dried parsley, oregano, rosemary, bay leaf, orange zest, salt, pepper, and chicken thighs. Cover and cook on low for 6 hours.

3. Use a slotted spoon to remove the thighs, cut the meat from the bone and into bite-sized pieces, and return it to the pot. Remove and discard the orange zest and bay leaf. Stir in the green beans, corn, and peas; cover and cook on low for 1 hour or until the vegetables are heated through. Taste for seasoning and add additional salt, pepper, and herbs if needed.

Or, if you prefer . . .

Transform the Herbed Chicken and Vegetable Soup recipe into a tomato-based meal by substituting 2 (15-ounce) cans diced tomatoes for the chicken broth.

Manhattan Scallop Chowder

Serve this chowder with oyster crackers or warm dinner rolls and a tossed salad.

1. Add the butter, celery, bell pepper, and carrot to the slow cooker; stir to coat the vegetables in the butter. Cover and cook on high for 15 minutes. Stir in the onion. Cover and cook on high for 30 minutes, or until the vegetables are soft.

2. Stir in the potatoes, tomatoes, tomato purée, clam juice, wine, water, thyme, dried parsley, bay leaf, and pepper. Cover, reduce the temperature to low, and cook for 7 hours or until the potatoes are cooked through.

3. Cut the scallops so that they are each no larger than 1-inch pieces. Add to the slow cooker, increase the temperature to high, cover, and cook for 15 minutes or until the scallops are firm. Remove and discard the bay leaf. Taste for seasoning and add salt or adjust other seasonings if necessary. Ladle into soup bowls. If desired, sprinkle minced fresh parsley over each serving and garnish with fresh basil.

Serves 6

Ingredients:

2 tablespoons butter, melted
2 stalks celery, finely diced
1 medium green bell pepper, seeded and diced
1 large carrot, peeled and finely diced
1 medium onion, peeled and diced
2 large potatoes, scrubbed and diced
1 (15-ounce) can diced tomatoes
1 (15-ounce) can tomato purée
2 cups (bottled) clam juice
1 cup dry white wine
¾ cup water
1 teaspoon dried thyme
1 teaspoon dried parsley
1 bay leaf
¼ teaspoon freshly ground black pepper
1½ pounds bay scallops
Salt, to taste
Optional: Fresh parsley, minced
Optional: Fresh basil

Clam Chowder

Serves 8

Ingredients:
8 strips bacon
2 large carrots, peeled and
  finely diced
2 stalks of celery, finely diced
2 large yellow onions, peeled
  and diced
2 tablespoons all-purpose
  flour
6 (6½-ounce) cans baby
  clams
8 medium red potatoes,
  scrubbed and diced
1 tablespoon dried parsley
1 bay leaf
1 tablespoon Worcestershire
  sauce
2 teaspoons dried thyme
5 cups water
3 cups heavy cream
1 cup whole milk
Salt and freshly ground black
  pepper, to taste
Hot sauce, to taste
Optional: Fresh parsley,
  minced

This chowder is even better if you sauté 1 small diced red pepper along with the carrots and celery. Serve the chowder with oyster crackers and a tossed salad.

1. Cut the bacon into bite-sized pieces and add to the slow cooker along with the carrots and celery. Cover and cook on high for 15 minutes. Stir in the onions; cover and cook on high for 30 minutes or until the onion is transparent. Stir in the flour; gradually add 1 can of the (undrained) clams; stir and cook to remove any lumps.

2. Add the remaining (undrained) clams, potatoes, parsley, bay leaf, Worcestershire sauce, thyme, and water to the slow cooker. Cover and cook on high for 4 hours.

3. Stir in the cream, milk, salt, pepper, and hot sauce. Cover, reduce the slow cooker heat setting to low, and cook for 30 minutes or until the soup is heated through. (You do not want to bring it to a boil after you've added the cream and milk.) Taste for seasoning and adjust if necessary. Ladle into soup bowls and sprinkle minced fresh parsley over each serving if desired.

Speed Things Up
It'll dirty another pan, but you can speed up the cooking process for the Clam Chowder recipe if you fry the bacon in a nonstick skillet over medium-high heat and then sauté the carrots, celery, and onion in the rendered bacon fat. If you do, stir in the flour and cook it in with the sautéed vegetables on the stove for 2 minutes before you add it to the slow cooker.

Beef-Vegetable Soup

Add a bit more flavor to this soup by substituting several strips of bacon cut into bite-sized pieces for the oil. Another alternative is substituting canned French Onion Soup for some of the beef broth.

1. Peel the carrots. Dice 6 of the carrots and grate 1. Add the grated carrot, celery, onion, mushrooms, oil, and butter to the slow cooker. Stir to coat the vegetables in the oil and butter. Cover and cook on high for 30 minutes or until the vegetables are soft.

2. Stir in the garlic. Add the broth, diced carrots, potatoes, dried parsley, oregano, rosemary, bay leaf, salt, and pepper. Trim the roast of any fat and cut into bite-sized pieces. Cover and cook on low for 6 hours or until the beef is tender and the potatoes are cooked through.

3. Remove and discard the bay leaf. Stir in the green beans, corn, and peas; cover and cook on low for 1 hour or until the vegetables are heated through. Taste for seasoning and add additional salt, pepper, and herbs if needed.

Or, if you prefer . . .
Make Beef-Vegetable Soup a tomato-based dish by substituting 2 (15-ounce) cans of diced tomatoes for the beef broth.

Serves 8

Ingredients:
7 large carrots
2 stalks celery, finely diced
1 large sweet onion, peeled and diced
8 ounces fresh mushrooms, cleaned and sliced
1 tablespoon extra-virgin olive oil
1 teaspoon butter, melted
1 clove of garlic, peeled and minced
4 cups beef broth
6 medium potatoes, peeled and diced
1 tablespoon dried parsley
¼ teaspoon dried oregano
¼ teaspoon dried rosemary
1 bay leaf
Salt and freshly ground black pepper, to taste
1 (3-pound) chuck roast
1 (10-ounce) package frozen green beans, thawed
1 (10-ounce) package frozen whole kernel corn, thawed
1 (10-ounce) package frozen baby peas, thawed
Optional: Fresh parsley

Fresh Vegetable Soup

Serves 8

Ingredients:

6 cups water or chicken broth

1 large yellow onion, peeled and diced

2 leeks—white part only, rinsed and sliced

1 (28-ounce) can whole plum tomatoes, crushed

4 large carrots, peeled and diced

1 acorn squash, peeled, seeded, and diced

2 large potatoes, peeled and diced

2 (15-ounce) cans garbanzo or white beans, rinsed and drained

¼ teaspoon dried thyme

¼ teaspoon dried basil

¼ teaspoon dried marjoram

2 teaspoons dried parsley

2 stalks celery, sliced

½ cup celery leaves, chopped

½ pound green beans, ends trimmed and cut into 2-inch pieces

½ pound zucchini, sliced

1 small cabbage, cored and shredded

Salt and freshly ground black pepper, to taste

If fresh herbs are available, you can replace the dried herbs with a bouquet garni made by tying a small bunch of parsley and a stalk each of thyme, basil, and marjoram together with kitchen twine and suspending it in the soup.

1. Add the water or broth, onion, leeks, tomatoes, carrots, acorn squash, potatoes, beans, thyme, basil, marjoram, and parsley to the slow cooker. Cover and cook on low for 6 hours or until the acorn squash and potatoes are tender.

2. Stir in the celery, celery leaves, green beans, zucchini, and cabbage. Add additional water or broth if needed. Cover and cook for 1 hour or until the newly added vegetables are cooked through. Ladle into soup bowls.

Notes on Fresh Vegetable Soup

This recipe is an adaptation of a French country soup that is served with toasted croutons or slices of French bread spread with (basil and Parmesan cheese) pesto and crème fraîche floating on top. You can replace the beans with other seasonal fresh vegetables (peas, corn cut from the cob, etc.) if you wish.

Oatmeal Soup

This recipe is a way to add fiber to your diet. You have the option of adding the cooked chicken breast back into the soup or into the tossed salad you serve with the soup.

1. Preheat oven to 350°F. Add the oatmeal and oat bran to a baking sheet lined with nonstick foil. Stirring the oatmeal mixture every 2 minutes, bake for 6 minutes or until the oatmeal is toasted and lightly browned. (Watch carefully, because it will go from browned to burnt in an instant!)

2. Melt the butter in a nonstick skillet over medium heat. Add the carrot and celery; sauté for 3 minutes or until the vegetables begin to soften. Stir in the onion and sauté for 5 minutes or until the onion is transparent. Remove the skin from the chicken breast pieces; place meat side down in the skillet and fry for 5 minutes. Transfer the meat and vegetables to the slow cooker. Season to taste with salt and pepper. Add the water. Cover and cook on low for 7 hours or until the chicken and oats are cooked through.

3. Use a slotted spoon and remove the chicken breast pieces from the slow cooker. Use an immersion blender to purée the vegetables and oatmeal into the broth if you wish. Stir in the cream. Cover and cook on low for 30 minutes, or until the soup is brought to temperature. Ladle into bowls. Garnish each serving with a tablespoon of minced fresh parsley if desired.

Oatmeal Choices
Use your choice of quick-cook oatmeal, old fashioned oatmeal, or steel-cut oats, according to your preference. Just keep in mind that you may need to add additional water during the cooking process if you use steel-cut oats.

Serves 4

Ingredients:
½ cup oatmeal
2 tablespoons oat bran
2 tablespoons butter
1 small carrot, peeled and grated
½ stalk celery, finely diced
1 medium sweet onion, peeled and diced
2 bone-in chicken breasts, cut in half
Salt and freshly ground black pepper, to taste
4 cups water
1 cup heavy cream
Optional: ¼ cup fresh parsley, minced

Potato Soup

This soup is a meal in itself.

Ingredients:
4 strips bacon
1 small carrot, peeled and
    grated
½ stalk celery, finely diced
1 large sweet onion, peeled
    and diced
1 (4-ounce) cooked ham steak,
    diced
Optional: 4 slices Canadian
    bacon
4 large potatoes, peeled and
    diced
5 cups chicken broth
Salt and freshly ground black
    pepper, to taste

1. Cut the bacon into 1-inch pieces and add it to the slow cooker along with the carrot, celery, and onion. Cover and cook on high for 15 minutes.

2. Stir in the diced ham. If using, cut the Canadian bacon into bite-sized pieces and stir into the vegetables. Cover and cook on high for 15 more minutes or until the fat begins to render from the bacon and the onion is transparent.

3. Stir the diced potatoes into the onion mixture. Cover and cook on high for 15 more minutes. Add the broth, salt, and pepper; reduce heat setting to low, cover, and cook for 4 hours or until the potatoes are cooked through.

Deluxe Cream of Potato Soup
Once the potatoes are cooked through, add 1 cup heavy cream, 4 ounces of cream cheese cut into cubes, and 1 cup (4 ounces) grated medium or sharp Cheddar cheese to the slow cooker. Stirring occasionally, cover and cook on low for 30 minutes or until the cheeses are melted and can be stirred into the soup.

Butternut Squash Soup

The apple will sweeten the soup a little, but you can add maple syrup if you want it sweeter. You can turn this into a cream soup by stirring in 1 cup of heavy cream after you've puréed the soup. Preheat the cream if you want to save yourself the step of needing to reheat the soup.

Serves 6

Ingredients:
2 tablespoons butter, melted
1 medium onion, peeled and
    diced
1 stalk celery, thinly diced
1 butternut squash, peeled,
    seeded, and diced
1 small Granny Smith apple,
    peeled, cored, and diced
2 (3-inch) cinnamon sticks
6 whole cloves
6 allspice berries
6 cups chicken broth
Salt and freshly ground black
    pepper, to taste
Optional: 1 or 2 tablespoons
    maple syrup
Freshly grated nutmeg

1. Add the butter, onion, and celery to the slow cooker. Cover and, stirring occasionally, cook on high for 30 minutes or until the onions begin to soften or are transparent. Add the diced squash (about 3 cups), apple, and cinnamon sticks. Place the cloves and allspice in a muslin cooking bag or tie them inside a piece of cheesecloth; add to the slow cooker along with the broth, salt, and pepper. Cover and cook on low for 6 hours or until the squash is tender.

2. Remove the cinnamon sticks, cloves, and allspice. Use an immersion blender to purée the soup. Taste for seasoning and adjust, adding maple syrup to taste if desired. Ladle into bowls. Grate fresh nutmeg to taste over each serving.

Easier Than Peeling and Dicing the Butternut Squash
Some supermarkets sell butternut squash that's already peeled and diced. Or, you can use a knife to pierce the squash several times, place it on a baking sheet, and bake it in a 350°F oven for an hour. Once it's cool enough to handle, cut it lengthwise. Scrape out and discard the seeds. Use a spoon to scrape the cooked flesh from the inside of the peel.

Cream of Broccoli Soup

Serves 4

Ingredients:

1 (12-ounce) bag frozen
broccoli florets, thawed

1 small onion, peeled and
diced

4 cups chicken broth

Salt and freshly ground black
pepper, to taste

Optional: 4 slices white bread,
crusts removed

1 cup heavy cream

*You can convert this to a rich broccoli-cheese soup by adding 2 to 4
ounces of cream cheese cut into cubes and 1 cup (4 ounces)
of grated Cheddar cheese when you add the cream.*

1. Add the broccoli, onion, broth, salt, and pepper to the slow cooker;
   cover and cook on low for 4 hours. If you prefer a thickened cream
   soup, tear the bread into pieces and stir them into the broth.

2. Use an immersion blender to purée the soup. Stir in the cream. Cover
   and, stirring occasionally to ensure that the bread remains blended in
   with the soup, cook on low for 30 minutes, or until the soup is brought
   to temperature.

Cream of Mushroom Soup

Serves 4

Ingredients:

8 ounces fresh mushrooms,
cleaned and sliced

1 small onion, peeled and
diced

4 cups chicken broth

Salt and freshly ground black
pepper, to taste

1 cup heavy cream or crème
fraîche

*For a thicker soup, use crème fraîche instead of cream. If you do,
watch the soup carefully while you bring it back to temperature
because if the soup comes to a boil, it can separate.*

1. Add the mushrooms, onion, broth, salt, and pepper to the slow cooker;
   cover and cook on low for 4 hours.

2. (Optional step: If you want to purée the cooked diced onion, first use a
   slotted spoon to remove some of the mushrooms and set aside. Use an
   immersion blender to purée and then return the reserved mushrooms
   to the slow cooker.)

3. Stir in the cream or crème fraîche. Cover and cook on low for 30 minutes or until the soup is brought to temperature.

Split Pea Soup

The combination of chicken broth and the different meats in this soup gives it a distinctive flavor. Because the sodium content in the broth and meats can affect the flavor, wait until the soup is cooked and, when you taste it for seasoning, add salt if it's needed.

1. Add the bacon and celery to the slow cooker; cover and cook on high while you prepare the carrots. Grate half of one of the carrots and dice the remaining carrots. Add the grated carrot and diced onion to the slow cooker; stir to mix them in with the bacon and celery. Cover and cook on high for 30 minutes or until the onions are transparent.

2. Add the diced carrots, split peas, broth, water, potatoes, ham hock, and smoked sausage or ham to the slow cooker. Cover and cook on low for 8 hours or until the peas are soft. Use a slotted spoon to remove the ham hock; remove the meat from the bone and return it to the slow cooker. Taste for seasoning and add salt and pepper if needed.

Adjustments to the Split Pea Soup Recipe

If you have homemade Ham Broth (page 107) available, you can substitute ½ cup of it for an equal amount of the water and omit the smoked ham hock. This is a soup that can also be enhanced by adding ½ cup of Pork Broth (page 106) instead of that much of the water, too.

Serves 6

Ingredients:
6 strips bacon, diced
2 stalks celery, finely diced
3 large carrots, peeled
1 large sweet onion, peeled and diced
2 cups dried split peas, rinsed and drained
4 cups chicken broth
3 cups water
2 large potatoes, peeled and diced
1 smoked ham hock
4 ounces smoked sausage or ham, diced
Salt and freshly ground black pepper, to taste

Thai-Spiced Chicken Soup

Serves 8

Ingredients:
2 tablespoons peanut or
   vegetable oil
2 carrots, peeled and thinly
   sliced
4 stalks celery, thinly sliced
1 small onion, thinly sliced
8 ounces fresh mushrooms,
   cleaned and sliced
2 cloves of garlic, peeled and
   minced
2 pounds boneless, skinless
   chicken breasts
8 cups chicken broth
2 cups frozen cross-cut green
   beans, thawed
1 tablespoon fresh ginger,
   grated
2 tablespoons red Thai curry
   paste
1 tablespoon fresh lemon
   juice
1 tablespoon fresh lime juice
½ teaspoon ground cumin
¼ teaspoon ground
   cardamom
¼ teaspoon ground
   cinnamon
¼ teaspoon ground dried
   coriander
⅛ teaspoon ground anise
   seed
1 tablespoon fish sauce
Optional: Fresh cilantro,
   minced

Thai red curry paste is a mixture of red chili peppers, shallots, garlic, galangal, lemon grass, coriander roots, peppercorns, salt, shrimp paste, and Kaffir lime zest. Fish sauce is a salty condiment and, much like soy sauce, a flavoring in Thai cuisine; it is made from fermented fish.

1. Add the oil, carrots, celery, and onion to the slow cooker; stir to coat the vegetables in the oil. Cover and cook on high for 30 minutes or until the onion is transparent. Stir in the mushrooms and garlic; cover and cook on high for 15 minutes.

2. Cut the chicken breast into bite-sized pieces. Add to the slow cooker along with all of the remaining ingredients except for the fresh cilantro. Cover and cook on low for 7 hours. Taste for seasoning, and add more Thai red curry paste (if you think the soup needs more heat) or more fish sauce (if you think the soup needs more salt). Ladle into soup bowls; sprinkle each serving with minced fresh cilantro if desired.

Borscht

When available, you can substitute about a pound of diced vine-ripened tomatoes for the canned.

Serves 6–8

Ingredients:

1½ tablespoons extra-virgin olive oil

1 clove of garlic, peeled and minced

½ pound chuck roast, cut into ½-inch pieces

1 small yellow onion, peeled and diced

1 pound red beets

1 small head cabbage, cored and chopped

1 (15-ounce) can diced tomatoes

7 cups beef broth

¼ cup red wine vinegar

2 bay leaves

1 tablespoon lemon juice

Beet greens

Salt and freshly ground black pepper, to taste

Sour cream

Optional: Fresh dill

1. Add the oil, garlic, beef, and onion to the slow cooker; stir to coat the beef and vegetables in the oil. Cover and cook on high for 30 minutes or until the onion is transparent.

2. Peel and dice the beets. (You may wish to wear gloves; beet juice can stain your hands and fingernails. Be careful, because it can also stain some countertops.) Save the beet greens; rinse well and cover them with cold water until needed.

3. Add the cabbage, tomatoes, beets, beef broth, vinegar, bay leaves, and lemon juice to the slow cooker. Cover and cook on low for 7 hours.

4. Chop the reserved beet greens and add to the soup; cover and cook on low for another 15 minutes, or until the greens are wilted. Taste for seasoning and add salt and pepper to taste. Ladle the soup into bowls and garnish each bowl with a heaping tablespoon of sour cream and some fresh dill if using.

Cauliflower and Cheese Soup

Serves 6

Ingredients:

1 (12-ounce) bag frozen
    cauliflower, thawed
1 small onion, peeled and
    diced
5 cups chicken broth
Salt and freshly ground black
    pepper, to taste
4 ounces cream cheese, cut
    into cubes
1 cup (4 ounces) medium
    Cheddar cheese, grated
1 cup heavy cream

Be sure to save any leftovers. This rich soup tastes even better when it's reheated and served the next day. Just remember to reheat it over low heat so that the cheese doesn't separate.

1. Add the cauliflower, onion, broth, salt, and pepper to the slow cooker; cover and cook on low for 4 hours. Use an immersion blender to purée the soup if desired.

2. Stir in the cream cheese, Cheddar cheese, and cream. Cover and, stirring occasionally, cook on low for 30 minutes or until the soup is brought to temperature.

Baked Beans Soup

Serves 6

Ingredients:

2 (16-ounce) cans baked
    beans
1 tablespoon molasses
1 tablespoon brown sugar
6 strips bacon, diced
1 large sweet onion, peeled
    and diced
1 (15-ounce) can stewed
    tomatoes
1 (2-pound) chuck roast
Salt and freshly ground
    pepper, to taste

You can increase the number of servings of this soup to 8 by adding 2 cans of stewed tomatoes. Serve over corn bread with a tossed salad.

1. Add the baked beans, molasses, brown sugar, bacon, onion, and stewed tomatoes to the slow cooker; stir to mix.

2. Trim the beef of any fat and cut it into 1-inch cubes. Add to the slow cooker and stir it into the beans. Cover and cook on low for 8 hours or until the beef is tender. Taste for seasoning; add salt and pepper if needed.

Southwestern Cheese Soup

Serve this soup with a tossed salad and corn chips. Use hot or mild green chilies, according to your personal preference.

1. Fry the ground beef in a large nonstick skillet over medium-high heat, breaking it apart as you do so. Drain and discard any fat rendered from the beef.

2. Transfer the ground beef to the slow cooker and stir the taco seasoning mix into the meat. Add the corn, beans, diced tomatoes, stewed tomatoes, and chilies to the slow cooker. Cover and cook on low for 4 hours.

3. Stir the cheese into the soup. Cover, and stirring occasionally, continue to cook on low for 30 minutes or until the cheese is melted and blended into the soup.

Serves 8

Ingredients:
2 pounds lean ground beef
1 envelope taco seasoning mix
1 (15¼-ounce) can whole kernel corn
1 (15-ounce) can kidney beans
1 (15-ounce) can diced tomatoes
2 (15-ounce) cans stewed tomatoes
1 (7-ounce) can green chilies, minced and drained
2 pounds Velveeta cheese, cut into cubes

Italian Wedding Soup

This is a main-course soup that you can serve with garlic bread and a tossed salad.

1. Add the meatballs, broth, and endive or escarole to the slow cooker; cover and cook on low for 4 hours. Use a slotted spoon to remove the meatballs to a serving bowl; cover and keep warm. Increase the setting of the slow cooker to high; cook uncovered while you whisk the eggs.

2. Add the eggs, cheese, salt, and pepper to a small bowl; whisk to blend. Stir the soup in the slow cooker in a circular motion, and then drizzle the egg mixture into the moving broth. Use a fork to separate the eggs into thin strands. Once the eggs are set, pour soup over the meatballs.

Serves 4

Ingredients:
1 pound frozen meatballs, thawed
6 cups chicken broth
1 pound curly endive or escarole, coarsely chopped
2 large eggs
2 tablespoons freshly grated Parmesan-Reggiano cheese
Salt and freshly ground black pepper, to taste

Cream of Winter Vegetables Soup

Serves 6

Ingredients:
2 tablespoons butter
4 leeks
1 large yellow onion, peeled
and diced
4 medium carrots, peeled and
sliced
4 medium potatoes, peeled
and diced
2 large turnips, peeled and
diced
6 cups boiling water or
chicken broth
Salt and freshly ground black
pepper, to taste
1¼ cups crème fraîche

*Serve this soup with a tossed salad, smoked sausage, and
French or artisan whole-grain bread.*

1. Coat the inside of the crock of the slow cooker with the butter. Slice
the white parts of the leeks and about an inch of the green parts into
½-inch thick slices; rinse well and drain. Add to the slow cooker along
with the onion, carrots, potatoes, and turnips. Pour the boiling water or
broth over the vegetables. Cover and cook on low for 8 hours or until
all the vegetables are tender.

2. Use an immersion blender to purée the soup. Taste for seasoning and
add salt and pepper if desired. Stir in the crème fraîche; cover and cook
on low for 15 minutes, or until the soup is brought back to temperature.

Crème Fraîche
*Add 1 cup of heavy cream, ⅓ cup sour cream, and 2 tablespoons plain
yogurt (with active acidophilus cultures) to a sterilized glass container.
Mix, cover with plastic wrap, and let sit for 8 hours at room temperature.
Refrigerate until ready to use or for up to a week.*

Chapter 16
Stews

Cuban Beef Stew

Ingredients:
2 pounds beef chuck roast
1 large onion, peeled and
    diced
2 cloves of garlic, peeled and
    minced
1 red bell pepper, seeded and
    diced
1 green bell pepper, seeded
    and diced
4 strips bacon, chopped
1 (7-ounce) can green chilies,
    minced and drained
½ teaspoon dried thyme
½ teaspoon ground allspice
¼ teaspoon freshly grated
    nutmeg
1 cup beef broth
1 cup tomato juice
Salt, to taste
¾ teaspoon freshly ground
    pepper
3 large sweet potatoes

Serve Cuban Beef Stew over cooked rice or cooked rice and beans. Seeded and diced fresh jalapeño peppers can be substituted for the canned chilies.

1. Trim the beef of any fat and cut into 1-inch cubes. Add it to the slow cooker along with all of the other ingredients except for the sweet potatoes. Stir to mix.

2. Peel and cut the sweet potatoes in half; add to the top of the other ingredients. Cover and cook on low for 8 hours or until the beef is tender.

Sweet Potato Choices

You can either serve a half slow-cooked sweet potato with each serving of the Cuban Beef Stew or, if you've added the sweet potato halves as instructed, cut them into cubes after they've cooked and carefully stir them into the stew. If you want sweet potatoes cubes that remain firm enough to stir into the stew without the risk of them falling apart, peel and dice the sweet potatoes and wait to stir them into the stew until the final 2 or 3 hours of the cooking time.

Brunswick Stew

This stew is often made with rabbit. This Americanized version uses the easier to obtain and work with boneless, skinless pieces of chicken.

1. Add the bacon, onion, and red bell pepper to the slow cooker; cover and cook on high for 30 minutes.

2. Put the flour, salt, pepper, and cayenne in a gallon-size food-storage bag. Cut the chicken into bite-sized pieces, add to the bag, close the bag, and shake to coat the pieces with the seasoned flour.

3. Add the floured pieces to the slow cooker and stir them into the bacon, onions, and red bell pepper.

4. Stir in the broth, tomatoes, thyme, parsley, and Worcestershire sauce. Cover and cook on low for 6–8 hours.

5. Add the lima beans, corn, and okra; cover and cook on low for 1 hour or until the vegetables are heated through.

Serves 8

Ingredients:
2 slices bacon, diced
3 small onions, peeled and thinly sliced
1 red bell pepper, seeded and diced
3 tablespoons all-purpose flour
1 teaspoon salt
½ teaspoon pepper
Pinch cayenne pepper
1 pound boneless, skinless chicken breast
1 pound boneless, skinless chicken thighs
1½-2 cups chicken broth
2 (15-ounce) cans diced tomatoes
½ teaspoon dried thyme, crushed
2 teaspoons dried parsley
1 tablespoon Worcestershire sauce
2 cups frozen lima beans, thawed
2 cups frozen whole-kernel corn, thawed
½ cup frozen sliced okra, thawed

Beef Stew with Root Vegetables and Raisins

Ingredients:

1 tablespoon vegetable oil

1 tablespoon butter, melted

1 large onion, peeled and
    diced

1 stalk celery, finely diced

2 tablespoons all-purpose
    flour

Salt, to taste

¼ teaspoon freshly ground
    black pepper

1 (2-pound) beef chuck roast,
    cut into 1-inch cubes

1 (1-pound) bag baby carrots

2 large parsnips, peeled and
    diced

2 large Yukon gold or red
    potatoes, peeled and
    diced

2 (14½-ounce) cans diced
    tomatoes, undrained

2 cups beef broth

2 cloves garlic, peeled and
    minced

1 bay leaf

1 teaspoon dried thyme,
    crushed

½ cup almond- or pimiento-
    stuffed green olives

⅓ cup golden raisins

The olives and raisins can either be stirred into the stew just before serving or you can have them at the table as condiments. Serve over or with hot biscuits.

1. Add the oil, butter, onion, and celery to the slow cooker. Cover and, stirring occasionally, cook on high for 30 minutes, or while you prepare the other ingredients.

2. Place the flour, salt, and pepper in a plastic bag and add the meat cubes; close and shake to coat the meat. Add half of the meat to the slow cooker, stirring it into the onion and celery.

3. Add the carrots, parsnips, potatoes, tomatoes, broth, garlic, bay leaf, and thyme to the cooker; stir to combine. Reduce the heat setting to low; cover and cook for 8 hours.

4. Remove and discard bay leaf. Serve warm.

Bouillabaisse

*Serve this stew with garlic toast. For extra flavor, you can drizzle
some extra-virgin olive oil over the top of each serving and
then sprinkled on some minced fresh parsley.*

1. Add the oil and onions to the slow cooker; cover and, stirring occasionally, cook on high for 30 minutes or until the onion slices are transparent.

2. Stir in the garlic, tomato juice or broth, tomatoes, wine, water or fish stock, bay leaf, pepper, tarragon, thyme, and parsley. Cover, reduce the slow cooker heat to low, and cook for 4 to 8 hours.

3. Gently stir in the fish pieces; cover and cook on low for 15 minutes. Stir in the shrimp, clams, and mussels; cover and cook on low for 15 minutes or until the fish is opaque and cooked through and all ingredients are brought to temperature.

Serves 8

Ingredients:

2 tablespoons extra-virgin olive oil

1 large yellow onion, peeled and sliced

4 green onions, cleaned and sliced

1 clove of garlic, peeled and minced

2 cups tomato juice or chicken broth

1 (14½-ounce) can diced tomatoes

1 cup Chardonnay or other dry white wine

2 cups water or fish stock

1 bay leaf

½ teaspoon freshly ground black pepper

1 teaspoon dried tarragon, crumbled

½ teaspoon thyme, crushed

1 tablespoon parsley, crushed

1 pound white fish (halibut, cod, snapper), cut into one-inch pieces

1 pound frozen cooked shrimp, thawed

2 (3.53-ounce) pouches of whole baby clams

1 (10-ounce) can boiled mussels, drained

African-Inspired Chicken Stew

Serves 6

Ingredients:
8 chicken thighs
8 chicken legs
1 large yellow onion, peeled
    and sliced
½ teaspoon dried dill
2 bay leaves
4 cups water or chicken broth
½ cup peanut butter
3 tablespoons cornstarch
½ cup cold water
Salt and freshly ground
    pepper, to taste
Optional: 3–6 cups cooked
    long-grain rice
Optional: 5 bananas, peeled
    and cut lengthwise, then
    browned in butter
Optional: Unsweetened
    pineapple chunks
Optional: 4 ounces
    unsweetened coconut,
    toasted
½ cup roasted peanuts,
    chopped fine

Serve African-Inspired Chicken Stew with all of the optional condiments and it's an all-in-one meal and dessert.

1. Add the chicken pieces, onion, dill, bay leaves, and water or chicken broth to the slow cooker. Cover and cook on low for 4 hours, or until the chicken is cooked through. Remove the chicken from the pot and keep warm; discard the skin if desired. Remove and discard the bay leaves.

2. Add ½ cup of the hot liquid from the slow cooker to the peanut butter; mix well, and then pour the resulting peanut butter sauce into the pan. In a small bowl, mix the cornstarch and water together; remove any lumps. Whisk the cornstarch mixture into the broth in the pan, continuing to cook and stir until the broth thickens enough to coat the back of a spoon. (If you prefer a thicker sauce, mix additional cornstarch in cold water and repeat the process, cooking it long enough to cook out the raw cornstarch taste from the sauce.)

3. Taste the sauce for seasoning and add salt and pepper if needed.

4. For each serving, place a chicken thigh and chicken leg over some cooked rice. Ladle the thickened pan juices over the chicken and rice. If desired, top with fried bananas, pineapple, toasted coconut, and chopped peanuts.

Toasting Coconut
Preheat oven to 350°F. Spread the coconut out over a jellyroll pan. Place the pan on a shelf positioned in the center of the oven and, watching it carefully and stirring it every minute or two, bake the coconut for 6 minutes or until it's a very light golden brown.

Seafood Stew

Serve the stew with warm garlic bread or topped with toasted garlic croutons.

1. Add the oil, onions, garlic, and sausage to the slow cooker; stir to coat the onions in the oil. Cover and, stirring occasionally, cook on high for 30 minutes or until the onion is transparent.

2. Add the thyme, oregano, bay leaf, and potatoes, stirring everything to mix the herbs and coat the potatoes in the oil.

3. Pour in the chicken broth. Cover and cook on low for 4 hours.

4. Stir in the kale and fish. Add enough hot water to cover the fish if needed. Cover and continue to cook on low for 15 minutes.

5. Add the drained clams and cook on low for an additional 15 minutes or until the fish is cooked and the clams are brought to temperature. Taste for seasoning and add salt and pepper if needed. Garnish with chopped parsley if desired, and drizzle with extra-virgin olive oil.

Why Water Is Optional
The heat at which you cook a dish makes a difference in how much of the liquid will evaporate during the cooking process. Some vegetables in a dish also sometimes absorb more liquid than do others. If such evaporation or absorption occurs, the broth will become concentrated. Thus, water only reintroduces more liquid; it doesn't dilute the taste.

Serves 8

Ingredients:
2 tablespoons extra-virgin olive oil, plus more for serving
2 medium onions, peeled and diced
4 garlic cloves, peeled and minced
1 pound smoked sausage, sliced
½ teaspoon dried thyme
¼ teaspoon dried oregano, crushed
1 bay leaf
8 large Yukon gold potatoes, peeled and diced
8 cups chicken broth
1 pound kale, chopped
Optional: Hot water
2 pounds perch, cod, or bass fillets, skin and pin bones removed
2 (28-ounce) cans boiled baby clams, drained
Sea salt and freshly ground black pepper, to taste
Optional: ¼ cup fresh flat-leaf parsley, minced

Marsala Beef Stew

Serves 6

Ingredients:

2 tablespoons extra-virgin
   olive oil
1 tablespoon butter or ghee
1 (2-pound) English-cut chuck
   roast, cut into bite-sized
   pieces
2 tablespoons all-purpose
   flour
1 small carrot, peeled and
   finely diced
1 celery stalk, finely diced
1 large yellow onion, peeled
   and diced
3 cloves of garlic, peeled and
   minced
8 ounces mushrooms,
   cleaned and sliced
½ cup dry white wine
1 cup Marsala wine
½ teaspoon dried rosemary
½ teaspoon dried oregano
½ teaspoon dried basil
2 cups beef broth
2 cups water
Salt and freshly ground black
   pepper, to taste

This rich stew is good served over mashed potatoes, polenta, or cooked rice alongside a tossed salad. Top things off with some warm dinner rolls or whole-grain country bread.

1. Add the oil and butter or ghee to a large nonstick skillet and bring it to temperature over medium-high heat.

2. Put the beef pieces and flour in a large plastic food-safe bag; close and toss to coat the meat in the flour. Add as many pieces of beef that will comfortably fit in the pan without crowding it and brown for 10 minutes or until the meat takes on a rich dark outer color. Transfer the browned meat to the slow cooker.

3. Reduce the heat to medium and add the carrot and celery; sauté for 3–5 minutes, or until soft. Add the onion and sauté until the onion is transparent. Add the garlic and sauté for an additional 30 seconds. Stir in the mushrooms; sauté until tender. Transfer the sautéed vegetables and mushrooms to the slow cooker.

4. Add the remaining flour-coated beef to the slow cooker; stir to mix.

5. Add the wines to the skillet, and stir to pick up any browned bits sticking to the pan. Pour into the slow cooker. Add the rosemary, oregano, basil, broth, water, salt, and pepper to the slow cooker. Cover and cook on low for 6–8 hours or until the meat is tender. (You may need to allow the stew to cook uncovered for an hour or so to evaporate any extra liquid to thicken the sauce.) Taste for seasoning and add salt and pepper if needed. The taste of the stew will benefit if you allow it to rest, uncovered, off of the heat for a half hour, and then put the crock back in the slow cooker over low heat long enough to bring it back to temperature, but that step isn't necessary; you can serve it immediately if you prefer.

Quick and Easy Stew

*A quick and easy way to thicken stew is to stir some leftover
mashed potatoes into the broth.*

Trim the fat from the roast and cut into bite-sized pieces. Add to the
slow cooker along with the soups and water; stir to mix. Add the vegetables and pepper. Cover and cook on low for 8 hours or until the beef
is tender and the vegetables are cooked through. Stir in vinegar (as a
flavor-enhancer) if desired.

Serves 8

Ingredients:
1 (2-pound) chuck roast
1 (10½-ounce) can condensed
    French onion soup
1 (10¾-ounce) can condensed
    tomato soup
4 cups water
1½ (1-pound) bags frozen
    soup vegetables, thawed
Freshly ground black pepper,
    to taste
Optional: 2 tablespoons red
    wine or balsamic vinegar

Quick and Easy Stew, Too

*Unless you use low-sodium or salt-free soup, you probably
won't need to add any salt to this stew.*

Trim the fat from the roast and cut into bite-sized pieces. Add to the
slow cooker along with the soups and water; stir to mix. Add the vegetables and pepper. Cover and cook on low for 8 hours or until the beef
is tender and the vegetables are cooked through.

Serves 8

Ingredients:
1 (2-pound) chuck roast
1 (10¾-ounce) can condensed
    cream of celery soup
1 (10¾-ounce) can condensed
    cream of mushroom soup
1 (10½-ounce) can condensed
    French onion soup
2 cups water
1½ (1-pound) bags frozen
    soup vegetables, thawed
Freshly ground black pepper,
    to taste

Green Chili Stew

Serve this stew with a salad and over corn bread. It also works as an enchilada filling. One way to accommodate different tastes would be to use mild green chili peppers in the stew and have hot green salsa at the table.

Serves 6

Ingredients:
1 stick butter, melted
¼ cup all-purpose flour
4 cups chicken broth
1 large yellow onion, peeled and diced
½ teaspoon dried oregano
½ tablespoon granulated garlic
1 tablespoon chili powder
1 (28-ounce) can heat-and-serve pork
3 (7-ounce) cans mild or hot green chilies, drained and chopped
Salt and freshly ground black pepper, to taste
Optional: Sour cream

1. Add the butter to the slow cooker and whisk in the flour, and then gradually whisk in the broth.

2. Stir in the onion, oregano, garlic, chili powder, pork, and canned chilies. Cover and cook on low for 6 hours. Stir well and taste for seasoning; add salt and pepper if needed. Add a dollop of sour cream over each serving if desired.

Or, if you prefer . . .
For the Green Chili Stew, you can substitute chicken for the pork, or use slow-cooked, pulled pork shoulder roast and part of its broth instead of the canned pork and some of the chicken broth.

Irish Coddle

Serve this stew with Irish soda bread.

1. Cut the bacon into 1-inch pieces and add to a large nonstick skillet along with the sausage. Cook the bacon and brown the sausage over medium-high heat for about 10 minutes, breaking apart the sausage as you do so. Add salt, pepper, and the onion; sauté the onion for 5 minutes or until it is transparent. Drain the meat and onion mixture of any excess fat; discard the fat.

2. Spread ⅓ of the meat-onion mixture over the bottom of the slow cooker. Add the potatoes in a layer, sprinkling them with salt and pepper if desired. Spoon another ⅓ of the meat-onion mixture over the potatoes. Top that with the carrots in a layer. Spread the remaining meat-onion mixture over the top of the carrots.

3. Pour in the beer, broth, hard cider, or water. Cover and cook on low for 6 hours or until the vegetables are tender. Stir to mix; taste for seasoning and adjust if necessary. Ladle into bowls to serve.

Serves 6

Ingredients:
6 strips bacon
1½ pounds pork sausage
Salt and freshly ground black pepper, to taste
1 large yellow onion, peeled and diced
3 large potatoes, peeled and diced
3 large carrots, peeled and diced
1 cup beer, chicken broth, hard cider, or water

Moroccan Chicken Stew

Serves 4

Ingredients:

8 small chicken thighs, skin removed

1 large yellow onion, peeled and diced

3 cloves of garlic, peeled and minced

1 teaspoon ground ginger

½ teaspoon turmeric

¼ teaspoon cinnamon

Salt, to taste

½ teaspoon freshly ground black pepper

1 (15-ounce) can diced tomatoes

1 preserved lemon, rinsed and diced

1 teaspoon dried parsley

1 teaspoon dried coriander

1 (7½-ounce) jar pimiento-stuffed olives, drained

2 cups cooked couscous or rice

You can substitute a cut-up, 3-pound whole chicken for the chicken thighs; if you do, remove as much of the skin as possible. When you season the dish, keep in mind that the olives and the preserved lemon will affect the saltiness.

1. Add the chicken, onion, garlic, ginger, turmeric, cinnamon, salt, and pepper to the slow cooker. Pour the tomatoes over the chicken and sprinkle the lemon over the tomatoes. Cover and cook on low for 6 hours or until chicken is tender.

2. Use a slotted spoon or tongs to remove the chicken from the slow cooker. Remove the meat from the bones; use two forks to shred it, and then return it to the slow cooker. Sprinkle the parsley, coriander, and olives over the top; cover and cook on low for an additional 5 minutes. Serve warm over cooked couscous or rice.

Preserved Lemons

To make 5 preserved lemons, cut 5 lemons into partial quarters (leaving them attached at one end); rub kosher salt over the outside and cut sides of the lemons, and then pack them tightly in a sterilized 1-quart glass jar. Add 2 tablespoons kosher salt and enough lemon juice to cover the lemons. Seal and let set at room temperature for 14 days, inverting the jar once a day to mix. Store indefinitely in the refrigerator.

Country Beef and Vegetable Stew

*Serve this country stew with French bread or biscuits and a
tossed or steamed vegetable salad.*

1. Add the celery, roast, salt, pepper, onion, garlic, broth, vinegar, Worcestershire sauce, thyme, marjoram, potatoes, turnips, carrots, and pearl onions to the slow cooker. Cover and cook on low for 8 hours or until the beef is tender and the vegetables are cooked through.

2. Optional: If you wish to thicken the pan juices, use a slotted spoon to transfer the meat and vegetables to a serving platter; cover and keep warm. Increase the temperature on the slow cooker to high. Skim and discard any fat from the pan juices. In a bowl, use a fork to blend together the butter and flour, and then whisk about a cup of the pan juices into the butter and flour. When the remaining pan juices begin to bubble around the edges, slowly whisk in the butter-flour mixture. Cook and stir for 10 minutes or until the mixture is thickened and the flour taste is cooked out of the sauce. Taste for seasoning and add salt and pepper if desired. Carefully stir the cooked vegetables into the thickened sauce. Cut the meat into bite-sized pieces and fold into the sauce and vegetables. Pour the thickened pan juices and vegetables into a tureen or serve directly from the slow cooker.

Steamed Vegetable Salad
Prepare a 12-ounce package of steam-in-the-bag frozen green beans according to package directions. When they're done, transfer them to a serving bowl and, before you've added the vegetables back into the thickened sauce in Step 2, mix some of the cooked potatoes, carrots, and pearl onions into the steamed beans. Dress the vegetables with red-wine vinaigrette. Salt and pepper to taste.

Serves 8

Ingredients:
2 stalks celery, diced
1 (3-pound) boneless beef
  chuck roast
Salt and freshly ground black
  pepper, to taste
1 large onion, peeled and
  diced
2 cloves garlic, peeled and
  minced
2 cups beef broth
¼ cup red wine vinegar
1 tablespoon Worcestershire
  sauce
½ teaspoon dried thyme
1 teaspoon dried marjoram
4 large potatoes, scrubbed
  and diced
2 medium turnips, scrubbed
  and diced
1 (2-pound) bag baby carrots
1 (1-pound) bag frozen pearl
  onions, thawed
Optional: ¼ cup butter,
  softened
Optional: ¼ cup all-purpose
  flour

Pork and Apple Stew

If you prefer a tart apple taste, you can substitute Granny Smith apples for the golden delicious. (You can also add more apples if you wish. Apples and pork were made for each other!)

Trim the roast of any fat; discard the fat and cut the roast into bite-sized pieces. Add the pork to the slow cooker along with the remaining ingredients in the order given. (You want to rest the sweet potato quarters on top of the mixture in the slow cooker.) Cover and cook on low for 6 hours or until the pork is cooked through and tender.

Herbs and Spice Test

If you're unsure about the herbs and spices suggested in a recipe, wait to add them until the end of the cooking time. Once the meat is cooked through, spoon out ¼ cup or so of the pan juices into a microwave-safe bowl. Add a pinch of each herb and spice (in proportion to how they're suggested in the recipe), microwave on high for 15–30 seconds, and then taste the broth to see if you like it. Season the dish accordingly.

Serves 8

Ingredients:

1 (3-pound) boneless pork shoulder roast

Salt and freshly ground black pepper, to taste

1 large sweet onion, peeled and diced

2 golden delicious apples, peeled, cored, and diced

1 (2-pound) bag baby carrots

2 stalks celery, finely diced

2 cups apple juice or cider

Optional: ¼ cup dry vermouth

Optional: 2 tablespoons brandy

Optional: 2 tablespoons brown sugar

½ teaspoon dried thyme

¼ teaspoon ground allspice

¼ teaspoon dried sage

2 large sweet potatoes, peeled and quartered

Pot-au-feu

Pot-au-feu is French for "pot on the fire." When this Americanized adaptation of this French boiled dinner is made in a large slow cooker, you can add the potatoes so that they sit atop the meat and steam during the cooking process.

Serves 8

Ingredients:
2 tablespoons butter
1 (1-pound) bag baby carrots
4 stalks celery, finely diced
2 large onions, peeled and
     sliced
2 cloves garlic, peeled
1 bouquet garni
1 (2-pound) boneless chuck,
     cut into 1-inch pieces
8 chicken thighs
1 pound Western-style pork
     ribs
Coarse sea salt and freshly
     ground black pepper, to
     taste
4 small turnips, peeled and
     quartered
1 medium rutabaga, peeled
     and cut into eighths
4 cups water
8 medium red or Yukon Gold
     potatoes

1. Add the butter to a large (6½-quart) slow cooker set on high heat. (You can make this dish in a 4-quart slow cooker, but you may need to omit the potatoes from the cooker and prepare them separately.) Finely dice 10 of the baby carrots and 2 of the onion slices. Add the diced carrots, celery, and onion to the slow cooker; cover and cook for 15 minutes.

2. In this order, add the garlic, bouquet garni, beef, chicken, and pork; sprinkle the salt and pepper over the meat and then layer in the onion slices, remaining carrots, turnips, and rutabaga.

3. Pour in the water. (If you're using a 4-quart slow cooker, you can add the water in stages throughout the cooking process. Start with about 2 cups of the water and check the cooker every 2 hours to see if you need to add more to prevent it from boiling dry.)

4. Arrange the potatoes on top of the rutabaga. Reduce the heat setting to low, cover, and cook for 8 hours.

5. For a casual supper, you can ladle servings directly from the crock. For a more formal dinner, use a slotted spoon to arrange the vegetables and potatoes around the outside of a large serving platter with the meats arranged in the center; ladle a generous amount of the broth over all. Strain the remaining broth; pour into a gravy boat.

Bouquet Garni
For the Pot-au-feu recipe, create the bouquet garni by wrapping 2 bay leaves, 1 teaspoon dried thyme, 1 tablespoon dried parsley, 1 teaspoon black peppercorns, and 4 cloves in cheesecloth, or add them to a muslin spice bag.

Veal Stew

Serves 8

Ingredients:

3 tablespoons all-purpose flour

½ teaspoon salt

¼ teaspoon black pepper

1 pound boneless veal shoulder, cut into 1" cubes

2 tablespoons butter

1 medium yellow onion, peeled and sliced

2 small cloves of garlic, peeled and minced

1 large green bell pepper, seeded and diced

1 medium eggplant, peeled and diced

1 medium zucchini, peeled and diced

1 cup leeks, white part only, rinsed and thinly sliced

2 small turnips, peeled and diced

1 cup celery root

2 small parsnips, peeled and diced

2 large carrots, peeled and sliced

½ cup beef broth

½ cup dry red wine

2 teaspoons dried parsley

¼ teaspoon dried thyme

¼ teaspoon dried marjoram

1 tablespoon tomato paste

1 (15-ounce) can diced tomatoes

1 small head cabbage, cored and thinly sliced

1 (14½-ounce) can French-style green beans, drained

¼ cup seedless green grapes, cut in half

This recipe lets you stretch a small amount of expensive veal into lots of servings. This stew is good if each bowl is garnished with a dollop of drained yogurt or sour cream.

1. Add the flour, salt, and pepper to a large food-storage bag; shake to mix. Add the veal cubes and toss to coat in flour. Melt the butter in a large nonstick skillet over medium-high heat. Add the veal and brown for 5 minutes. Add the onions and sauté, stirring frequently, for 5 minutes or until the onions are transparent. Add the garlic and sauté for an additional 30 seconds. Transfer to the slow cooker.

2. Add the green bell pepper, eggplant, zucchini, leeks, turnips, celery root, parsnips, and carrots to the slow cooker. Stir to mix together with the meat and sautéed vegetables.

3. Add the broth, wine, parsley, thyme, marjoram, tomato paste, and diced tomatoes to a bowl or measuring cup; stir to mix, and then pour into the slow cooker. Add as much of the cabbage as will sit on top of the ingredients already in the slow cooker. Cover and begin to cook on low for up to 8 hours. As the cabbage wilts, add the rest, stirring it into the stew about halfway through the cooking time. An hour before the end of the cooking time, add the green beans and green grapes. The stew is done when the meat and all of the vegetables are cooked through and tender.

Enchilada Chili

Fresh cilantro should top each serving. If you're using freeze-dried cilantro, add a tablespoon to the slow cooker near the end of the cooking time and stir it into the chili.

1. Add the beef, beans, tomatoes, broth, enchilada sauce, onion, garlic, and water to the slow cooker. Cover and cook on low for 8 hours.

2. In a small bowl, whisk the cornmeal together with enough cold water to make a paste; stir some of the liquid from the slow cooker into the cornmeal paste and then whisk it into the chili. Cook and stir on high for 15–30 minutes or until chili is thickened and the raw cornmeal taste is cooked out of the chili.

3. Top each serving with minced cilantro and grated cheese.

Enchilada Chili Dip
To serve this chili as a dip, after Step 3, reduce the heat to low and stir in the cheese; continue to stir until cheese is melted. Reduce the heat setting to warm. Serve with baked corn tortilla chips. (According to your tastes, you may wish to increase the amount of cheese.)

Serves 8

Ingredients:

2 pounds boneless beef chuck roast, cut into bite-sized pieces

1 (15-ounce) can pinto and/or red kidney beans, rinsed and drained

1 (15-ounce) can diced tomatoes, undrained

1 (10½-ounce) can condensed beef broth

1 (10-ounce) can enchilada sauce

1 large onion, peeled and chopped

2 cloves of garlic, peeled and minced

1 cup water

4 tablespoons fine cornmeal or masa harina (corn flour)

2 tablespoons fresh cilantro, minced

1 cup (4 ounces) Queso Blanco or Monterey jack cheese, grated

Portuguese Beef Stew

Serves 8

Ingredients:

2 tablespoons extra-virgin
  olive oil
3 pounds beef bottom round
Salt and freshly ground black
  pepper, to taste
1 large onion, peeled and
  diced
2 cloves of garlic, peeled and
  minced
1 cup Zinfandel or other dry
  red wine
1 (6-ounce) can tomato paste
1 (28-ounce) can diced
  tomatoes
1 cup beef broth
1½ tablespoon pickling spices
1 bay leaf
2 teaspoons dried mint

*Serve this stew over pieces of torn French bread. You'll want about an ounce
of bread for each serving, or about 2 generous slices, depending
on the circumference of the loaf.*

1. Add the oil to the slow cooker. Trim the beef of any fat and cut it into bite-sized pieces. Add the meat to the cooker along with the salt, pepper, onion, and garlic. Stir to coat the meat and vegetables in the oil.

2. Add the wine, tomato paste, undrained tomatoes, and broth to a bowl or measuring cup. Stir to mix. Pour into the slow cooker. Add the pickling spices and bay leaf. Cover and cook on low for 7 hours or until the beef is cooked through and tender. Skim and discard any fat from the surface of the stew in the slow cooker. Remove and discard the bay leaf.

3. Stir in the dried mint; cover and continue to cook on low for 15 minutes to allow the mint to blend into the stew. (If you have fresh mint available, you can instead sprinkle about 1 teaspoon of minced fresh mint over each serving. Garnish each serving with a sprig of mint as well if desired.)

Handling Pickling Spices
When pickling spices are used in a dish, they're usually added to a muslin cooking bag or a tea ball or tied into a piece of cheesecloth. After the cooking time, they're pulled from the pot and discarded. For the Portuguese Beef Stew recipe, if you wish, you can simply stir them in with the other ingredients.

Chapter 17
Legumes and Grains

Fat-Free Refried Beans

Serves 8

Ingredients:

3 cups dried pinto beans

1 large onion, peeled and halved

½ fresh jalapeño pepper, seeded and chopped

6 cloves of garlic, peeled and minced

⅛ teaspoon ground cumin, optional

9 cups water

Salt and freshly ground black pepper, to taste

Some cooks like to mash the onion, jalapeño pepper, and garlic into the cooked beans; others prefer to discard them once the beans are cooked. (They've pretty much given up their flavors to the beans at this point anyhow.)

1. Rinse and drain the amount of beans called for in the recipe and then add them to a bowl or saucepan. Add enough water to cover the beans by 2 inches. Cover and let soak overnight or for 8 hours. Drain the beans, then rinse and drain again.

2. Add the beans, onion, jalapeño, garlic, and cumin to the slow cooker. Pour in the water and stir to combine. Cover and, stirring occasionally and adding more water as needed, cook on high for 8 hours or until the beans are cooked through and tender. (If you have to add more than 1 cup of water during cooking, lower the temperature to low or simmer.)

3. Once the beans are cooked, strain them, reserving the liquid. Mash the beans with a potato masher, adding some of the reserved water as needed to attain desired consistency. Add salt and pepper to taste.

Reheating Fat-Free Refried Beans

Fat-Free Refried Beans can be reheated in the microwave or using any other traditional method that you use to warm up leftovers. However, if you want to add a touch of authentic flavor (and fat) to them, melt some lard in a nonstick skillet over medium heat, stir in the beans, and sauté until heated through.

Barley and Bean Soup with Beef

You can substitute a 15-ounce rinsed and drained can of cannelini beans for the dried; if you do, you can add the tomatoes along with the other ingredients and omit the last hour of cooking time.

1. Rinse and drain the dried beans. Put in a bowl and add enough water to cover the beans by 2 inches. Cover and let soak for 8 hours or overnight. Drain the beans, rinse, and add to the slow cooker.

2. Trim off and discard any fat from the chuck roast and then cut it into bite-sized pieces; add to the slow cooker along with the rinsed pearl barley.

3. Remove the stems from the spinach; chop it and add to the slow cooker along with the garlic, beef broth, water or vegetable broth, celery, onion, carrots, parsnip, and turnip. Stir to combine. Cover and cook on low for 8 hours, or until the beans are cooked through.

4. Stir in the undrained diced tomatoes. Cover and cook for an additional hour. Taste for seasoning and add salt and pepper if needed.

Serves 8

Ingredients:
½ cup dried cannelini (white kidney) beans
2 pounds beef chuck
½ cup pearl barley, rinsed
2 cups fresh spinach
2 cloves of garlic, peeled and minced
2 cups beef broth
2 cups water or vegetable broth
1 stalk celery, sliced
1 large onion, peeled and diced
1 cup baby carrots, sliced
1 parsnip, peeled and diced
1 turnip, peeled and diced
1 (15-ounce) can diced tomatoes
Salt and freshly ground black pepper, to taste

Mock Enchiladas

Serves 8

Ingredients:

2 pounds lean ground beef
1 large onion, peeled and
    diced
1 (4½-ounce) can chopped
    chilies
1 (12-ounce) jar mild
    enchilada sauce
1 (10½-ounce) can golden
    mushroom soup
1 (10½-ounce) can Cheddar
    cheese soup
1 (10½-ounce) can cream of
    mushroom soup
1 (10½-ounce) can cream of
    celery soup
2 cups refried beans
Plain corn tortilla chips, to
    taste

To make this a one-dish meal, serve this dish over shredded lettuce and topped with chopped green onion, a dollop of sour cream, and some guacamole.

1. Add the ground beef and diced onion to a nonstick skillet over medium heat; brown the hamburger for 15 minutes, until cooked through, breaking it apart and stirring it into the onions as you do so. Drain and discard any fat that is rendered from the ground beef.

2. Add the cooked beef and onions to the slow cooker. Stir in the chilies, enchilada sauce, soups, and refried beans. Cover and cook on low for 6 hours.

3. Stir 8 ounces or more tortilla chips into the mixture in the slow cooker. Cover and cook on low for 15 minutes or until the tortilla chips are soft.

Corn Tortilla Casserole

Serve this casserole along with a tossed salad. Have some taco or enchilada sauce at the table along with an assortment of optional condiments, like chopped jalapeño peppers, diced green onions, sour cream, and guacamole.

1. Add the ground beef and onion to a nonstick skillet over medium heat; brown the hamburger for 15 minutes, until cooked through, breaking it apart and stirring it into the onions as you do so. Drain and discard any fat that is rendered from the ground beef.

2. Stir the garlic, taco seasoning, salt, black pepper, diced tomatoes, tomato paste, and refried beans into the ground beef and onions. Bring to a simmer, and, stirring occasionally, cook for 5 to 10 minutes.

3. Treat the crock of the slow cooker with nonstick spray. Add enough of the beef and tomato sauce to the slow cooker to cover the bottom of the crock. Lay one of the corn tortillas over the beef and tomato sauce, and then ladle more of the sauce over the top; sprinkle with Cheddar cheese. Repeat until all of the corn tortillas, sauce, and Cheddar cheese are in the slow cooker, ending with a tortilla topped with sauce. Cover and cook on low for 8 hours. Cut into 8 wedges and serve.

Cheese Warning

Some less expensive or store brands of Cheddar cheese contain a higher oil content and therefore tend to separate during the slow-cooking process. The only failed recipe test done for this cookbook was done using a store brand. After that, all recipes calling for Cheddar cheese were tested using Kraft mild or medium Cheddar.

Serves 8

Ingredients:
2 pounds lean ground beef
1 small onion, peeled and
    diced
1 clove of garlic, minced
1 envelope taco seasoning
Salt and freshly ground black
    pepper, to taste
1 (15-ounce) can diced
    tomatoes
1 (6-ounce) can tomato paste
2 cups refried beans
Nonstick spray
9 corn tortillas
2 cups (8 ounces) Cheddar
    cheese, grated

Preparing Great Northern Beans for the Slow Cooker

Yield varies according to the recipe

Ingredients:
Great northern beans
Water

Presoaking beans removes the enzymes that make them difficult for some people to digest. Some claim that this method of soaking the beans is more effective at removing those enzymes than the quick-soaking method. The biggest advantage, however, is that the overnight soaking method results in beans that cook more evenly.

1. Rinse and drain the amount of beans called for in the recipe and then add them to a bowl or saucepan. Add enough water to cover the beans by 2 inches. Cover and let soak overnight or for 8 hours.

2. Drain the beans, then rinse and drain again. Add them to the slow cooker according to the recipe instructions unless the slow cooker recipe calls for tomatoes or sugar. Do not add salt to the slow cooker until the beans are cooked through either.

3. If the recipe calls for tomatoes or sugar, speed up the slow-cooking process by cooking the beans together with enough water to cover the beans by 2 inches in a saucepan. Bring to a boil over high heat, and then reduce the heat and simmer the beans for 40 minutes to an hour or until they just begin to become tender. Drain, reserving the amount of cooking liquid to equal the amount of water called for in the slow cooker recipe, and add to the slow cooker. Continue to cook according to recipe instructions.

Cooking Beans Isn't an Exact Science
The amount of time it will take to cook (or slow-cook) beans depends on the size and variety of beans used and, due to the age of the beans and other factors, can even vary from bag to bag of the same variety of beans.

Quick-Soaking Great Northern Beans

This quick-soaking method will work with most beans, except for cannellini (white kidney beans), which will become mushy.

Yield varies according to the recipe

Ingredients:
Great northern beans
Water

1. Rinse and drain the amount of beans called for in the recipe and then add them to a saucepan. Add enough water to cover the beans by 2 inches. Bring to a boil over high heat. Boil for 2 minutes. Remove the pan from the heat; cover and let sit for an hour.

2. Follow the instructions in Steps 2 and 3 in the Preparing Great Northern Beans for the Slow Cooker recipe (page 218).

Barbecue Beef and Bean Soup

You can serve this soup as a main dish with a tossed salad and over or along with corn bread.

Serves 8

Ingredients:
1 pound great northern beans, soaked
1 large onion, peeled and diced
⅛ teaspoon freshly ground black pepper
2 pounds beef short or Western ribs
6 cups water
¾ cup barbecue sauce
Salt and freshly ground black pepper, to taste
Optional: 1 tablespoon brown sugar

1. Soak the beans overnight and then precook them on the stovetop according to the instructions given in Preparing Great Northern Beans for the Slow Cooker (page 218).

2. Once the beans are precooked, add them to the slow cooker. Stir in the onion and pepper. Add the beef ribs and pour in the water. Cover and cook on low for 8 hours or until the beans are cooked through.

3. Remove the short ribs and cut the meat from the bones. Stir the meat and barbecue sauce into the beans. Cover and cook on low for 1 hour. Taste for seasoning and add salt, pepper, and brown sugar if desired.

Crushed Red Pepper Beef and Pinto Beans

Serves 6

Ingredients:

1 pound dried pinto beans
6 cups cold water
½ pound bacon, diced
1 pound beef chuck or sirloin steak
½ teaspoon dried red pepper flakes, crushed
1 large onion, peeled and diced
4 cloves of garlic, peeled and minced
1 (6-ounce) can tomato paste
1½ tablespoons chili powder
Salt and freshly ground black pepper, to taste
1 teaspoon ground cumin
½ teaspoon dried marjoram or cilantro

Serve this as a main dish along with a tossed salad and corn bread or as a side dish at your next cookout.

1. Rinse and drain the dried beans. Put in a bowl and add enough water to cover the beans by 2 inches. Cover and let soak for 8 hours or overnight. Drain the beans, rinse, and add to the slow cooker along with the water.

2. Add bacon to a nonstick skillet over medium heat. Trim the steak of any fat, cut into bite-sized pieces, and add to the skillet along with the crushed red pepper flakes and onion; sauté for 15 minutes or until the onion is just beginning to brown. Stir in the garlic and sauté for 30 seconds. Stir the sautéed mixture into the beans and water in the slow cooker. Cover and cook on low for 8 hours.

3. Stir in the tomato paste, chili powder, salt, pepper, cumin, and marjoram or cilantro. Cover and cook on low for 2 hours or until the beans are cooked through. Taste for seasoning and adjust if necessary.

Americanized Moussaka

This adaptation would probably make a Greek cuisine purist shudder, but it's a way to hide vegetables in a kid-friendly meal. With the addition of the optional Cheddar cheese it can also serve as a hummus-style party dip or spread, a baked potato topper, or even a warm salad dressing. As a bonus, it freezes well.

1. Prepare the Meatless Moussaka recipe according to the instructions on page 145.

2. Stir in the cooked and drained ground beef. Cut the cream cheese into cubes and stir into the moussaka. Add the heavy cream and eggs to a bowl or measuring cup; whisk until the eggs are beaten into the cream and then stir into the moussaka. Cover and cook on low for an additional 1 to 2 hours.

3. If using the optional Cheddar cheese, gradually stir it into the mixture; cover and cook on low for 15 minutes or until the cheese is melted and can be completely stirred into the moussaka. If you won't be serving the moussaka immediately, reduce the heat on slow cooker to warm.

Serves 12

Ingredients:
Meatless Moussaka (page 145)
3 pounds lean ground beef, cooked and drained of fat
1 (8-ounce) package cream cheese
1 cup heavy cream
2 large eggs
Optional: 4 cups (1 pound) medium Cheddar cheese, grated

Dueling Flavors Chili

Serves 8–10

Ingredients:

1 pound ground chuck
1 pound ground pork
2 large yellow onions, peeled and diced
6 cloves of garlic, peeled and minced
1 teaspoon whole cumin seeds
2 tablespoons chili powder
¼ teaspoon oregano
1 (28-ounce) can diced tomatoes
¼ cup ketchup
¼ teaspoon cinnamon
¼ teaspoon ground cloves
2 tablespoons brown sugar
2 (15-ounce) cans kidney beans, rinsed and drained
1 (14-ounce) can lower sodium beef broth
Optional: 1 tablespoon Worcestershire sauce
Water, if needed
Optional: Hot sauce to taste
Salt and freshly ground black pepper, to taste

This is a sweet and hot chili. The longer you cook it, the richer the flavor.

1. Add the ground chuck, pork, onion, garlic, cumin seeds, chili powder, and oregano to a nonstick skillet; cook over medium heat until the beef and pork are browned and cooked through. Drain off any excess fat and discard. Transfer to the slow cooker.

2. Stir in the tomatoes, ketchup, cinnamon, cloves, brown sugar, kidney beans, beef broth, and Worcestershire sauce if using. Add enough water, if needed, to bring the liquid level to the top of the beans and meat. Cover and cook on low for 8 hours.

3. Taste for seasoning and add hot sauce, if desired, and salt and pepper if needed. You may also wish to add more brown sugar or chili powder, according to your taste.

Chapter 18
Pasta

Pasta and Bean Soup

You can substitute a smoked turkey thigh for the ham hocks.

Serves 8

Ingredients:

1 (1½-pound) pork shoulder
    roast
2 (15-ounce) cans cannelloni
    or small white beans
2 smoked ham hocks
1 bay leaf
2 cloves of garlic, peeled and
    minced
1 small yellow onion, peeled
    and diced
1 cup baby carrots, cut into
    thirds
¼ cup lovage or celery leaves,
    minced
1 (15-ounce) can diced
    tomatoes
Pinch dried red pepper flakes
¼ teaspoon dried oregano
Pinch dried rosemary
½ teaspoon dried basil
1 teaspoon dried parsley
½ teaspoon sugar
1 cup water
2 cups chicken broth
Salt and freshly ground black
    pepper, to taste
1 cup small pasta, like orzo
    or stars

1. Trim and discard any fat from the pork roast and cut the roast into bite-sized pieces. Add the pork and all of the other ingredients except for the pasta to the slow cooker. Cover and cook on low for 8 hours.

2. Remove the bay leaf and discard. Remove the ham hocks and set aside to cool enough to remove the meat from the bones. Use two forks to shred the ham and return it to the slow cooker.

3. Optional step: Remove several cups of the soup and purée in a blender or food processor. Return puréed beans to the pot. Return the soup to a simmer.

4. Cook the pasta according to package directions. Drain and add to the slow cooker. Stir to mix into the soup. Taste for seasoning and add additional salt and pepper if needed.

Cheese-Lover's Tortellini

All it takes to make this dish a meal is a tossed salad and some garlic bread.

Serves 8

Ingredients:
2 pounds lean ground beef
1 medium onion, peeled and
   diced
2 cloves of garlic, peeled and
   minced
1 (26-ounce) jar pasta sauce
2 (15-ounce) cans diced
   tomatoes, drained
½ teaspoon sugar
1 (10-ounce) box frozen
   spinach, thawed
2 cups ricotta cheese
½ cup freshly grated
   Parmesan-Reggiano
   cheese
1 (1-pound) bag frozen
   cheese tortellini
Salt and freshly ground black
   pepper, to taste

1. Add the ground beef and onion to a nonstick skillet over medium-high heat; stir and fry for 8 minutes or until the onions are transparent and the meat is broken apart and no longer pink. Stir in the garlic and sauté for 30 seconds. Drain and discard any fat rendered from the meat.

2. Transfer to the slow cooker. Stir in the pasta sauce, drained tomatoes, and sugar. Cover and cook on low for 8 hours.

3. Skim any additional fat from the surface of the pasta sauce in the slow cooker and discard. Squeeze the thawed spinach to remove any excess moisture and stir it into the pasta sauce along with the ricotta and Parmesan-Reggiano cheeses. Cover and cook on low while you cook the pasta.

4. Cook the tortellini according to package directions. Drain and fold into the pasta sauce in the slow cooker. Taste for seasoning and add salt and pepper if needed. Serve directly from the slow cooker.

Easy Mac and Cheese

Serves 8

Ingredients:
Nonstick spray
2 cups milk
4 cups elbow macaroni
1 (2-pound) box Velveeta
    cheese
Salt and freshly ground black
    pepper, to taste

This is a popular dish for a carry-in supper or buffet.

1. Treat the slow cooker with nonstick spray. Pour the milk into the slow cooker. To bring the milk to temperature, cover and cook on high while you cook the macaroni.

2. Cook the macaroni according to the package directions. Drain and add to the slow cooker. Stir into the milk. Reduce the temperature of the slow cooker to low.

3. Cut the cheese into small cubes. Stir into the macaroni and milk. Cover and cook on low for 1 hour. Stir. Add additional milk if needed.

4. Cover and cook on low for another hour, or until the cheese is completely melted and you can stir it into the macaroni. To serve, ladle the mac and cheese directly from the slow cooker.

Mexican-Style Macaroni and Cheese

Use mild or hot salsa, according to taste. Serve with a tossed salad and baked corn tortilla chips.

1. Add the butter, onion, and bell pepper to the slow cooker. Cover and cook on high for 30 minutes, or until the onion is transparent.

2. Stir in the flour, salt, cilantro, and cumin. Cook and stir for 3 minutes, adding a little of the milk, if necessary, to form a loose paste. Whisk in the milk. Cover and continue to cook on high while you cook the pasta.

3. Cook the macaroni according to package directions; drain.

4. Whisk the milk mixture in the slow cooker. Reduce heat to low. Stir in the drained macaroni, Colby cheese, Monterey jack cheese, salsa, and olives. Cover and cook on low for 2 hours or until cheese is melted and can be stirred into the sauce completely.

5. Taste for seasoning. Add salt and pepper, if needed, and chili powder, to taste if desired. To serve, ladle from the slow cooker onto a dinner plate.

Serves 8

Ingredients:
3 tablespoons butter
1 medium onion, peeled and diced
1 red bell pepper, seeded and diced
⅓ cup all-purpose flour
½ teaspoon salt
1 teaspoon dried cilantro, crushed
½ teaspoon ground cumin
3 cups milk
4 cups dried elbow macaroni
2 cups (8 ounces) Colby cheese, cubed
2 cups (8 ounces) Monterey jack cheese, grated
1 cup bottled salsa
⅔ cup halved pitted green and/or ripe olives
Salt and freshly ground black pepper, to taste
Optional: Chili powder, to taste

Mushroom Chicken

Serve this delicious chicken with spinach salad and garlic bread.

Serves 6

Ingredients:

2 cups sliced fresh
mushrooms

1 (15-ounce) can diced
tomatoes with basil,
garlic, and oregano

1 red bell pepper, seeded and
diced

1 medium onion, peeled and
thinly sliced

¼ cup dry red wine or beef
broth

2 tablespoons quick-cooking
tapioca

2 tablespoons balsamic
vinegar

3 cloves of garlic, peeled and
minced

2½ pounds meaty chicken
pieces (breasts, thighs,
and/or drumsticks), skin
removed

¼ teaspoon salt

¼ teaspoon paprika

¼ teaspoon freshly ground
black pepper

1 (9-ounce) package fresh or
frozen cheese tortellini or
ravioli

Optional: Parmesan-
Reggiano, grated

1. Add the mushrooms, undrained tomatoes, red pepper, onion, wine or broth, tapioca, balsamic vinegar, and garlic to the slow cooker. Stir to combine. Place the chicken pieces on top of the sauce. Sprinkle the salt, paprika, and black pepper over the chicken. Cover and cook on low for 8 hours.

2. Remove the chicken pieces and keep warm. (Or, if you prefer, once the chicken is cool enough to handle, remove the chicken from the bones; shred the chicken and discard the bones.)

3. Add the tortellini or ravioli to the sauce; cover and cook on high for 10 to 15 minutes or until the pasta is done. If using shredded chicken, stir it into the pasta and sauce. If using chicken pieces, arrange them on a serving platter and top with the pasta and sauce. Serve with additional grated cheese if desired.

Pasta and the Slow Cooker

While it's possible to cook fresh (or fresh refrigerated) pasta in the slow cooker, unless you can stay close enough to keep an eye on the slow cooker, don't attempt it. It only takes a few minutes and one more dirty pan to cook pasta according to the package directions. That's the foolproof way to fix it.

Freezer to the Plate Chicken Pasta Sauce

Serve over your choice of cooked pasta along with a tossed salad and garlic bread. Have salt, a pepper grinder, and freshly grated Parmesan-Reggiano cheese at the table for those who want it.

1. Add the marinara sauce to the slow cooker. Add the chicken, pushing each piece down into the sauce. Cover and cook on low for 8 hours.

2. Use tongs or a slotted spoon to remove the chicken to a cutting board. Use two forks to shred the chicken. Return to the slow cooker and stir into the sauce.

Serves 4

Ingredients:
1 (26-ounce) jar marinara sauce
8 frozen chicken tenders

Tortellini Soup

Opening a few cans is the most labor involved in making this dish. The result tastes like you've been cooking all day.

1. Add the oil and onion to the slow cooker. Stir to coat the onion in oil. Cover and cook on high for 30 minutes, or until the onions are transparent.

2. Stir in the broth, tomatoes, and spinach. Reduce the temperature of the slow cooker to low, cover, and cook for 4 hours.

3. Cook the tortellini according to package directions; drain and stir into the soup. Serve topped with grated cheese if desired.

Serves 6

Ingredients:
1 tablespoon extra-virgin olive oil
1 small onion, peeled and finely diced
2 (14-ounce) cans of chicken broth
1 (15-ounce) can of stewed Italian tomatoes
1 (15-ounce) can of chopped spinach, drained
1 (16-ounce) package of fresh or frozen tortellini, your preferred flavor
Optional: Parmesan-Reggiano cheese

Tuxedo Soup

This soup, which gets its name from the bowtie pasta, is one that the kids will love. Serve it with a tossed salad and garlic bread.

Serves 8

Ingredients:

1 pound lean ground beef

1 medium onion, peeled and diced

1 small green pepper, seeded and diced

1 stalk celery, diced

1 medium carrot, peeled and diced

4 cloves of garlic, peeled and minced

2 (15-ounce) cans diced tomatoes, undrained

1 cup water

1 (26-ounce) jar spaghetti sauce

1 tablespoon sugar

½ teaspoon dried Italian seasoning, crushed

Dash dried red pepper flakes

1 cup bowtie pasta

Salt and freshly ground black pepper, to taste

Parmesan-Reggiano or mozzarella cheese, grated

Optional: Fresh flat-leaf parsley, minced

1. Add the ground beef, onion, green pepper, celery, and carrot to a non-stick skillet and, stirring frequently, sauté over medium-high heat for 8 minutes or until the vegetables are tender and the meat is no longer pink. Stir in the garlic and sauté for 30 seconds. Drain and discard any excess fat. Transfer to the slow cooker.

2. Stir in the undrained tomatoes, water, spaghetti sauce, sugar, Italian seasoning, and red pepper flakes. Cover and cook on low for 8 hours.

3. Cook the pasta according to package directions. Drain and stir into the slow cooker. Thin the soup with additional hot water if necessary. Taste for seasoning and add salt and pepper if desired. Ladle into soup bowls. Sprinkle cheese to taste over each serving. Garnish with parsley if using.

Extra Vegetables
Thanks to the spaghetti sauce, you can hide more vegetables in Tuxedo Soup and the kids won't even notice. For example, dice a few more carrots and stir them in with the other ingredients in Step 2.

Chapter 19
Rice

Shrimp Risotto

Serves 6

Ingredients:
1 tablespoon olive oil
2 tablespoons butter, melted
2 medium white onions,
   peeled and diced
2 cups Arborio rice
½ cup dry white wine
1 cup Shrimp-Infused Broth
   (see sidebar)
5 cups chicken broth
1½ pounds shrimp, peeled
   and deveined
½ cup freshly grated
   Parmesan-Reggiano
   cheese
3 tablespoons fresh flat-leaf
   parsley, minced
Salt, to taste

Shrimp-Infused Broth will give this risotto a flavor boost. If you don't want to take the time to make it, substitute 1 cup of additional chicken broth and stir a pinch of crushed saffron threads directly into the slow cooker.

1. Add the oil, butter, and onion to the slow cooker. Stir to coat the onions in the oil. Cover and cook on high for 30 minutes or until the onion is transparent.

2. Stir in the rice; continue to stir for several minutes or until the rice turns translucent. Add the white wine and broths. Cover and cook on high for 2½ hours or until the rice is cooked al dente.

3. Add the shrimp to the slow cooker, atop the risotto. Cover and cook on high for 20 minutes or until the shrimp is pink. Stir in the cheese and parsley. Taste for seasoning and add salt if needed. Serve immediately.

Shrimp-Infused Broth
Add 1 cup of chicken broth and the shrimp shells from 1½ pounds of shrimp to a saucepan. Bring to a boil over medium-high heat; reduce the heat and maintain a simmer for 15 minutes or until the shells are pink. Strain; crush a pinch of saffron threads and stir it into the broth.

Breakfast Risotto

Serve this like you would cooked oatmeal: topped with additional brown sugar, raisins or other dried fruit, and milk.

1. Add the butter and rice to the slow cooker; stir to coat the rice in the butter.

2. Add the remaining ingredients and stir to combine. Cover and cook on low for 9 hours or until the rice is cooked through.

Arborio Rice
Arborio rice is a short-grain rice used in risotto because it has a creamy texture when cooked. Other varieties used in risotto are Vialone Nano and Carnaroli rice.

Serves 6

Ingredients:
¼ cup butter, melted
1½ cups Arborio rice
3 small apples, peeled, cored, and sliced
1½ teaspoons ground cinnamon
⅛ teaspoon freshly ground nutmeg
⅛ teaspoon ground cloves
⅛ teaspoon salt
⅓ cup brown sugar
1 cup apple juice
3 cups milk

Beans and Rice

You can add an additional boost to the flavor of this dish by substituting spicy tomato-vegetable juice for the broth or water.

1. Treat the slow cooker with nonstick spray. Add the oil and rice; stir to coat the rice in the oil.

2. Add the black beans, pinto beans, salt, Italian seasoning, onion flakes, tomatoes, and vegetable broth or water to the slow cooker. Stir to combine. Cover and cook on low for 6 hours or until the rice is tender.

Serves 6

Ingredients:
Nonstick spray
1 tablespoon olive oil
1 cup converted long-grain rice
1 (15-ounce) can black beans, rinsed and drained
1 (15-ounce) can pinto beans, rinsed and drained
½ teaspoon salt
1 teaspoon Italian seasoning
½ tablespoon dried onion flakes
1 (15-ounce) can diced tomatoes
1¼ cups vegetable broth or water

Zesty Peanut Soup

Serves 8

Ingredients:

1 large sweet onion, peeled and diced

2 green onions, cleaned and diced

2 red bell peppers, seeded and diced

4 cloves of garlic, peeled and minced

1 (28-ounce) can diced or crushed tomatoes

8 cups vegetable broth

¼ teaspoon freshly ground black pepper

½ teaspoon chili powder

½ cup brown rice

1 cup peanut butter

Salt

Optional: Sour cream

Optional: Roasted or dry-roasted peanuts, chopped

Optional: Hot sauce, to taste

This soup is one that you can make ahead because it tastes even better the next day. The rice cooks into the soup and acts as a thickener.

1. Add the onions, bell peppers, garlic, tomatoes, broth, black pepper, chili powder, and rice to the slow cooker. Stir to combine. Cover and cook on low for 8 hours or until the onion is transparent and the red bell pepper is tender.

2. Stir in the peanut butter. Increase the heat to high, cover, and cook for 30 minutes or until heated through. Taste for seasoning; add salt and additional black pepper if needed.

3. To serve, ladle into soup bowls. If desired, add a dollop of sour cream and chopped peanuts to each serving. Have hot sauce available for those who wish to add it to their soup.

Pepper Pork and Rice

This stew is good garnished with strips of green onion. (Only add the poblano and jalapeño peppers if you want a hot, spicy stew; otherwise, omit them entirely or substitute chopped green pepper.)

1. Trim and discard fat from the pork; cut the pork into 1-inch cubes.

2. Add the oil to the slow cooker and bring it to temperature over high.

3. Add the pork; cover and cook for 15 minutes. Stir the pork and brown for another 15 minutes. Drain off and discard any excess fat rendered from the meat.

4. Add the remaining ingredients (except for the cilantro or parsley; stir to combine. Reduce the slow cooker heat to low, cover, and cook for 8 hours or until the meat and rice are cooked through.

5. Discard cinnamon stick. Stir in additional chicken broth if the stew is too thick and bring it to temperature. Stir in the cilantro or parsley if desired. Taste for seasoning and add salt if needed. Serve warm.

Serves 8

Ingredients:
2 pounds boneless pork shoulder
1 tablespoon cooking oil
1 large onion, peeled and diced
Optional: 2 fresh poblano peppers, seeded and cut into 1-inch pieces
Optional: 1 fresh jalapeño pepper, seeded and chopped
4 cloves garlic, minced
1 (2-inch) cinnamon stick
2 cups converted rice
3 cups water
4 cups chicken broth
2 (15-ounce) cans diced tomatoes
1 tablespoon chili powder
1 teaspoon dried oregano, crushed
¼ teaspoon black pepper
Optional: ¼ cup snipped fresh cilantro or parsley
Optional: Salt, to taste

Rice and Vegetables

Serves 8

Ingredients:
1 cup long-grain rice
1 cup tomato juice
1 pound ground beef,
    browned and drained
½ pound ground lamb or
    pork, browned and
    drained
1 large yellow onion, peeled
    and diced
1 tablespoon dried parsley
¼ teaspoon salt
Freshly ground black pepper,
    to taste
1 teaspoon paprika
⅛ teaspoon ground allspice
Pinch ground cinnamon
1 teaspoon sugar
2 (15-ounce) cans diced
    tomatoes
4 green peppers, seeded and
    diced
1 cup beef broth
2 tablespoons lemon juice
Water or additional broth if
    needed

This dish has all of the elements of a stuffed peppers and tomatoes recipe, but it saves you some time because instead of making a filling for the peppers and tomatoes, you instead prepare it in layers in the slow cooker.

1. In a large mixing bowl, combine the rice, tomato juice, beef, lamb or pork, onion, parsley, salt, black pepper, paprika, allspice, cinnamon, and sugar. Set aside.

2. Add one can of the diced tomatoes to a 4-quart or larger slow cooker. Add half of the meat-rice mixture. Spread the diced green peppers over the top of the meat-rice mixture, then top the peppers with the rest of the meat. Add the other can of diced tomatoes.

3. Pour in the beef broth and add the lemon juice. If needed, add additional water or broth to bring the liquid to almost the top of the solid ingredients. Cover and cook for 8 hours on low. Taste for seasoning and add additional salt and pepper if needed.

Soupy to Succulent
If too much liquid remains in the slow cooker, cook uncovered long enough to allow some of the liquid to evaporate.

Polynesian Pork Chops

You can substitute pork steaks for the pork chops. (Because pork steaks tend to have more marbling, there's actually less chance of pork steaks being dry when prepared this way.)

1. Treat the slow cooker with nonstick spray. Trim and discard any fat from the pork chops and then cut them into bite-sized pieces. Arrange half of the pork over the bottom of the slow cooker. Top with the bell pepper, onion, and rice. Sprinkle the salt and place the remaining pork over the rice.

2. Add the entire can of pineapple, barbecue sauce, water, and black pepper to a bowl or measuring cup; stir to mix and then pour into the slow cooker. Cover and cook on low for 8 hours or until the pork is cooked through and the rice is tender.

3. Stir the mixture in the slow cooker to fluff the rice. Taste for seasoning and add additional salt, barbecue sauce, and pepper if needed. Top each serving with chopped macadamia nuts if desired.

Serves 6

Ingredients:
Nonstick spray
6 (6-ounce) boneless pork chops
1 green bell pepper, seeded and diced
1 large onion, peeled and diced
2 cups converted rice
1 teaspoon sea salt
1 (20-ounce) can crushed pineapple
1 cup honey-mustard barbecue sauce
3 cups water
Freshly ground black pepper, to taste
Optional: Dry-roasted macadamia nuts, chopped

Tex-Mex Chili

Serves 6

Ingredients:

1 pound turkey or chorizo
    sausage

Nonstick spray

1 medium onion, peeled and
    diced

1 (15-ounce) can Tex-Mex-
    style chili beans

1 (11-ounce) can whole
    kernel corn with peppers,
    drained

1 (6-ounce) package Spanish-
    style rice mix

6 cups water

*Serve this chili with warm flour tortillas or baked corn tortilla chips. It's
good topped with a dollop of guacamole and sour cream.*

1. Remove casings from the sausage, if present, and add to a nonstick skil-
    let. Breaking apart the sausage as you do so, fry over medium-high heat
    for 8 minutes or until the sausage is no longer pink. Drain and discard
    any rendered fat. Treat the slow cooker with nonstick spray and add the
    onion and browned sausage.

2. Stir in the undrained beans, corn, and seasoning packet from the rice.
    Pour in the water. Cover and cook on low for 6 hours.

3. Stir the rice mix into the contents of the slow cooker. Cover and cook
    on low for 1 hour.

Old World Cabbage Rolls

You won't use an entire head of cabbage in this recipe, but a large one gives you leaves large enough to make bigger cabbage rolls. If you prefer, substitute a small to medium head of cabbage and make smaller rolls.

Serves 8

Ingredients:
1 large head of cabbage
1 large egg
1 (8-ounce) can tomato sauce
½ cup brown rice
1 envelope onion soup mix
1 pound lean ground turkey
⅓ cup Parmesan-Reggiano cheese, grated
3 cups vegetable or tomato juice

1. Remove and discard the outer leaves of the cabbage. Peel off 8 large leaves. (Refrigerate the unused cabbage for another use.) Soften the cabbage leaves (see sidebar).

2. Add the egg, tomato sauce, uncooked rice, soup mix, ground turkey, and cheese to a bowl; mix well.

3. Spoon about ¼ cup of the meat mixture into the center of each cabbage leaf. Fold the ends of the leaf over the filling, and then roll the sides over the ends. Place seam side down in the slow cooker.

4. Pour the vegetable or tomato juice over the cabbage rolls. Cover and cook on low for 6 hours.

Softening Cabbage Leaves
To soften the cabbage leaves, one option is to layer them in a microwave-safe bowl and microwave on high for 2 minutes. The other alternative is to put them in a bowl, pour boiling water over the top of them and let them rest in the water for 2 minutes; use tongs to remove the cabbage leaves and pat them dry with paper towels or drain them on a clean, cotton cloth.

Greek Meatballs

Serves 8

Ingredients:
1½ pounds lean ground beef
1 cup converted rice
1 small yellow onion, peeled
    and finely diced
3 cloves garlic, peeled and
    minced
2 teaspoons dried parsley
½ teaspoon oregano
1 teaspoon ground cumin
2 teaspoons dried mint
1 large egg
All-purpose flour
2 cups tomato juice or
    tomato-vegetable juice
2 tablespoons Greek extra-
    virgin olive oil
½ teaspoon ground
    cinnamon
1 tablespoon honey
4 cups water
Salt and freshly ground black
    pepper, to taste

Serve this youvarlakia (Greek-style meatball) adaptation like a soup with some crusty bread. To complete the meal, add a salad tossed with a lemon juice and extra-virgin olive oil vinaigrette and topped with feta cheese.

1. Make the meatballs by mixing the ground beef together with the rice, onion, garlic, parsley, oregano, cumin, mint, and egg; shape into small meatballs and roll each one in flour.

2. Add the tomato or tomato-vegetable juice, olive oil, cinnamon, and honey to the slow cooker. Carefully add the meatballs. Pour in the water. (The water should take the liquid level up to where it completely covers the meatballs.)

3. Cover and cook on low for 6 hours or until the meatballs are cooked through. Taste for seasoning and add salt and pepper if needed.

Spanish Chicken and Rice

Have Spanish extra-virgin olive oil at the table for those who wish to drizzle a little over the rice. For more heat, sprinkle some additional dried red pepper flakes on top, too.

Serves 4

Ingredients:
1 tablespoon olive or
    vegetable oil
4 chicken thighs
4 split chicken breasts
2 tablespoons lemon juice
4 ounces smoked ham, cubed
1 medium onion, peeled and
    diced
1 red bell pepper, seeded and
    diced
4 cloves of garlic, peeled and
    minced
Nonstick spray
2½ cups water
1¾ cups chicken broth
1 teaspoon oregano
½ teaspoon salt
¼ teaspoon saffron threads,
    crushed
⅛ teaspoon dried red pepper
    flakes, crushed
2 cups converted long-grain
    rice

1. Bring the oil to temperature in a large nonstick skillet over medium-high heat. Put the chicken in the skillet skin side down and fry for 5 minutes or until the skin is browned. Transfer the chicken to a plate and sprinkle the lemon juice over the chicken.

2. Pour off and discard all but 2 tablespoons of the fat in the skillet. Reduce the heat under the skillet to medium. Add the ham, onion, and bell pepper; sauté for 5 minutes or until the onion is transparent. Stir in the garlic and sauté for 30 seconds.

3. Treat the slow cooker with nonstick spray. Pour the cooked ham and vegetables into the slow cooker. Add the water, broth, oregano, salt, saffron, red pepper flakes, and rice. Stir to combine.

4. Place the chicken thighs, skin side up, in the slow cooker and add the breast pieces on top of the thighs. Cover and cook on low for 6 hours or until the rice is tender and the chicken is cooked through. Place a split chicken breast and thigh on each serving plate. Stir and fluff the rice mixture and spoon it onto the plates.

Adding a Vegetable to Spanish Chicken and Rice
After you've removed the chicken from the slow cooker in Step 4, stir in 1 cup (or more) of thawed baby peas. Stir into the mixture remaining in the cooker when you fluff the rice. The heat from the rice should be sufficient to warm the peas so you can serve immediately.

Chapter 20
Casseroles

Chicken, Broccoli, and Rice Casserole

This is one of the few recipes cooked on high in this book. Using minute rice means the rice will be cooked correctly, and the shorter 4-hour cooking time makes this the perfect meal to put in the slow cooker to have ready for when you and the family get home from church or an afternoon at the kids' ball games.

1. Treat the slow cooker with nonstick spray. Add the mushroom soup, Cheez Whiz, mayonnaise, lemon juice, water, and milk; stir to combine.

2. Cut the chicken breasts into bite-sized pieces and chop the water chestnuts; stir into the soup mixture in the slow cooker along with the broccoli florets, rice, onion, celery, and sliced mushrooms if using. Cover and cook on high for 4 hours or until the rice is cooked through.

3. Taste the casserole for seasoning; stir in salt and pepper if needed. Sprinkle paprika over the casserole, if desired, and top with the almonds.

Disguise the Leftovers

Preheat oven to 350°F. Transfer the leftover Chicken, Broccoli, and Rice Casserole to a casserole dish treated with nonstick spray. Bake for 20 minutes while you pulse 2 slices of bread in the food processor until they're fine bread crumbs; mix together with 1 tablespoon melted butter. Top the casserole with the buttered bread crumbs and bake for 10 more minutes or until the casserole is heated through and the bread crumbs are golden brown.

Ham and Potato Casserole

At 12 servings, this recipe obviously feeds a crowd, which makes it a great dish to take to a carry-in dinner.

1. Treat the slow cooker with nonstick spray. Add the sour cream, soup, and dried onion to the slow cooker; mix well.

2. Stir in the hash brown potatoes, cheese, and ham.

3. In a bowl, toss the stuffing mix together with the melted butter. Evenly sprinkle over the hash brown potatoes mixture in the slow cooker. Cover and cook on low for 6 hours.

Serves 12

Ingredients:
Nonstick spray
1 cup sour cream
1 (10¾-ounce) can condensed cream of chicken soup
1 tablespoon dried minced onion
2 (16-ounce) bags frozen hash brown potatoes, thawed
2 cups (8 ounces) Cheddar cheese, grated
2 cups cooked ham, diced
1 (6-ounce) package herb-seasoned stuffing mix
¼ cup butter, melted

Hamburger-Vegetable Casserole

When you taste this casserole for seasoning at the end of the cooking time, you can also stir in some dried herbs to add some additional flavor. For example, oregano and red pepper flakes work well with tomato soup, or parsley and thyme go well with mushroom soup. When in doubt, some Mrs. Dash Table Blend is almost always a good choice.

1. Treat the slow cooker with nonstick spray. Add the potatoes, carrots, peas, onion, celery, and cooked and drained ground beef in layers in the order given.

2. Mix the soup with the water and pour over the layers. Cover and cook on low for 8 hours. Stir and taste for seasoning; add salt and pepper if needed.

Serves 4

Ingredients:
Nonstick spray
2 large potatoes, scrubbed and sliced
3 large carrots, peeled and thinly sliced
1 cup frozen baby peas, thawed
1 large onion, peeled and diced
2 stalks of celery, sliced
1 pound lean ground beef, browned and drained
1 (15¾-ounce) can of cream of tomato soup or cream of mushroom soup
1 soup can water
Salt and freshly ground black pepper, to taste

Beef and Green Bean Casserole

Serves 6

Ingredients:

1½ pounds round or sirloin
   steak
⅓ cup all-purpose flour
Salt, to taste
¼ teaspoon freshly ground
   black pepper
1 green bell pepper, seeded
   and sliced
1 (15-ounce) can diced
   tomatoes
3 tablespoons soy sauce
1 large onion, peeled and
   sliced
8 ounces fresh mushrooms,
   cleaned and sliced
1 (10-ounce) package frozen
   French-style green beans,
   thawed

*Serve this casserole with a tossed salad, steamed baby
potatoes or rice, and warm dinner rolls.*

1. Trim and discard any fat from the beef; cut the meat into short, thin strips.

2. Add the steak strips, flour, salt, and pepper to the slow cooker; stir to coat the steak in the seasoned flour.

3. Add the bell pepper, tomatoes, soy sauce, onion, mushrooms, and green beans. Stir to combine. Cover and cook on low 8 hours. Stir and taste for seasoning; add additional salt and pepper if needed.

Turkey and Dressing Casserole

Serves 4

Ingredients:

Nonstick spray
2 cups leftover turkey
4 cups leftover stuffing
2 cups leftover gravy
2 tablespoons heavy cream

*If you want to add a vegetable to this casserole, stir in a can of creamed
corn or a thawed box of frozen baby peas and pearl onions in
sauce along with the gravy and cream.*

1. Treat the slow cooker with nonstick spray.

2. Cut the turkey and dressing into bite-sized pieces. Add to the slow cooker along with the gravy and cream. Stir to mix. Cover and cook on low for 3 hours, or until heated through.

Pizza Casserole

This casserole is easy to adjust according to your preferences. You can add ingredients like sliced green or black olives, roasted red peppers, and additional mushrooms. Likewise, you can add or substitute bacon or other meat toppings for what's called for in the recipe.

1. Add the ground beef, sausage, and onion to a nonstick skillet over medium-high heat. Sauté for 10 minutes, or until the meat is cooked through and the onion is transparent. Drain and discard any fat rendered from the meat. Stir in the garlic and sauté for 30 seconds. Treat the slow cooker with nonstick spray, and then transfer the cooked meat and onions to the slow cooker.

2. Add the soup and sauce to the slow cooker. Stir to mix into the meat. Fold in the cooked rigatoni, pepperoni, mushrooms, and cheese.

3. Cover and cook on low for 4 hours. Stir and taste for seasoning; add salt and pepper if needed.

Serves 8

Ingredients:
1½ pounds lean ground beef
½ pound ground sausage
1 large onion, peeled and diced
4 cloves of garlic, peeled and minced
Nonstick spray
1 (10¾-ounce) can cream of mushroom soup
1 (26-ounce) jar pizza or pasta sauce
1 (16-ounce) box rigatoni, cooked
1 (4-ounce) package sliced pepperoni
8 ounces mushrooms, sliced
4 cups (1 pound) mozzarella cheese, grated
Salt and freshly ground black pepper, to taste

Pork and Beans Casserole

Serves 8

Ingredients:
4 strips bacon
1 (3-pound) pork roast
1 (10½-ounce) can condensed French onion soup
1 cup ketchup
¼ cup cider vinegar
3 tablespoons brown sugar
2 (15-ounce) cans pork and beans
Optional: Barbecue sauce, to taste

You can serve this casserole with mashed potatoes or steamed cabbage and corn bread. Grind a generous amount of black pepper over each serving.

1. Cut the bacon into 1-inch pieces and add the bacon to the slow cooker. Cover and cook on high for 15 minutes, or until the bacon begins to render its fat. Add the pork roast, fat side down. Cover and cook for ½ hour. Turn the roast; cover and cook for another ½ hour.

2. Mix together the soup, ketchup, vinegar, and brown sugar. Pour over the meat. Reduce the slow cooker setting to low and cook covered for 6 hours or until meat pulls apart and registers 165°F in the center of the roast.

3. Lift the meat from the slow cooker crock and transfer it to a cutting board; shred the meat using two forks, removing and discarding any fat.

4. Skim and discard any fat from the top of the meat juices in the slow cooker, and then remove and discard all but 1 cup of those juices. Stir the shredded meat and pork and beans into the juices. Cover and cook on low for 2 hours. Taste for seasoning and add barbecue sauce to taste if desired.

Freshly Ground Black Pepper
Ground black pepper contains anticaking agents that can cause stomach upset for some people and can also change the flavor. In addition, whole peppercorns retain the succulent black pepper flavor, which tends to dissipate once the pepper is ground, which is why dishes always taste better when you grind the pepper yourself.

Ground Pork and Eggplant Casserole

Serve this casserole with some toasted garlic bread and a tossed salad.

1. Add the ground pork, oil, onion, celery, and bell pepper to a large non-stick skillet over medium-high heat; sauté for 15 minutes or until the pork is cooked through, breaking it apart as it cooks. Remove and discard any fat rendered from the meat, and transfer the meat and sautéed vegetables to the slow cooker.

2. Add the garlic, eggplant, thyme, parsley, tomato paste, Worcestershire sauce, salt, pepper, and egg to the slow cooker. Stir to combine. Cover and cook on low for 8 hours, or until the eggplant is cooked through. Taste for seasoning and add additional salt and pepper, if needed, and hot sauce if desired.

Serves 8

Ingredients:

2 pounds lean ground pork

1 tablespoon peanut or olive oil

2 large yellow onions, peeled and diced

3 stalks celery, diced

1 green bell pepper, seeded and diced

6 cloves of garlic, peeled and minced

4 medium eggplants, cut into ½-inch pieces

⅛ teaspoon dried thyme, crushed

1 tablespoon freeze-dried parsley

3 tablespoons tomato paste

2 teaspoons Worcestershire sauce

Salt and freshly ground black pepper, to taste

1 large egg, beaten

Optional: Hot sauce, to taste

Salisbury Steak Casserole

Ingredients:
1 (10½-ounce) can condensed French onion soup
1½ pounds lean ground beef
½ cup dry bread crumbs
1 large egg
Salt and freshly ground pepper, to taste
Nonstick spray
1 (1-pound) bag frozen hash browns, thawed
1 (1-pound) bag frozen broccoli, green beans, onions and peppers, thawed
¼ cup ketchup
¼ cup water
1 teaspoon Worcestershire sauce
½ teaspoon prepared mustard
1 tablespoon all-purpose flour
1 tablespoon butter, softened
2 tablespoons heavy cream

To make this a complete meal, all you have to do is add a salad or coleslaw and some warm dinner rolls.

1. In a bowl, mix together half of the soup with the beef, bread crumbs, egg, salt, and pepper. Shape into 6 or 8 patties.

2. Add the patties to a nonstick skillet; brown on both sides over medium-high heat, and then pour off and discard any excess fat.

3. Treat the slow cooker with nonstick spray. Spread the hash browns over the bottom of the slow cooker. Top with the frozen vegetable mix. Arrange the browned meat patties over the vegetables.

4. In the soup can, mix the remaining soup together with the ketchup, water, Worcestershire sauce, and mustard. Add the butter and flour to a small bowl; mix into a paste and then whisk in the heavy cream. Add the flour mixture to the soup can and whisk to combine. Pour over the patties. Cover and cook on low for 8 hours.

Chapter 21
Comfort Food Classics

Hamburger-Potato Soup

Ingredients:

1½ pounds lean ground beef

2 cloves of garlic, peeled and minced

¼ teaspoon freshly ground black pepper

½ teaspoon dried thyme

1 tablespoon butter

6 medium potatoes, peeled and sliced

Salt, to taste

2 large onions, peeled and diced

1 (10¾-ounce) can condensed cream of mushroom soup

½ cup milk

Serve this with a tossed salad and a steamed vegetable.

1. Add the ground beef to a nonstick skillet over medium-high heat; breaking apart the meat as you do so, fry for 5 minutes or until the beef is lightly browned. Stir in the garlic, pepper, and thyme; sauté for 30 seconds. Remove and discard any excess fat rendered from the meat.

2. Butter the inside of the slow cooker. Put half of the sliced potatoes in a layer over the bottom of the slow cooker; lightly salt the potatoes. Top the potatoes with half of the diced onions. Add half of the browned beef. Add the remaining potatoes, another light sprinkling of salt, remaining onions, and remaining browned beef.

3. Add the mushroom soup and milk to a bowl or measuring cup; stir to combine. Pour the soup mixture over the contents of the slow cooker. Cover and cook on low for 8 hours or until the potatoes are cooked through.

Cheeseburger-Potato Casserole

After the 8 hours of cooking time, or when the potatoes are cooked through, sprinkle 1 cup (4 ounces) of grated Cheddar cheese over the top of the casserole. Cover and cook on low for 30 minutes or until the cheese is melted.

Chicken-Noodle Soup

You can substitute a cut-up 3-pound whole chicken for the chicken pieces. Bone-in chicken adds additional flavor to the soup broth. Stirring in the beaten eggs when you add the chicken back into the soup will give it a homemade noodles taste.

1. Add the chicken thighs and breasts, carrots, onion, celery, salt, parsley, marjoram, basil, poultry seasoning, black pepper, bay leaf, and 6 cups of the water to the slow cooker. Cover and cook on low for 8 hours. Move the chicken to a cutting board. Remove and discard the bay leaf.

2. Increase the temperature of the slow cooker to high. Add the remaining 2 cups of water. Stir in the noodles and cook, covered, on high for 20 minutes or until the noodles are cooked through.

3. While the noodles cook, remove the meat from the bones. Cut the chicken into bite-sized pieces or shred it with two forks.

4. Ladle about ½ cup of the broth from the slow cooker into a bowl. Add the eggs and whisk to mix; stir the egg mixture into the slow cooker along with the chicken. Cover and cook for 15 minutes.

Serves 8

Ingredients:
4 bone-in chicken thighs, skin removed
2 bone-in chicken breasts, skin removed
4 large carrots, peeled and sliced
1 large sweet onion, peeled and diced
2 stalks of celery, diced
1 teaspoon salt
2 teaspoons dried parsley
¾ teaspoon dried marjoram
½ teaspoon dried basil
¼ teaspoon poultry seasoning
¼ teaspoon freshly ground black pepper
1 bay leaf
8 cups water
2½ cups medium egg noodles, uncooked
2 large eggs

Chicken and Dumplings

Water quality can affect the taste of this dish. If your tap water has a heavy chlorine taste, use a water filter or bottled water.

Serves 6

Ingredients:
2 cups plus 2 tablespoons all-purpose flour
1¼ teaspoons salt
½ teaspoon poultry seasoning
4 chicken thighs
2 split chicken breasts
1 tablespoon vegetable oil
4 large carrots
1 stalk of celery, diced
1 large yellow onion, peeled and diced
2 cups water
¼ teaspoon freshly ground black pepper
1 cup frozen baby peas, thawed
1 tablespoon baking powder
3 tablespoons butter
1 cup milk
Optional: ¼ cup fresh flat-leaf parsley, minced

1. Add 2 tablespoons of the flour, 1 teaspoon of the salt, poultry seasoning, and the chicken pieces to a large plastic food storage bag. Close the bag and shake to coat the chicken in the flour.

2. Bring the oil to temperature in a large nonstick skillet over medium-high heat. Add the chicken pieces; fry the chicken for 4 minutes on each side. Use tongs to transfer the chicken to the slow cooker. Cover and turn the heat setting of the slow cooker to low.

3. Peel the carrots. Grate 1 carrot. Slice the other 3 and add the slices to the slow cooker. Add the grated carrot, celery, and onion to the skillet; sauté for 5 minutes or until the onion is transparent and the celery is soft. Pour the sautéed vegetables and water into the slow cooker. Cover and cook on low for 6 hours or until the chicken is cooked through.

4. Use tongs to move the chicken pieces to a cutting board. Remove and discard the skin from the chicken. Remove the chicken from the bone and use two forks to shred it. Add the chicken back into the slow cooker. Stir in the pepper and peas. Cover and increase the heat setting to high.

5. To make the dumplings, add the remaining 2 cups of flour, the baking powder, and the remaining ½ teaspoon of salt to a bowl; stir to combine. Add the milk and butter to a microwave-safe bowl. Microwave on high for 1 minute or until the butter is melted. Pour the milk and butter into the flour mixture; stir with a fork to mix the batter, which will be stiff and dry. Evenly divide and shape the batter into 6 ovals that are 2 inches in diameter. Place the dumplings on top of the chicken mixture in the slow cooker. Cover and cook on high for 30 minutes or until a toothpick inserted into a dumpling comes out clean.

6. Serve topped with minced fresh parsley if desired.

North Carolina–Inspired Barbecue

Cooking the pork in beer with apples adds a German influence to these sandwiches. The North Carolina influence comes from the ketchup-based coleslaw served as the condiment on the sandwiches. To continue the comfort-food theme, serve with baked beans and warm German potato salad.

Serves 12

Ingredients:
3 pounds pork Western ribs
1 (12-ounce) can beer
2 large Golden Delicious
  apples
1 large sweet onion, peeled
  and sliced
2 tablespoons brown sugar
Optional: 1 cup peach
  marmalade (see Chapter 5)
½ teaspoon freshly ground
  black pepper
Salt, to taste
12 hamburger buns

1. Add the pork to the slow cooker. (Do not trim the fat from the ribs; it's what helps the meat cook up moist enough to shred for sandwiches. A lot of the fat will melt out of the meat as it cooks.)

2. Pour the beer over the pork. Peel, core, and slice the apples and add them to the slow cooker along with the onion, brown sugar, marmalade (if using), black pepper, and salt. Cover and cook on low for 6 hours or until the pork is cooked through and tender.

3. Use a slotted spoon to move the pork to a cutting board. Remove and discard any fat still on the meat. Use two forks to shred the meat.

4. Spoon the meat onto hamburger buns. Top the meat with a heaping tablespoon of North Carolina-Style Coleslaw (see below).

5. Optional: Have the onion slices that were cooked in with the meat available for those who want to add them to their sandwiches.

North Carolina-Style Coleslaw
Add ¾ cup cider vinegar, 1 tablespoon ketchup, 1 tablespoon brown sugar, 1 teaspoon salt, ⅛ teaspoon dried red pepper flakes, and ¾ teaspoon freshly ground black pepper to a large bowl. Whisk to mix, and then stir in a 2-pound bag of coleslaw mix. Add hot sauce, to taste. (This coleslaw is tart by itself; to best decide how to adjust the seasoning, taste it with some of the meat. Stir in some mayonnaise or extra-virgin olive oil if you think it's too tart.)

Lamb Chops

Serves 6

Ingredients:

1 tablespoon olive or
    vegetable oil
6 (8-ounce) lamb rib chops,
    cut 1-inch thick
12 small new potatoes,
    scrubbed
6 medium carrots, peeled and
    cut into 1-inch pieces
2 cups water
½ teaspoon dried dill
½ teaspoon salt
¼ teaspoon ground black
    pepper
4 teaspoons butter, softened
4 teaspoons all-purpose flour
¼ cup red currant jelly
½ cup plain regular or low-fat
    yogurt

The red currant jelly gives the gravy a fruity taste reminiscent of wine.

1. Bring the oil to temperature in a large nonstick skillet over medium-high heat. Add the lamb to the skillet; brown for 3 minutes on each side.

2. Remove a narrow strip of peel from center of each new potato. Place potatoes, carrots, water, dill, salt, and pepper in a large slow cooker. Add the lamb to the slow cooker over the vegetables. Cover and cook on low for 8 hours.

3. Transfer the lamb chops and vegetables to a serving platter; cover and keep warm.

4. For the sauce, strain the cooking liquid; skim off any fat and discard. Pour all but ½ cup of the cooking liquid back into the slow cooker; turn the heat setting to high.

5. Whisk the butter, flour, and jelly into the reserved ½ cup of cooking liquid; remove any lumps, and then whisk the flour mixture into the liquid in the slow cooker. Cook and stir for 15 minutes or until the gravy is thickened and bubbly. Stir in the yogurt. Taste for seasoning and add additional salt, pepper, and jelly if needed. Serve chops and vegetables with the sauce.

Country Meatloaf

*The grated carrots and butter-style crackers make
this a sweeter-tasting meatloaf.*

1. Add the ground beef and pork, salt, pepper, onion, celery, carrot, green pepper, egg, ketchup, tomato sauce, oatmeal, and cracker crumbs into a large bowl and mix well.

2. Treat the slow cooker with nonstick spray. Add the meat mixture and shape the meatloaf into a shape to fit the crock of the slow cooker.

3. In a small bowl, mix together the ketchup, brown sugar, and mustard; spread it over the top of the meatloaf. Cover and cook on low for 7 hours or until the meat is cooked through. Use paper towels to blot and remove any fat that's rendered from the meat. Let the meatloaf sit for 30 minutes and then slice and serve.

One-Pot Meatloaf Meal
There will be room on top of the Country Meatloaf to add 3 large, peeled and sliced carrots and 6 medium peeled potatoes. You may need to increase the cooking time to 8 hours if you add the vegetables.

Serves 6

Ingredients:
1 pound lean ground beef
½ pound lean ground pork
¾ teaspoon salt
¼ teaspoon ground black
    pepper
1 medium yellow onion,
    peeled and finely
    chopped
1 stalk celery, very finely
    chopped
½ cup carrot, grated
1 small green pepper, seeded
    and finely chopped
1 large egg
½ cup ketchup
½ cup tomato sauce
½ cup quick-cooking oatmeal
½ cup butter-style crackers,
    crumbled
Nonstick spray
⅓ cup ketchup
2 tablespoons brown sugar
1 tablespoon prepared
    mustard

Scalloped Potatoes

Serves 6

Ingredients:
Nonstick spray
1½ (16-ounce) packages
    frozen hash brown
    potatoes, thawed
1 cup milk
½ cup sour cream
1 (10¾-ounce) can condensed
    cream of mushroom soup
1 cup (4 ounces) Cheddar
    cheese, grated
1 small green bell pepper,
    seeded and diced
½ cup butter, melted
1 small onion, peeled and
    diced
2 tablespoons pimientos,
    minced
⅛ teaspoon freshly ground
    black pepper
1 cup cheese cracker crumbs,
    divided

*This recipe employs all sorts of laborsaving tricks. You use thawed
frozen hash browns and therefore skip peeling and slicing the
potatoes. You add soup, which lets you skip making a roux to
thicken the sauce. You can even stir in a pound of diced ham
if you want to turn it into a one-pot meal to serve along with a salad.*

1. Treat the slow cooker with nonstick spray. Add the hash browns, milk, sour cream, soup, cheese, green pepper, butter, onion, pimiento, black pepper, and ½ cup of the cracker crumbs. Stir to combine.

2. Top the mixture in the slow cooker with the remaining cracker crumbs.

3. Cover and cook on low for 7 hours or until the mixture is bubbly and the potatoes are cooked through. Serve ladled from the slow cooker.

Meatball Sandwiches

A 38-ounce bag of Rosina Italian Style frozen fully cooked meatballs (www.rosina.com) contains 72 meatballs, so you can stretch this beyond 8 sandwiches. In fact, there's enough for making 8 sandwiches and later warming up the leftovers to serve over pasta. Serve the sandwiches along with a romaine hearts salad tossed together with Italian dressing.

Serves 8

Ingredients:
*1 (38-ounce) bag frozen, fully
    cooked meatballs*
1 (48-ounce) jar pasta sauce
French bread or garlic toast
*Freshly grated Parmesan-
    Reggiano cheese, to taste*

1. Put the frozen meatballs in the slow cooker. Pour the pasta sauce over the meatballs. Cover and cook on low for 8 hours or until the meatballs are thawed and heated through.

2. Serve the meatballs and sauce between 2 slices of French bread or garlic toast. Grate Parmesan-Reggiano cheese to taste over the meatballs.

French Dip Sandwiches

Serves 12

Ingredients:
1 large onion
1 (3-pound) beef bottom
   round roast
½ cup dry white or red wine
   or water
1 envelope au jus gravy mix
⅛ teaspoon freshly ground
   black pepper
Salt, to taste
Hard rolls or French bread

Using lean bottom round not only cuts the fat, it lets you slow-cook the meat long enough that you can put it on before you go to bed and have it ready for a lunch buffet the next day. If you're serving it at a buffet, simply stir the sliced meat back into the onions and broth and serve it directly from the slow cooker.

1. Peel, quarter, and slice the onion. Line bottom of the slow cooker with the onion slices.

2. Trim and discard any visible fat from the roast and add it to the slow cooker on top of the onion.

3. Add the wine or water, au jus mix, and black pepper to a small bowl; mix well and then pour the mixture over the roast. Cook on low for 2 hours or until the meat is very tender.

4. Remove the meat from the slow cooker and let stand for 10 minutes. Cut the meat across the grain into thin slices. Serve the meat on hard rolls or French bread.

5. Taste the broth and add salt if needed. Use the broth for dipping.

Seafood and Chicken Gumbo

Filé powder is made from ground dried sassafras leaves; it helps flavor and thicken the gumbo. If you're using homemade chicken broth, you can skip Steps 1 and 2; simply omit the oil and add the bacon, chicken, onion, and celery to the slow cooker and proceed to Step 3.

1. Bring the oil to temperature in a nonstick skillet over medium-high heat. Add the bacon and chicken; fry the chicken for 3 minutes on each side. Use tongs to move the chicken to a plate.

2. Add the onion and celery to the skillet; sauté for 10 minutes or until the onion is lightly browned.

3. Add the rice to the slow cooker and spread it over the bottom of the crock. Place the chicken pieces over the rice. Pour in the sautéed onion and celery. Add the tomatoes, bell pepper, okra, broth, water, and bay leaf. Cover and cook on low for 6 hours.

4. Add the shrimp, scallops, crab, thyme, and parsley. Cover and cook on low for 15 minutes.

5. Turn off the heat to the slow cooker. Stir in the filé powder. Cover and let rest for 15 minutes or until the shrimp is pink and the scallops are opaque. Salt to taste. Ladle into bowls and serve immediately.

Serves 4

Ingredients:
1 tablespoon olive or vegetable oil
2 strips bacon, diced
4 chicken thighs, skin removed
1 large onion, peeled and diced
2 stalks of celery, diced
½ cup aromatic brown rice
1 (15-ounce) can diced tomatoes
1 green bell pepper, seeded and diced
1 cup frozen okra, thawed
2 cups chicken broth
2 cups water
1 bay leaf
⅓ pound shrimp, peeled and deveined
⅓ pound scallops, quartered
⅓ pound cooked crabmeat
¼ teaspoon dried thyme
1 teaspoon dried parsley
2 teaspoons filé powder
Salt, to taste

Chapter 22
Dishes Worth the Extra Effort

Stuffed Grape Leaves

Serves 4–6

Ingredients:
Nonstick spray
1 pound lean ground lamb
1 cup long-grain rice
¼ teaspoon ground
    cinnamon
¼ teaspoon ground allspice
Salt and freshly ground
    pepper, to taste
1 (1-pound) jar of grape
    leaves
Water or chicken broth
6 tablespoons fresh lemon
    juice (juice of 2 lemons)

This dish is often used as an appetizer, but it's also good as a light supper.
Serve it with a Cucumber-Yogurt Salad (see sidebar on page 148).

1. Treat the inside of the slow cooker with nonstick spray.

2. In a large bowl, mix together the lamb, rice, cinnamon, allspice, salt, and pepper.

3. Drain the grape leaves. Use any small leaves to line the bottom of the slow cooker. Lay each larger leaf on a flat surface, vein side up; trim off any stem. Spoon some of the lamb mixture onto the center of each grape leaf. To form each roll, fold the stem end over the filling, and then fold the sides over each other, and lastly fold down the tip. Carefully place each roll, seam side down, in the slow cooker. Place the rolls close together in the crock to prevent them from unrolling while they cook. You will have several layers of rolls, depending on how tightly you roll them.

4. Place a plate over the rolls and then add enough water or broth to cover the plate. Cover and cook on low for 6 hours.

5. Add the lemon juice; cover and continue to cook on low for an additional 30 minutes. The stuffed grape leaves (dolmades) are done when they're tender when pierced with a fork. You can serve them warm, at room temperature, or cool.

"Corn"-It-Yourself Corned Beef, Brine Method

Rather than being granulated, the salt used in processing corned beef used to be pieces the size of a kernel of corn. Corned beef got its name because this method of preserving the meat was referred to as corning.

1. Add the water to a 4-quart or larger stockpot along with salt, brown sugar, saltpeter, cinnamon stick, mustard seeds, peppercorns, cloves, allspice, juniper berries, bay leaf, and ginger. Stir and cook over high heat for 10 minutes or until the salt and sugar have dissolved. Remove from the heat and add the ice. Stir until the ice has melted.

2. When the brine has cooled to 45°F, place the brisket in a 2-gallon zip-closure bag or large covered container. (The container you choose needs to allow the brisket to be completely submerged in the brine.) Pour in the brine. Seal or close the container, cover, and place in the refrigerator for 10 days. Daily turn the meat over in the brine, stirring the brine as you do so.

3. At the end of the 10 days, remove the meat from the brine and rinse it well under cool water.

4. Add the brisket to the slow cooker along with the onion, carrot, and celery. Add enough water to cover the meat. Cover and cook on low for 10 hours, or until the meat is fork tender. Remove the meat from the slow cooker to a cutting board; cover and allow it to rest for 30 minutes. To serve, thinly slice the brisket across the grain.

Tender and Juicy Corned Beef

Corned beef (or any slow-cooked beef or pork roast, for that matter) will actually be most tender if you allow it to cool completely in the cooking broth. Cool for an hour so that the meat and broth reach room temperature, and then refrigerate overnight. Either reheat the corned beef in the broth, or slice and reheat just the meat itself.

Yields 1 (about 3-pound) corned beef brisket

Ingredients:
4 cups water
½ cup kosher salt
¼ cup brown sugar
1 tablespoon saltpeter
1 (3-inch) cinnamon stick, broken in half
½ teaspoon mustard seeds
½ teaspoon black peppercorns
4 whole cloves
4 whole allspice berries
6 whole juniper berries
1 bay leaf, crumbled
¼ teaspoon ground ginger
1 pound ice
1 (3-pound) beef brisket, trimmed
1 small onion, peeled and quartered
1 large carrot, peeled and sliced
1 stalk of celery, diced

"Corn"-It-Yourself Corned Beef, Salt-Rub Method

Yields 1 (about 3-pound) corned beef brisket

Ingredients:
½ cup kosher salt
1 tablespoon black peppercorns, cracked
1 tablespoon dried thyme
2 teaspoons allspice
2 teaspoons paprika
2 bay leaves, crumbled
1 (3-pound) beef brisket, trimmed
1 small onion, peeled and quartered
1 large carrot, peeled and sliced
1 stalk of celery, diced

This method of making corned beef is less cumbersome than dealing with brine, but it results in meat that's much saltier. If salt is a concern, you can remove some of it by rinsing the meat and then submerging it in cold water for an hour before you add it to the slow cooker. There's also an optional cooking step to this recipe that will help.

1. Add the salt, cracked black pepper, thyme, allspice, paprika, and crumbled bay leaves to a bowl or sandwich bag; mix well.

2. Use a fork to prick the beef brisket on both sides. Rub half of the salt mixture into each side of the meat. Seal in a large zip-closure bag, forcing out as much air as possible. Place that bag inside of another bag. Place in the refrigerator and put a weight (such as a gallon of milk) on top. Refrigerate for 5–7 days, turning once a day. At the end of the 5–7 days, remove the meat from the food storage bag and rinse it well under cool water.

3. Add the brisket to the slow cooker along with the onion, carrot, and celery. Add enough water to cover the meat. Cover and cook on low for 10 hours, or until the meat is fork tender.

4. Optional Step: To remove more of the salt from the meat, remove it from the slow cooker and discard the cooking liquid and cooked vegetables. Place the cooked brisket back in the slow cooker and cover completely with fresh water. Cover and cook on low for 1 to 2 hours.

5. Remove the meat from the slow cooker to a cutting board; cover and allow it to rest for 30 minutes. Thinly slice the brisket across the grain.

Pastrami Instead
To make pastrami, after you've rinsed the brine or salt cure from the meat, cook the cured brisket according to the recipe instructions on page 92.

Kicked-Up Corned Beef and Cabbage

If you want (and there is room in the slow cooker), you can add 6 medium peeled potatoes when you add the cabbage wedges in Step 4.

1. Treat the inside of the slow cooker with nonstick spray. Arrange the onion slices across the bottom of the crock.

2. Trim and discard excess fat from the brisket and place it on top of the onions.

3. Add the apple juice, brown sugar, orange zest, mustard, and cloves to a bowl and stir to mix; pour over the brisket. Cover and cook on low for 8 hours.

4. Place the cabbage on top of the brisket. Cover and cook on low for 2 more hours or until the cabbage is cooked through and the brisket is tender. Move the cabbage and meat to a serving platter. Cover and let rest for 15 minutes. Carve the brisket by slicing it against the grain.

Serves 6

Ingredients:
Nonstick spray
2 medium onions, peeled and sliced
1 (3-pound) corned beef brisket
1 cup apple juice
¼ cup brown sugar, packed
2 teaspoons orange zest, finely grated
2 teaspoons prepared mustard
6 whole cloves
6 cabbage wedges

Lemon-Butter Roast Chicken

Serves 4

Ingredients:

1 (2½-pound) chicken
2 cloves of garlic, peeled and
  minced
2 tablespoons butter
Mrs. Dash Lemon Pepper
  Seasoning Blend, to taste
¼ cup water
3 tablespoons fresh lemon
  juice

*This is a salt-free way to fix chicken. Because of the lemon juice and
the herbs in the seasoning blend, you won't even miss it!*

1. Rinse the chicken under cool running water and pat dry. Place the chicken on a broiling pan; broil for about 10 minutes on each side, or until the skin is lightly browned.

2. In a small bowl, stir the garlic into the butter. Rub the garlic-butter over the outside of the chicken. Generously sprinkle Mrs. Dash Lemon Pepper Seasoning Blend over all sides of the chicken.

3. Pour the water into the slow cooker. Position the cooking rack in the slow cooker and place the chicken on top of the rack, breast side up.

4. Cover and cook on low for 7 hours. Add the lemon juice to the water in the slow cooker. Cover and cook for 1 more hour on low.

5. Transfer the chicken to a cutting board. Cover and let rest for 10 minutes before carving. Skim any fat from the juice in the slow cooker and then pour it into gravy boat. Carve the chicken and serve it with some juice poured over the chicken.

Fusion Chicken

Serve with cooked rice and a steamed vegetable.

Serves 8

Ingredients:
2 tablespoons frozen orange juice concentrate
2 cups chicken broth
Salt, to taste
¼ teaspoon freshly ground black pepper
1 (4-ounce) can tomato paste
2 tablespoons soy sauce
2 tablespoons brown sugar
2 cloves of garlic, peeled and minced
Dash allspice
3 pounds boneless, skinless chicken breasts and thighs
2 tablespoons butter
8 ounces fresh mushrooms, cleaned and sliced
1 (11-ounce) can mandarin orange sections, drained
1 small green bell pepper, seeded and sliced lengthwise
¼ teaspoon ground ginger
3 tablespoons cornstarch
¼ cup cold milk
¼ cup cold water

1. The night before or at least 8 hours before you plan to begin slow-cooking this dish, make the marinade by adding the orange juice concentrate, broth, salt, black pepper, tomato paste, soy sauce, brown sugar, garlic, and allspice to a closable container large enough to also hold the chicken pieces. Thoroughly mix the marinade, add the chicken, close container, and refrigerate overnight or for 8 hours.

2. Place the chicken in the slow cooker; pour the marinade over the chicken. Cover and cook on low while you prepare the mushrooms.

3. Bring the butter to temperature over medium heat; add the mushrooms and sauté for 6 minutes. Add the mushrooms and pan juices to the slow cooker along with the orange sections, green pepper, and ginger. Cover and cook on low for 6 hours. Turn the cooker to high.

4. Add the cornstarch, milk, and cold water to a bowl; whisk to mix. Slowly add the cornstarch mixture into the slow cooker and stir for 5 minutes or until the juices begins to thicken. Cover and cook for 15 minutes or until the mixture is thickened and the cornstarch taste is cooked out of sauce.

Pork Loin Braised in Milk

Serves 8

Ingredients:

1 tablespoon butter

1 tablespoon olive oil

1 (3-pound) boneless pork
  loin

Salt and freshly ground black
  pepper, to taste

1 medium onion, peeled and
  diced

1 medium carrot, peeled and
  diced

2 cloves of garlic, peeled and
  minced

2 cups whole milk

½ teaspoon dried rosemary

1 bay leaf

Optional: 1 or 2 tablespoons
  heavy cream

*The extra effort required by this dish is reducing the pan juices and then
using an immersion blender to help turn the milk that separates
during the cooking process into a creamy, succulent sauce.*

1. Bring the butter and oil to temperature in a large nonstick skillet over medium-high heat. Add the pork loin to the skillet and, turning the pork, brown on all sides. Season the loin with salt and pepper; transfer it to the slow cooker. Cover and cook on low while you sauté the vegetables.

2. Reduce the heat setting under the skillet to medium. Add the onion and carrot to the skillet; sauté for 5 minutes or until the onion is transparent. Stir in the garlic and sauté for 30 seconds.

3. Pour ½ cup of the milk into the skillet. Add the rosemary and bay leaf. Stir to scrape the browned bits from the bottom of the skillet. Pour into the slow cooker along with the remaining milk. Cover and cook on low for 6 hours or until the pork is cooked through and tender. Transfer the loin to a serving platter; tent with foil and keep warm.

4. Remove and discard the bay leaf. Skim any fat from the milk and pan juices in the slow cooker. Increase the heat setting to high and cook uncovered until the pan juices are reduced to 1 cup. (Alternatively, you can pour the pan juices into a saucepan and bring to a boil over medium heat; boil until reduced to 1 cup.)

5. Use an immersion blender to process the pan juices until smooth. Taste for seasoning and add salt and pepper if needed. If desired, add the cream and blend. Carve the roast and pour the thickened sauce over the slices or serve it on the side.

Tzimmes

Serves 8

Ingredients:
1 (3-pound) beef brisket
1 large yellow onion, peeled
    and diced
Salt and freshly ground black
    pepper, to taste
2 stalks celery, diced
1 large carrot, peeled and
    diced
1 (12-ounce) box pitted
    prunes (dried plums)
1 tablespoon dried or freeze-
    dried parsley
3 cups beef broth
3 tablespoons fresh lemon
    juice
¼ teaspoon ground cloves
1 teaspoon ground cinnamon
1 tablespoon honey
2 tablespoons white or white
    wine vinegar
4 large sweet potatoes,
    peeled and quartered
Optional: 2 tablespoons
    butter

*If there's room in the slow cooker, at the beginning of Step 3 you can add a
1-pound bag of thawed frozen cut green beans along with the sweet potatoes.*

1. Add the brisket, onion, salt, pepper, celery, carrot, prunes, and parsley
   to the slow cooker.

2. Mix the broth, lemon juice, cloves, cinnamon, honey, and vinegar
   together and pour over the meat. Cover and cook on low for 6 hours or
   until the meat is cooked through.

3. Add the sweet potatoes. Cover and cook on low for another 2 hours
   or until the brisket and sweet potatoes are tender. Use a slotted spoon
   to move the vegetables and meat to a serving platter. Tent with foil or
   otherwise cover and keep warm. Allow the meat to rest for 15 minutes
   before you carve it, slicing it against the grain.

4. For a richer sauce, after you remove the meat and vegetables to a serving platter, whisk the butter into the pan juices a teaspoon at a time
   before spooning it over the dish.

A Touch More Cinnamon?
*Taste the broth at the end of Step 2. That's the ideal time to add more
ground cloves and cinnamon to taste if you think it could use more.*

Herbed Chicken with Root Vegetables

Serves 4

Ingredients:
1 tablespoon olive or
    vegetable oil
1 tablespoon butter
8 chicken thighs
4 small turnips, peeled and
    diced
4 medium carrots, peeled and
    sliced
1 medium onion, peeled and
    diced
Nonstick spray
1 small head cabbage
1 teaspoon garlic powder
½ teaspoon dried rosemary
½ teaspoon dried thyme
½ teaspoon dried basil
1 teaspoon dried parsley
⅛ teaspoon salt
¼ teaspoon freshly ground
    black pepper

Once you've browned the chicken and root vegetables, you slow-roast this dish in your slow cooker. Browning the chicken and root vegetables in this dish adds to the overall flavor. You can substitute peeled and quartered medium potatoes for all or some of the turnips.

1. Bring the oil and butter to temperature in a large nonstick skillet over medium-high heat. Add the chicken thighs skin side down; fry for 4 minutes or until the skin is golden brown. Turn and brown on the other side for an equal amount of time. Transfer chicken to a plate or cutting board until needed.

2. Add the turnips, carrots, and onion to the skillet. Reduce the heat under the skillet to medium; sauté for 5 minutes or until the onion just begins to brown. Treat the slow cooker with nonstick spray. Scrape the sautéed vegetables from the pan into the slow cooker.

3. Remove and discard the outer leaves from the cabbage. Cut it into 8 wedges; cut away and discard the core. Set aside.

4. Add the garlic powder, rosemary, thyme, basil, parsley, salt, and black pepper to a small bowl. Stir to mix. Sprinkle half of the herb mixture over the vegetables in the slow cooker. Arrange the cabbage wedges over the vegetables.

5. Place the chicken thighs skin side up over the top of the cabbage wedges. Sprinkle with the remaining herb mixture. Cover and cook on low for 7 hours or until the chicken and cabbage are cooked through.

Pork Ragout

Serve this dish with a tossed salad, steamed vegetable, and warm dinner rolls.

Serves 8

Ingredients:
Nonstick spray
1 large yellow onion, peeled
  and diced
3 large carrots, peeled and
  sliced
3 cloves of garlic, peeled and
  minced
3 pounds boneless pork
  shoulder
3 tablespoons olive or
  vegetable oil
3 tablespoons all-purpose
  flour
1½ cups chicken broth
1½ cups dry white wine
½ teaspoon dried rosemary
½ teaspoon dried thyme
¼ teaspoon salt
⅛ teaspoon freshly ground
  black pepper
4 tablespoons butter
1 pound fresh mushrooms,
  cleaned and sliced
¼ cup fresh flat-leaf parsley,
  minced
2 tablespoons fresh lemon
  juice
1 pound medium egg noodles
2 large eggs
2 tablespoons cold water

1. Treat the slow cooker with nonstick spray. Arrange the onion, carrots, and garlic over the bottom. Cover and set heat to low.

2. Trim and discard any fat from the pork; cut the meat into bite-sized pieces. Pat dry with paper towels. Bring the oil to temperature in a large nonstick skillet over medium-high heat. Add half of the pork pieces to the skillet; stir and cook for 5 minutes or until the meat is browned on all sides. Use a slotted spoon to move the browned meat to the slow cooker. Repeat with the remaining meat.

3. Sprinkle the flour in the skillet and stir into the oil in the pan for 1 minute. Whisk in the broth and 1 cup of the wine, scraping up any browned bits from the bottom of the pan. Stir in the rosemary, thyme, salt, and black pepper. Continue to cook and stir for 5 minutes or until the mixture just begins to thicken. Pour over the meat and vegetables in the slow cooker. Cover and cook on low for 6 hours.

4. Melt 2 tablespoons of the butter in a large nonstick skillet. Add the mushrooms; sauté for 5 minutes or until soft. Pour into the slow cooker. Stir in the remaining wine, parsley, and lemon juice. Cover and continue to cook on low for 30 minutes.

5. Cook the egg noodles according to package directions. Drain well.

6. Add the eggs and water to a small bowl; whisk to combine.

7. Over medium heat, melt the remaining 2 tablespoons of butter in the large nonstick skillet you used to sauté the mushrooms. Stir the egg noodles into the butter.

8. Pour the egg mixture over the noodles; stirring quickly, coat the egg noodles in the eggs. Cook and stir for 3 minutes, and then immediately transfer the noodles to a serving bowl. Serve topped with the ragout.

Chapter 23
Side Dishes

Bourbon Baked Beans

Serves 8

Ingredients:
4 strips bacon
1 large sweet onion, peeled and diced
3 (15-ounce) cans cannellini, great northern, or navy beans
2 ounces lean smoked ham, cubed
1 (15-ounce) can diced tomatoes
¼ cup maple syrup
3 tablespoons apple cider vinegar
4 cloves of garlic, peeled and minced
2 tablespoons dry mustard
1½ teaspoons freshly ground black pepper
½ teaspoon ground ginger
¼ teaspoon dried red pepper flakes
2 tablespoons bourbon
Salt, to taste

Serve these at your next cookout or as a side dish for a ham or pork loin dinner.

1. Dice the bacon and add it to the slow cooker along with the onion. Cover and cook on high for 15 minutes; stir and cook for an additional 15 minutes or until the bacon is rendering its fat and the onion is getting soft.

2. Drain and rinse the beans. Add the beans to the slow cooker along with the remaining ingredients. Stir to mix. Reduce the setting on the slow cooker to low; cover and cook for 6 hours. Taste for seasoning and add additional salt if needed.

Or, if you prefer . . .
This Bourbon Baked Beans recipe doesn't have as much tomato as some versions. If you prefer more tomato, you can add a 4-ounce can of tomato paste or some ketchup when you stir in all of the other ingredients.

Grandma's Green Beans

This recipe is easy to double if you need extra servings for a church social or buffet. Serve these green beans with meatloaf or any grilled meat.

Serves 6

Ingredients:
1 (1-pound) bag frozen green
   beans, thawed
1 medium sweet onion,
   peeled and diced
6 medium red potatoes
1 teaspoon sugar
Salt and freshly ground black
   pepper, to taste
6 strips of bacon

1. Add the green beans and onion to the slow cooker. Depending on your preference, you can either scrub and dice the potatoes or peel and dice them. Add the potatoes to the slow cooker along with the sugar, salt, and pepper.

2. Dice the bacon and add ⅔ of it to the slow cooker. Stir to mix well. Sprinkle the remaining bacon pieces over the top of the beans mixture. Cover and cook on low for 4 hours or until the potatoes are cooked through. Taste for seasoning and add additional salt and pepper if needed.

Fresh Green Beans
You can substitute a pound to a pound and a half fresh washed, trimmed, and cut green beans for the frozen. Increase the cooking time to 6 hours if you do.

Fresh Artichokes

*Preparing artichokes takes some work, but they're good served
with an avocado salad and poached salmon.*

Serves 4

Ingredients:
2 large fresh artichokes
6 cups hot water
1 lemon
¼ cup butter, melted
*Optional: ¼ teaspoon
   seasoned salt*

1. Rinse the artichokes under cool running water. Use a sharp knife to slice about an inch off the top of each artichoke; cut off the stem near the base. Use kitchen shears to trim about ½ inch off the top of each leaf. Use the knife to cut each artichoke in half vertically. Use a spoon or melon baller to scoop out and discard the fuzzy center, or choke.

2. Place the artichoke halves in the slow cooker. Pour in the hot water. Cut 4 thin slices from the center of the lemon and add to the slow cooker; reserve the remaining lemon. Cover and cook on high for 4 hours or until the artichoke heart is tender when pierced with a knife. Use a slotted spoon to remove the artichoke halves from the slow cooker.

3. To prepare the butter sauce, add the melted butter to a bowl. Add the juice from the reserved portions of the lemon. Stir in seasoned salt if desired. Evenly drizzle over the artichoke halves. Serve immediately.

Sweet Potato Casserole

This is a welcome side dish at almost any holiday buffet.

1. Treat the slow cooker with nonstick spray.

2. Drain the sweet potatoes, add to a bowl, and mash them together with ⅓ cup of the butter, the white sugar, and 2 tablespoons of the brown sugar. Stir in the orange juice, eggs, and milk. Transfer the sweet potato mixture to the slow cooker.

3. Add the pecans, ⅓ cup of the brown sugar, the flour, and the remaining 2 tablespoons of butter to a bowl; use a fork to blend. Sprinkle over the sweet potatoes. Cover and cook on low for 6 hours.

Serves 8

Ingredients:
Nonstick spray
2 (29-ounce) cans sweet potatoes
⅓ cup plus 2 teaspoons butter, melted
2 tablespoons white sugar
2 tablespoons plus ⅓ cup brown sugar
1 tablespoon orange juice
2 large eggs, beaten
½ cup milk
⅓ cup chopped pecans
2 tablespoons all-purpose flour

Creamed Corn

This recipe is definitely not for somebody on a low-fat or low-carb diet. The cream cheese helps make the rich sauce for the corn. In fact, because of the cream cheese there will be enough sauce that if you need extra servings for a carry-in buffet, you can double the amount of corn you use and still have enough sauce.

1. Add the corn to the slow cooker. Cube the cream cheese and slice the butter; add them to the slow cooker along with the milk, sugar, salt, and pepper. Stir to combine.

2. Cover and cook on low for 4 hours. (After 2 hours, stir the corn mixture and watch carefully. Switch the slow cooker to the warm setting as soon as the cream sauce is thickened; keep warm until ready to serve. Otherwise, the corn can scorch and change flavor if the heat is left too high for too long.)

Serves 12

Ingredients:
4 cups frozen whole-kernel corn, thawed
1 (8-ounce) package cream cheese
½ cup butter
½ cup milk
1 tablespoon white sugar
Salt and freshly ground black pepper, to taste

Boston Brown Bread

Serves 8

Ingredients:
½ cup rye flour
½ cup stone-ground
    cornmeal
½ cup whole wheat flour
½ teaspoon baking powder
¼ teaspoon fine salt
¼ teaspoon baking soda
½ cup dark molasses
½ cup buttermilk
1 large egg
Butter (for coating pan)
Boiling water

This classic steamed bread goes perfectly with Boston baked beans or a hearty stew.

1. Add the rye flour, cornmeal, whole wheat flour, baking powder, salt, and baking soda to a mixing bowl. Stir to combine.

2. Add the molasses, buttermilk, and egg to another mixing bowl. Whisk to mix and pour into the flour mixture. Mix until a thick batter is formed.

3. Butter the inside of the container in which you'll be steaming the bread. Add enough batter to fill the container three-fourths full. Place the lid (see sidebar) over the container; center the container on the cooking insert inside the slow cooker.

4. Pour enough boiling water into the slow cooker to come to about halfway up the container. Cover and cook on high for 2½ hours or until the bread springs back to the touch. (To test it, carefully remove the lid or foil and touch the top of the bread; if your finger leaves an indentation, place the cover back over the bread and continue to cook and test in ½ hour intervals.

5. Remove the container from the water bath inside the slow cooker. Set on a cooling rack. When the bread is completely cooled, remove it from the container, slice, and serve.

Boston Brown Bread Steaming Container
You'll need a heatproof (stainless-steel or ceramic) bowl, pudding mold, 13-ounce coffee can, or other container that can sit on the cooking insert in the slow cooker and still have an inch of clearance between the top of the container and the lid of the slow cooker. Only fill the container three-fourths full. If the container doesn't have a lid, butter one side of a piece of foil large enough to fit over the entire top of the container and over the side far enough to press down to make a seal.

Vinegar-Braised Red Cabbage

This is a tart dish. Adding additional jelly or serving the cabbage with some additional butter melted on top can cut the tartness. Be sure to refrigerate any leftovers; the cabbage tastes better the next day and can be reheated and served warm or used cold as a pickle-replacement condiment on a sandwich.

1. Remove and discard the tough outer leaves of the cabbage. Cut the cabbage in half and remove the core; finely slice or shred the cabbage.

2. Add the shredded cabbage, butter, sugar, salt, water, vinegar, and apple to the slow cooker. Cover and cook on low for 6 hours or until the cabbage is cooked through.

3. Stir and taste for seasoning. Add additional salt and jelly if desired.

Serves 8

Ingredients:
1 medium head of red
   cabbage
4 tablespoons butter
1 tablespoon sugar
¼ teaspoon salt
⅓ cup water
⅓ cup white or white wine
   vinegar
1 small apple, peeled and
   grated
1 tablespoon red currant jelly,
   or to taste

Hot German Potato Salad

Ingredients:
6 baking potatoes
1 small red onion, peeled and
    diced
3 stalks celery, diced
1 small green bell pepper,
    seeded and diced
¼ cup apple cider vinegar
½ cup water
¼ cup light olive or vegetable
    oil, or bacon fat
2 tablespoons sugar
½ teaspoon celery seeds
¼ cup fresh flat-leaf parsley,
    minced
6 strips bacon, cooked until
    crisp, drained, and
    crumbled
Salt and freshly ground black
    pepper, to taste

Serve this with bratwurst sandwiches and chilled mugs of ice cold beer.

1. Scrub the potatoes; slice them into ¼-inch slices and add to the slow cooker. Add the onion, celery, and bell pepper; stir to mix.

2. Add the vinegar, water, oil, sugar, and celery seeds to a bowl or measuring cup; whisk to mix and then pour into the slow cooker.

3. Cover and cook on low for 4 hours or until the potatoes are cooked through.

4. Stir in the parsley and crumbled bacon. Season with salt and pepper, to taste. Serve hot.

Or, if you prefer . . .
You can omit the oil and bacon in the Hot German Potato Salad and instead add 8 ounces of diced smoked sausage in Step 1. The fat that renders from the sausage should be sufficient to offset the vinegar; however, if you think it's too tart when you taste the dish for seasoning, you can stir in a little vegetable oil when you add the salt and pepper.

Chapter 24
Fabulous Fruits

Applesauce

Yields about 4 cups

Ingredients:
12 apples
½ to 1 cup pure cane sugar
Pinch salt
Optional: 1 tablespoon
    lemon juice

You'll need about 4 pounds of apples for this size batch of applesauce, or enough to fill the slow cooker three-fourths full. The amount of sugar that you use will depend on the sweetness of the apples and your personal taste.

1. Wash, peel, core, and slice the apples. Add to the slow cooker. Cover and cook on low for 5 hours.

2. Stir in the sugar and salt. Use an immersion blender to purée the apples. Cover and cook on low for an additional 30 minutes or until the sugar is dissolved.

3. Optional: If the applesauce is too sweet, stir in the lemon juice to help balance the sweetness.

4. Serve warm as an accompaniment to pork chops or over pancakes. For leftovers, cool and store in the refrigerator for 2 or 3 days, or pour into appropriate covered containers and freeze for up to 3 months.

Spiced Applesauce
In Step 1, cook on low for 4 hours and then stir in 1 teaspoon ground cinnamon, ½ teaspoon ground cloves, ¼ teaspoon ground ginger, ¼ teaspoon allspice, and a pinch of freshly ground nutmeg. Cover and cook for another hour before proceeding to Step 2. Taste the applesauce after you've added the sugar and increase the amounts of spices if desired.

Cinnamon-Spiced Apple Butter

If you're using a less tart apple, add the brown sugar ¼ cup at a time until you reach desired sweetness. Serve over homemade biscuits or bread.

1. Wash, peel, core, and quarter the apples. Add to the slow cooker along with the cider or juice. Cover and cook on high for 4 hours.

2. Use an immersion blender to purée the apples. Stir in the brown sugar, cinnamon, allspice, cloves, and salt. Taste for seasoning and adjust if necessary.

3. Reduce the temperature of the slow cooker to low. Cook uncovered for 2 hours or until the apple butter is thick and dark. Store in the refrigerator for several weeks or freeze until needed.

Yields about 3 cups

Ingredients:
8 large or 12 medium Granny Smith apples
½ cup apple cider or juice
¾ cup dark brown sugar
2 teaspoons ground cinnamon
½ teaspoon allspice
½ teaspoon ground cloves
Pinch salt

Crustless Apple Pie

Adjust the cooking time depending on the type of apple you use. A softer golden delicious should be cooked through and soft in the recommended cooking times, but a crisper Granny Smith apple may take longer.

1. Treat the slow cooker with nonstick spray. Wash, core, and slice the apples and arrange them over the bottom of the slow cooker.

2. Add the orange juice and water to a small bowl or measuring cup; stir to mix. Evenly drizzle over the apples.

3. Add the pecans, brown sugar, butter, and cinnamon to a bowl. Mix well. Evenly crumble the pecan mixture over the apples. Cover and cook on high for 2 hours or on low for 4 hours. Serve warm or chilled topped with whipped cream or topping if desired.

Serves 8

Ingredients:
Nonstick spray
8 medium apples cored and sliced
3 tablespoons orange juice
3 tablespoons water
½ cup pecans, chopped
⅓ cup brown sugar
¼ cup butter, melted
½ teaspoon cinnamon
Optional: Whipped cream or topping

Cranberry Sauce

Serve this warm cranberry sauce directly from the slow cooker at your next holiday buffet. You can make it several days in advance, store it in the refrigerator, and then bring it back to temperature in the slow cooker. Or pour it into a mold and refrigerate until ready to remove it from the mold and serve it chilled.

Serves 10

Ingredients:
2 (12-ounce) bags fresh cranberries
2 cups sugar
2 tablespoons frozen orange juice concentrate
Pinch salt
Optional: Cinnamon and ground cloves, to taste

1. Rinse and drain the cranberries. Remove and discard any stems or blemished cranberries.

2. Add the cranberries to the slow cooker along with the sugar, orange juice concentrate, and salt. Stir to combine, adding the cinnamon and cloves if using. Cover and cook on low for 4 hours.

3. Remove the cover. Stir well, breaking the cranberries apart with a spoon or mashing them slightly with a potato masher. Taste for seasoning and adjust if necessary.

4. Cover and cook on low for another hour or until the cranberries are cooked through and soft and the sugar is completely dissolved.

5. If storing the cranberry sauce in a mold, allow it to cool to room temperature before pouring it into the mold and refrigerating.

In the Spirits Cranberry Sauce
For additional flavor, stir in a couple of tablespoons of orange liqueur, bourbon, or brandy if desired.

Baked Stuffed Apples

You can serve these baked apples as a warm dessert with some vanilla ice cream or along with some coffee cake for breakfast.

Serves 4

Ingredients:
4 large tart baking apples
½ cup light brown sugar
Optional: 4 teaspoons orange zest, grated
1 teaspoon cinnamon
¼ cup golden seedless raisins
4 teaspoons frozen orange juice concentrate
4 teaspoons butter
½ cup apple cider or juice

1. Wash the apples and remove the core and the stem, but don't peel them. Add the brown sugar, orange zest if using, and cinnamon to a small bowl; stir to mix.

2. Fill each apple with a tablespoon of raisins, a teaspoon of orange juice concentrate, and a generous tablespoon of the brown sugar mixture. Top the filling in each apple with a teaspoon of butter.

3. Pour the cider or juice into the slow cooker. Carefully place the apples upright in the slow cooker. Cover and cook on low for 5 hours or until the apples are cooked through and tender. Use tongs and a spatula to remove the apples to dessert plates. Serve warm.

Cherries Jubilee

You can substitute apple or peach pie filling for the cherry. (You can even sprinkle some chopped pecans or walnuts over the cake mix if you wish.) Serve warm directly from the slow cooker along with some ice cream, whipped cream, or whipped topping.

Serves 12

Ingredients:
Nonstick spray
2 (21-ounce) cans cherry pie filling
1 (18-ounce) package yellow cake mix
½ cup melted butter

1. Treat the slow cooker with nonstick spray. Spread the pie filling over the bottom of the slow cooker. Sprinkle the dry cake mix over the cherries. Drizzle the melted butter over the cake mix.

2. Cover and cook on high for 2 hours or on low for 4 hours.

Banana Bread

Serves 8

Ingredients:
1½ cups all-purpose flour
½ cup oat bran
¾ cup sugar
¾ cup baking soda
½ teaspoon salt
3 ripe bananas, mashed
6 tablespoons (¾ stick) butter,
    softened
2 large eggs, beaten
¼ cup plain yogurt
1 teaspoon vanilla
1¼ cups walnuts
Nonstick spray

Oat bran adds extra fiber to this recipe, making it a heart-healthier bread. The bananas impart a hearty enough flavor that few will notice the difference, but if the sweet taste of oat bran isn't to your liking, you can omit it and use 2 cups of flour instead.

1. Add the flour, oat bran, sugar, baking soda, and salt to a mixing bowl. Stir to mix.

2. Add the bananas, butter, eggs, yogurt, and vanilla to a food processor; pulse to cream together.

3. Add the walnuts and flour mixture to the food processor. Pulse to combine and chop the walnuts. Scrape down the sides of the container with a spatula and pulse until mixed.

4. Treat the slow cooker with nonstick spray. Add the batter to the slow cooker, using a spatula to spread it evenly across the bottom of the crock. Cover and cook on high for 3 hours, or until a toothpick inserted in the center of the bread comes out clean. Allow to cool uncovered before removing it from the slow cooker.

Spiced Banana Bread
For cinnamon-spiced banana bread, in Step 1 add a teaspoon of ground cinnamon; ¼ teaspoon each of ground cloves, ground ginger, and allspice; and nutmeg to the flour.

Cranberry Pear Compote

You can serve this compote warm over pound cake or cooled with whipped cream. You can layer the chilled compote in parfait glasses with whipped cream and pieces of pound cake, broken fig-filled cookies, or graham cracker crumbs.

1. Add the water, wine, sugar, allspice and cardamom to the slow cooker. Cover and cook on high for 30 minutes or until the liquid is bubbling around the edges. Stir to dissolve the sugar in the liquid.

2. Rinse and drain the cranberries. Remove and discard any stems or blemished cranberries. Stir into the liquid in the slow cooker. Cover and cook on high for 30 minutes or until the cranberries pop.

3. Wash, peel, core, and cut the pears into quarters. Stir into the other ingredients in the slow cooker. Cover and cook on low for 6 hours or on high for 3 hours.

4. Remove and discard the allspice berries and the cardamom pods. Serve warm from the slow cooker or allow to come to room temperature and pour into a covered container and refrigerate until chilled.

Serves 8

Ingredients:
1 cup water
½ cup port or Madeira wine
½ cup sugar
6 allspice berries
4 cardamom pods, crushed
1 cup cranberries
4 large pears, cored, peeled, and sliced into quarters

Pineapple Upside-Down Cake

Admittedly, it's a trick to invert this cake onto a serving plate. It's much easier to allow the cake to cool, cut it into 8 slices, and serve it from the crock of the slow cooker. Invert each slice as you place it on the dessert plate.

1. Prepare the cake mix according to the package directions.

2. Treat the bottom and sides of the slow cooker with nonstick spray. Pour the butter into the slow cooker, lifting and tilting the crock to evenly coat the bottom. Evenly sprinkle the brown sugar over the butter. Carefully spoon the crushed pineapple over the brown sugar, and then pour in any juice remaining in the can. If using, cut the maraschino cherries in half and arrange as many as you want cut side up over the pineapple.

3. Carefully pour (or ladle) the prepared cake batter over the mixture on the bottom of the slow cooker. Cover and cook on low for 4 hours or until a toothpick inserted into the cake comes out clean. If the cake is too moist on top, remove the cover and cook for another 15 to 30 minutes. Allow to cool and then serve.

Pineapple Upside-Down Cream Cheese Cake
Instead of using the cake mix recommended in the recipe, substitute the Cream Cheese Cake batter, instructions for which are given on page 292.

Chapter 25
Desserts

Cream Cheese Cake

Serve it as a shortcake topped with your favorite fresh or stewed fruit. It's also good topped with Butterscotch Caramel Sauce (see page 26) and is dense enough to dip into dessert fondue.

Serves 8

Ingredients:
Nonstick spray
1 (8-ounce) package cream cheese, softened
1 stick butter, softened
1 (5.1-ounce) package instant vanilla pudding
3 large eggs
½ cup heavy cream
2 teaspoons vanilla
1 (18-ounce) package yellow or butter cake mix

1. Treat the slow cooker with nonstick spray. (Or if you want to remove the cake from the crock to cut it into layers, generously butter the inside and sides of the crock and dust the butter with some of the dry cake mix.)

2. Cream the cream cheese and butter together in a mixing bowl. Beat in the pudding, eggs, cream, and vanilla. Fold in the cake mix. (The resulting batter will be thick—like cookie dough.)

3. Drop the batter into the slow cooker and lightly pat it down so it's evenly distributed. Cover and cook on high for 3 hours or until a toothpick inserted in the center comes out clean. Serve warm by scooping it out of the slow cooker, or if you want to spoon fruit over the entire cake and cut it into wedges, let the cake cool, cut around the edges with a knife, and invert the cake onto a plate.

Freeze Leftovers
This cake works well as the cake portion for fruit, whipped cream, and chopped toasted nuts parfaits or in a trifle.

Lemon Sugar-Crusted Cake

This cake is good with blueberry sauce, or you can add a cup of fresh blueberries to the batter before you cook it.

1. Add the cake mix, eggs, sour cream, ¾ cup of the butter, milk, pudding mix, and lemon oil or extract to a mixing bowl. Stir by hand to mix.

2. Use the remaining butter to grease the bottom and halfway up the sides of the slow cooker. Pour the sugar into the slow cooker and turn the crock until the sugar is coating all of the butter.

3. Carefully spread the batter in the slow cooker. Cover and cook on low for 4 hours or until a toothpick inserted into the center of the cake comes out clean.

Serves 8

Ingredients:
1 (18-ounce) lemon cake mix
4 large eggs
1 cup sour cream
¾ cup plus 1 tablespoon butter
1 cup milk
1 (3-ounce) package instant lemon pudding mix
3 drops lemon oil or ¼ teaspoon lemon extract
¼ cup sugar

Bread Pudding

Serve this bread pudding by itself or top it with some warm Butterscotch Caramel Sauce (see page 26) and toasted chopped pecans or walnuts.

1. Add the eggs to a mixing bowl and beat lightly, and then whisk in the milk, vanilla, cinnamon, salt, and brown sugar. Fold in the bread cubes and raisins or dates.

2. Pour the bread pudding mix into a 1½-quart baking dish that will fit on the cooking rack inside the slow cooker.

3. Place the rack in slow cooker. Pour in the hot water. Set the baking dish on the cooking rack. Cover and cook on high for about 2 hours or until the eggs are set. Serve warm or cool.

Serves 4

Ingredients:
2 large eggs
2¼ cups milk
1 teaspoon vanilla
½ teaspoon cinnamon
¼ teaspoon salt
½ cup brown sugar
2 cups of 1-inch bread cubes
½ cup raisins or chopped dates
½ cup hot water

Orange Pudding Cake

Serves 6

Ingredients:
4 large eggs, separated
⅓ cup fresh orange juice
1 tablespoon orange zest, grated
3 tablespoons butter, softened
1½ cups milk
1 cup all-purpose or cake flour
1 cup sugar
Pinch salt

Creamsicle and Orange Julius fans will love this dessert. It also works well with lemon juice and lemon zest instead of the orange. The beaten egg whites act as the leavening; the pudding forms on the bottom as the cake cooks.

1. Add the egg yolks, orange juice, orange zest, and butter to a food processor; process for 30 seconds to cream the ingredients together. Continue to process while you slowly pour in the milk.

2. Add the flour, sugar, and salt to a mixing bowl. Stir to mix. Pour the egg yolk mixture into the bowl and combine it with the dry ingredients. Add the egg whites to a separate chilled bowl; whip until stiff peaks form. Fold into the cake batter.

3. Pour into the slow cooker. Cover and cook on low for 2 to 2½ hours, or until the cake is set on top.

Banana Coconut Cake

Serves 8

Ingredients:
1 stick butter
1 (8-ounce) package cream cheese, softened
1½ cups granulated white sugar
3 large eggs
½ cup heavy cream
1 tablespoon lemon juice
2 small ripe bananas, sliced
1⅓ cups all-purpose flour
1 teaspoon baking powder
¼ teaspoon salt
¾ teaspoon baking soda
½ cup unsweetened grated coconut
½ cup pecans, chopped
Nonstick spray

You can substitute an equal amount of buttermilk for the cream and lemon juice.

1. Add the butter, cream cheese, sugar, eggs, cream, lemon juice, and banana slices to a food processor. Process until well mixed.

2. Add the flour, baking powder, salt, and baking soda to a mixing bowl. Stir to mix. Scrape in the butter-banana mixture. Stir to combine. Fold in the coconut and pecans.

3. Line the bottom of the slow cooker with a round of parchment paper, coat the paper and the sides of the crock with nonstick spray, and pour in the batter. Cover and cook on low for 4 hours or until a toothpick inserted in the center comes out clean.

Fruit Crisp

Serve with ice cream or with a dollop of whipped cream on top.

Serves 4

Ingredients:
*6 large peaches
¼ cup sugar
2 teaspoons ground
    cinnamon
Nonstick spray
¾ cup rolled oats
¼ cup all-purpose flour
½ cup brown sugar, packed
6 tablespoons butter
1 cup pecans*

1. Wash and peel the peaches. Cut them in half, remove the pits, and slice the peaches. Toss together with the sugar and cinnamon.

2. Treat the slow cooker with nonstick spray. Arrange the peaches over the bottom of the slow cooker.

3. To make the topping, add the oats, flour, brown sugar, and butter to a food processor. Pulse until the topping is the consistency of coarse cornmeal. Add the pecans and pulse a couple of times to rough-chop the nuts and mix them into the topping.

4. Sprinkle the topping evenly over the fruit in the slow cooker. Cover and cook on high for 2 hours or until the peaches are tender and the topping is crisp. Serve warm or chilled.

Quicker and Easier Fruit Crisp

Fruit Crisp is a versatile dessert. You don't have to limit yourself to fresh fruit. If you need to throw together a dessert in a hurry, you can thaw some frozen peaches or open a can of any pie filling and use one of those instead.

Mocha Custard

If you're impatient and indulgent, spoon this custard directly from the slow cooker and add even more calories by using the custard as hot sauce over ice cream. Otherwise, serve chilled according to the recipe instructions.

Serves 4

Ingredients:
¼ cup instant espresso powder
2 tablespoons unsweetened cocoa powder
⅔ cup sugar
Pinch salt
4 cups half-and-half
6 large eggs
½ teaspoon pure vanilla or maple extract
Nonstick spray
Optional: Whipped cream
Optional: Additional cocoa powder

1. Add the espresso powder, cocoa powder, sugar, and salt to a blender or food processor. Pulse to mix and remove any lumps.

2. Add the half-and-half, eggs, and extract to the blender or food processor. Process until blended.

3. Treat the slow cooker with nonstick spray. Pour in the custard mixture. Cover and cook on low for 2½ hours, or until the edges of the custard begin to puff and a knife inserted in the center comes out clean.

4. Remove the crock from the slow cooker; place it on hot pads or a rack. Let the custard stand at room temperature for an hour or until cooled. Cover the top of the crock with plastic wrap or the slow cooker lid; refrigerate for 4 hours. Serve spooned into custard cups or your favorite dessert stemware. Top with a dollop of whipped cream dusted with cocoa powder if desired.

Date Pudding

*This is a rich, decadent dessert that, when served with the quick sauce
(see sidebar) or Butterscotch Caramel Sauce (see page 26), is in the
tradition of an English sticky toffee pudding. In fact, you can double the
number of servings if you layer the pudding in parfait glasses with your
choice of sauce, chopped toasted pecans, and whipped cream.*

1. Add the dates to a mixing bowl and toss them together with the baking
   soda. Pour the boiling water over the dates. Set aside.

2. Add the brown sugar and butter to a food processor. Process to cream
   them together, and then continue to process while you add the eggs
   and vanilla.

3. Use a spatula to scrape the brown sugar mixture into the bowl with the
   dates. Stir to mix.

4. Add the flour, baking powder, and salt to a bowl; stir to mix. Fold into
   the date and brown sugar mixture.

5. Treat the slow cooker with nonstick spray. Pour the batter into the slow
   cooker. Cover and cook on low for 4 hours or until the center of the
   pudding cake is set but is still moist. Serve warm with your choice of
   sauce and a dollop of whipped cream if desired.

Quick Sauce

*Add 1½ cups packed brown sugar, ½ cup butter, and 3 cups of heavy
cream to a saucepan over medium heat. Stirring constantly, bring to a
boil and then, while continuing to stir constantly, reduce the heat and
maintain a simmer for 6 minutes.*

Serves 8

Ingredients:

2½ cups dates, pitted and
  snipped
1½ teaspoons baking soda
1⅔ cups boiling water
2 cups dark brown sugar,
  packed
½ cup butter, softened
3 large eggs
2 teaspoons vanilla
3½ cups all-purpose or cake
  flour
4 teaspoons baking powder
Pinch salt
Nonstick spray

Not Your Grandma's Chocolate Cake

Serve this pudding cake warm with ice cream.

Serves 8

Ingredients:
1 (21-ounce) package
    brownie mix
2 cups water
2 large eggs
¼ cup butter, melted
½ cup semisweet chocolate
    chips
Nonstick spray
1 cup sugar
¼ cup unsweetened cocoa
    powder

1. Add the brownie mix, ½ cup of the water, the eggs, and the melted butter to a bowl; stir to mix. Fold in the chocolate chips.

2. Treat the slow cooker with nonstick spray. Scrape the brownie mix batter into the slow cooker and spread evenly into the crock.

3. Add sugar and cocoa to a small bowl; stir to mix well. Add the remaining water to a saucepan over medium heat. Stir in the sugar-cocoa mixture. Bring to a boil and then pour over the brownie batter in the slow cooker. Cover and cook on high for 2 to 2½ hours.

Not Your Grandma's Banana Split
Serve the warm chocolate pudding cake over a banana sliced in half lengthwise. Add a scoop of strawberry ice cream; sweetened crushed pineapple; toasted, chopped peanuts, walnuts, cashews, pistachios, or pecans; and whipped cream. Top with a maraschino cherry.

Carrot Cake

*Ice this cake with cream cheese frosting or glaze the cake
while it's still warm (see sidebar).*

1. Add the flour, baking soda, baking powder, salt, cinnamon, cloves, and nutmeg to a mixing bowl; stir to combine.

2. Add the eggs, sugar, and butter to a food processor; process to cream together. Scrape into the flour mixture.

3. Pour in the water and add the grated carrots to the mixing bowl. Stir and fold to combine all ingredients. Fold in the nuts if using.

4. Treat the slow cooker with nonstick spray. Add the carrot cake batter and use a spatula to spread it evenly in the crock. Cover and cook on low for 2 hours or until cake is firm in the center.

Carrot Cake Glaze

Repeatedly pierce the top of the cake with a fork. Add ½ cup lemon, orange, or unsweetened pineapple juice; 1 teaspoon freshly grated lemon or orange zest; and 1½ cups of sifted powdered sugar to a microwave-safe measuring cup. Stir to combine. Microwave on high for 30 seconds. Stir and repeat until sugar is dissolved. Evenly pour over the cake.

Serves 8

Ingredients:
1½ cups all-purpose flour
½ teaspoon baking soda
1 teaspoon baking powder
¼ teaspoon salt
¾ teaspoon cinnamon
¼ teaspoon ground cloves
⅛ teaspoon freshly grated
    nutmeg
2 large eggs
¾ cups sugar
⅓ cup butter
¼ cup water
1 cup carrots, grated
Optional: ½ cup walnuts,
    chopped
Nonstick spray

Appendix A
Ingredients Sources

American Spoon
American Spoon Foods specialty
foods, such as:

• Cherry Peach Salsa • Fruit Butter
• Ginger Pear Butter
www.spoon.com

Birds Eye Foods
Frozen Vegetable Blends
www.birdseyefoods.com

BOCA
Frozen Ground Burger Crumbles
meat substitute
www.bocaburger.com

Brownwood Acres Foods, Inc.
Tart cherry juice concentrate
www.brownwoodacres.com

Cascadian Farm
Organic frozen hashbrowns;
vegetables
www.cascadianfarm.com

Crown Prince
Boiled baby clams and
other canned seafood
www.crownprince.com

Dik Jaxon Products Company
Cornmeal Mush (available in the
supermarket refrigerator case)
6195 Webster Street

Dayton, OH 45414
(937) 890-7350

Yoder's
Cornmeal Mush (available in the
supermarket refrigerator case)
I&K Distributors, Inc.
Delphos, OH 45833
(800) 869-6337, ext. 888

Dole Food Company, Inc.
Salad Mix
www.dole.com

Hormel
Hormel Less Sodium Chili (canned)
www.hormel.com

King Orchards
Tart cherry juice concentrate
www.mi-cherries.com

Nutty Guys
Dried fruit; nuts
www.nuttyguys.com

Minor's
Broth bases
www.soupbase.com

Mrs. Dash
Mrs. Dash Salt-Free Seasoning
and Grilling Blends
www.mrsdash.com

Muir Glen
Organic canned tomatoes
www.muirglen.com

Pillsbury
• Refrigerated Peel-and-Unroll Pie
  Crusts • Refrigerated Pizza Crust
• Refrigerated Biscuits and Dinner
  Rolls • Frozen Pie Crust • Frozen
  Biscuits
www.pillsbury.com

Redi-Base
Broth bases
www.redibase.com

Rosina Food Products, Inc.
Frozen Italian specialty food
products
www.rosina.com

Sea Star Salt
Celtic gray (sea) salt; fleur de sel
www.seastarseasalt.com

The Spice House
• Freeze-dried shallots • Spices
www.thespicehouse.com

Wellshire Farms
Nitrate-free bacon, corned beef,
ham, and other meats
www.wellshirefarms.com

Appendix B
Equipment Sources

Chicago Metallic Bakeware

Chicago Metallic Professional and Professional Nonstick Bakeware

www.chicagometallicbakeware.com

Cuisinart

Probably best known for their innovative food processors, Cuisinart also has a wide selection of countertop appliances and cookware:

- Cuisinart Brick Oven Toaster Oven with Rotisserie
- Cuisinart CleanWater Countertop Filtration System
- Cuisinart (countertop) Microwave Oven
- Cuisinart PowerPrep Plus 14-Cup Food Processor
- Cuisinart 4-quart and 6½-quart Programmable Slow Cookers

www.cuisinart.com

General Electric

Slow cookers

www.gehousewares.com

Hamilton Beach

Slow cookers

www.hamiltonbeach.com

Kaiser Bakeware

Baking sheets

www.kaiserbakeware.com

Pleasant Hill Grain

A full-service distributor for a wide variety of helpful cooking appliances, which include:

- BAMIX Hand Mixer (immersion blender)
- Berkey Stainless Water Purifier System
- Nutrimill Grain Mill

www.pleasanthillgrain.com

Reynolds Consumer Products Company

Reynolds Slow Cooker Liners

Reynolds Handi-Vac Vacuum Sealing System

www.reynoldskitchens.com

Rival

Slow cookers

www.crock-pot.com

Taylor Precision Products LP

Taylor Digital Oven Thermometer/ Timer

www.taylorusa.com

Index

Note: Page numbers in **bold** indicate recipe category lists.

THE EVERYTHING SERIES!

BUSINESS & PERSONAL FINANCE

Everything® Accounting Book
Everything® Budgeting Book, 2nd Ed.
Everything® Business Planning Book
Everything® Coaching and Mentoring Book, 2nd Ed.
Everything® Fundraising Book
Everything® Get Out of Debt Book
Everything® Grant Writing Book, 2nd Ed.
Everything® Guide to Buying Foreclosures
Everything® Guide to Fundraising, $15.95
Everything® Guide to Mortgages
Everything® Guide to Personal Finance for Single Mothers
Everything® Home-Based Business Book, 2nd Ed.
Everything® Homebuying Book, 3rd Ed., $15.95
Everything® Homeselling Book, 2nd Ed.
Everything® Human Resource Management Book
Everything® Improve Your Credit Book
Everything® Investing Book, 2nd Ed.
Everything® Landlording Book
Everything® Leadership Book, 2nd Ed.
Everything® Managing People Book, 2nd Ed.
Everything® Negotiating Book
Everything® Online Auctions Book
Everything® Online Business Book
Everything® Personal Finance Book
Everything® Personal Finance in Your 20s & 30s Book, 2nd Ed.
Everything® Personal Finance in Your 40s & 50s Book, $15.95
Everything® Project Management Book, 2nd Ed.
Everything® Real Estate Investing Book
Everything® Retirement Planning Book
Everything® Robert's Rules Book, $7.95
Everything® Selling Book
Everything® Start Your Own Business Book, 2nd Ed.
Everything® Wills & Estate Planning Book

COOKING

Everything® Barbecue Cookbook
Everything® Bartender's Book, 2nd Ed., $9.95
Everything® Calorie Counting Cookbook
Everything® Cheese Book
Everything® Chinese Cookbook
Everything® Classic Recipes Book
Everything® Cocktail Parties & Drinks Book
Everything® College Cookbook
Everything® Cooking for Baby and Toddler Book
Everything® Diabetes Cookbook
Everything® Easy Gourmet Cookbook
Everything® Fondue Cookbook
Everything® Food Allergy Cookbook, $15.95
Everything® Fondue Party Book
Everything® Gluten-Free Cookbook
Everything® Glycemic Index Cookbook
Everything® Grilling Cookbook
Everything® Healthy Cooking for Parties Book, $15.95
Everything® Holiday Cookbook
Everything® Indian Cookbook
Everything® Lactose-Free Cookbook
Everything® Low-Cholesterol Cookbook

Everything® Low-Fat High-Flavor Cookbook, 2nd Ed., $15.95
Everything® Low-Salt Cookbook
Everything® Meals for a Month Cookbook
Everything® Meals on a Budget Cookbook
Everything® Mediterranean Cookbook
Everything® Mexican Cookbook
Everything® No Trans Fat Cookbook
Everything® One-Pot Cookbook, 2nd Ed., $15.95
Everything® Organic Cooking for Baby & Toddler Book, $15.95
Everything® Pizza Cookbook
Everything® Quick Meals Cookbook, 2nd Ed., $15.95
Everything® Slow Cooker Cookbook
Everything® Slow Cooking for a Crowd Cookbook
Everything® Soup Cookbook
Everything® Stir-Fry Cookbook
Everything® Sugar-Free Cookbook
Everything® Tapas and Small Plates Cookbook
Everything® Tex-Mex Cookbook
Everything® Thai Cookbook
Everything® Vegetarian Cookbook
Everything® Whole-Grain, High-Fiber Cookbook
Everything® Wild Game Cookbook
Everything® Wine Book, 2nd Ed.

GAMES

Everything® 15-Minute Sudoku Book, $9.95
Everything® 30-Minute Sudoku Book, $9.95
Everything® Bible Crosswords Book, $9.95
Everything® Blackjack Strategy Book
Everything® Brain Strain Book, $9.95
Everything® Bridge Book
Everything® Card Games Book
Everything® Card Tricks Book, $9.95
Everything® Casino Gambling Book, 2nd Ed.
Everything® Chess Basics Book
Everything® Christmas Crosswords Book, $9.95
Everything® Craps Strategy Book
Everything® Crossword and Puzzle Book
Everything® Crosswords and Puzzles for Quote Lovers Book, $9.95
Everything® Crossword Challenge Book
Everything® Crosswords for the Beach Book, $9.95
Everything® Cryptic Crosswords Book, $9.95
Everything® Cryptograms Book, $9.95
Everything® Easy Crosswords Book
Everything® Easy Kakuro Book, $9.95
Everything® Easy Large-Print Crosswords Book
Everything® Games Book, 2nd Ed.
Everything® Giant Book of Crosswords
Everything® Giant Sudoku Book, $9.95
Everything® Giant Word Search Book
Everything® Kakuro Challenge Book, $9.95
Everything® Large-Print Crossword Challenge Book
Everything® Large-Print Crosswords Book
Everything® Large-Print Travel Crosswords Book
Everything® Lateral Thinking Puzzles Book, $9.95
Everything® Literary Crosswords Book, $9.95
Everything® Mazes Book
Everything® Memory Booster Puzzles Book, $9.95

Everything® Movie Crosswords Book, $9.95
Everything® Music Crosswords Book, $9.95
Everything® Online Poker Book
Everything® Pencil Puzzles Book, $9.95
Everything® Poker Strategy Book
Everything® Pool & Billiards Book
Everything® Puzzles for Commuters Book, $9.95
Everything® Puzzles for Dog Lovers Book, $9.95
Everything® Sports Crosswords Book, $9.95
Everything® Test Your IQ Book, $9.95
Everything® Texas Hold 'Em Book, $9.95
Everything® Travel Crosswords Book, $9.95
Everything® Travel Mazes Book, $9.95
Everything® Travel Word Search Book, $9.95
Everything® TV Crosswords Book, $9.95
Everything® Word Games Challenge Book
Everything® Word Scramble Book
Everything® Word Search Book

HEALTH

Everything® Alzheimer's Book
Everything® Diabetes Book
Everything® First Aid Book, $9.95
Everything® Green Living Book
Everything® Health Guide to Addiction and Recovery
Everything® Health Guide to Adult Bipolar Disorder
Everything® Health Guide to Arthritis
Everything® Health Guide to Controlling Anxiety
Everything® Health Guide to Depression
Everything® Health Guide to Diabetes, 2nd Ed.
Everything® Health Guide to Fibromyalgia
Everything® Health Guide to Menopause, 2nd Ed.
Everything® Health Guide to Migraines
Everything® Health Guide to Multiple Sclerosis
Everything® Health Guide to OCD
Everything® Health Guide to PMS
Everything® Health Guide to Postpartum Care
Everything® Health Guide to Thyroid Disease
Everything® Hypnosis Book
Everything® Low Cholesterol Book
Everything® Menopause Book
Everything® Nutrition Book
Everything® Reflexology Book
Everything® Stress Management Book
Everything® Superfoods Book, $15.95

HISTORY

Everything® American Government Book
Everything® American History Book, 2nd Ed.
Everything® American Revolution Book, $15.95
Everything® Civil War Book
Everything® Freemasons Book
Everything® Irish History & Heritage Book
Everything® World War II Book, 2nd Ed.

HOBBIES

Everything® Candlemaking Book
Everything® Cartooning Book
Everything® Coin Collecting Book
Everything® Digital Photography Book, 2nd Ed.

Everything® Drawing Book
Everything® Family Tree Book, 2nd Ed.
Everything® Guide to Online Genealogy, $15.95
Everything® Knitting Book
Everything® Knots Book
Everything® Photography Book
Everything® Quilting Book
Everything® Sewing Book
Everything® Soapmaking Book, 2nd Ed.
Everything® Woodworking Book

HOME IMPROVEMENT

Everything® Feng Shui Book
Everything® Feng Shui Decluttering Book, $9.95
Everything® Fix-It Book
Everything® Green Living Book
Everything® Home Decorating Book
Everything® Home Storage Solutions Book
Everything® Homebuilding Book
Everything® Organize Your Home Book, 2nd Ed.

KIDS' BOOKS

All titles are $7.95
Everything® Fairy Tales Book, $14.95
Everything® Kids' Animal Puzzle & Activity Book
Everything® Kids' Astronomy Book
Everything® Kids' Baseball Book, 5th Ed.
Everything® Kids' Bible Trivia Book
Everything® Kids' Bugs Book
Everything® Kids' Cars and Trucks Puzzle and Activity Book
Everything® Kids' Christmas Puzzle & Activity Book
Everything® Kids' Connect the Dots
Puzzle and Activity Book
Everything® Kids' Cookbook, 2nd Ed.
Everything® Kids' Crazy Puzzles Book
Everything® Kids' Dinosaurs Book
Everything® Kids' Dragons Puzzle and Activity Book
Everything® Kids' Environment Book $7.95
Everything® Kids' Fairies Puzzle and Activity Book
Everything® Kids' First Spanish Puzzle and Activity Book
Everything® Kids' Football Book
Everything® Kids' Geography Book
Everything® Kids' Gross Cookbook
Everything® Kids' Gross Hidden Pictures Book
Everything® Kids' Gross Jokes Book
Everything® Kids' Gross Mazes Book
Everything® Kids' Gross Puzzle & Activity Book
Everything® Kids' Halloween Puzzle & Activity Book
Everything® Kids' Hanukkah Puzzle and Activity Book
Everything® Kids' Hidden Pictures Book
Everything® Kids' Horses Book
Everything® Kids' Joke Book
Everything® Kids' Knock Knock Book
Everything® Kids' Learning French Book
Everything® Kids' Learning Spanish Book
Everything® Kids' Magical Science Experiments Book
Everything® Kids' Math Puzzles Book
Everything® Kids' Mazes Book
Everything® Kids' Money Book, 2nd Ed.
Everything® Kids' Mummies, Pharaoh's, and Pyramids Puzzle and Activity Book
Everything® Kids' Nature Book
Everything® Kids' Pirates Puzzle and Activity Book
Everything® Kids' Presidents Book
Everything® Kids' Princess Puzzle and Activity Book
Everything® Kids' Puzzle Book

Everything® Kids' Racecars Puzzle and Activity Book
Everything® Kids' Riddles & Brain Teasers Book
Everything® Kids' Science Experiments Book
Everything® Kids' Sharks Book
Everything® Kids' Soccer Book
Everything® Kids' Spelling Book
Everything® Kids' Spies Puzzle and Activity Book
Everything® Kids' States Book
Everything® Kids' Travel Activity Book
Everything® Kids' Word Search Puzzle and Activity Book

LANGUAGE

Everything® Conversational Japanese Book with CD, $19.95
Everything® French Grammar Book
Everything® French Phrase Book, $9.95
Everything® French Verb Book, $9.95
Everything® German Phrase Book, $9.95
Everything® German Practice Book with CD, $19.95
Everything® Inglés Book
Everything® Intermediate Spanish Book with CD, $19.95
Everything® Italian Phrase Book, $9.95
Everything® Italian Practice Book with CD, $19.95
Everything® Learning Brazilian Portuguese Book with CD, $19.95
Everything® Learning French Book with CD, 2nd Ed., $19.95
Everything® Learning German Book
Everything® Learning Italian Book
Everything® Learning Latin Book
Everything® Learning Russian Book with CD, $19.95
Everything® Learning Spanish Book
Everything® Learning Spanish Book with CD, 2nd Ed., $19.95
Everything® Russian Practice Book with CD, $19.95
Everything® Sign Language Book, $15.95
Everything® Spanish Grammar Book
Everything® Spanish Phrase Book, $9.95
Everything® Spanish Practice Book with CD, $9.95
Everything® Spanish Verb Book, $9.95
Everything® Speaking Mandarin Chinese Book with CD, $19.95

MUSIC

Everything® Bass Guitar Book with CD, $19.95
Everything® Drums Book with CD, $19.95
Everything® Guitar Book with CD, 2nd Ed., $19.95
Everything® Guitar Chords Book with CD, $19.95
Everything® Guitar Scales Book with CD, $19.95
Everything® Harmonica Book with CD, $15.95
Everything® Home Recording Book
Everything® Music Theory Book with CD, $19.95
Everything® Reading Music Book with CD, $19.95
Everything® Rock & Blues Guitar Book with CD, $19.95
Everything® Rock & Blues Piano Book with CD, $19.95
Everything® Rock Drums Book with CD, $19.95
Everything® Singing Book with CD, $19.95
Everything® Songwriting Book

NEW AGE

Everything® Astrology Book, 2nd Ed.
Everything® Birthday Personology Book
Everything® Celtic Wisdom Book, $15.95
Everything® Dreams Book, 2nd Ed.
Everything® Law of Attraction Book, $15.95
Everything® Love Signs Book, $9.95
Everything® Love Spells Book, $9.95
Everything® Palmistry Book
Everything® Psychic Book
Everything® Reiki Book

Everything® Sex Signs Book, $9.95
Everything® Spells & Charms Book, 2nd Ed.
Everything® Tarot Book, 2nd Ed.
Everything® Toltec Wisdom Book
Everything® Wicca & Witchcraft Book, 2nd Ed.

PARENTING

Everything® Baby Names Book, 2nd Ed.
Everything® Baby Shower Book, 2nd Ed.
Everything® Baby Sign Language Book with DVD
Everything® Baby's First Year Book
Everything® Birthing Book
Everything® Breastfeeding Book
Everything® Father-to-Be Book
Everything® Father's First Year Book
Everything® Get Ready for Baby Book, 2nd Ed.
Everything® Get Your Baby to Sleep Book, $9.95
Everything® Getting Pregnant Book
Everything® Guide to Pregnancy Over 35
Everything® Guide to Raising a One-Year-Old
Everything® Guide to Raising a Two-Year-Old
Everything® Guide to Raising Adolescent Boys
Everything® Guide to Raising Adolescent Girls
Everything® Mother's First Year Book
Everything® Parent's Guide to Childhood Illnesses
Everything® Parent's Guide to Children and Divorce
Everything® Parent's Guide to Children with ADD/ADHD
Everything® Parent's Guide to Children with Asperger's Syndrome
Everything® Parent's Guide to Children with Anxiety
Everything® Parent's Guide to Children with Asthma
Everything® Parent's Guide to Children with Autism
Everything® Parent's Guide to Children with Bipolar Disorder
Everything® Parent's Guide to Children with Depression
Everything® Parent's Guide to Children with Dyslexia
Everything® Parent's Guide to Children with Juvenile Diabetes
Everything® Parent's Guide to Children with OCD
Everything® Parent's Guide to Positive Discipline
Everything® Parent's Guide to Raising Boys
Everything® Parent's Guide to Raising Girls
Everything® Parent's Guide to Raising Siblings
Everything® Parent's Guide to Raising Your Adopted Child
Everything® Parent's Guide to Sensory Integration Disorder
Everything® Parent's Guide to Tantrums
Everything® Parent's Guide to the Strong-Willed Child
Everything® Parenting a Teenager Book
Everything® Potty Training Book, $9.95
Everything® Pregnancy Book, 3rd Ed.
Everything® Pregnancy Fitness Book
Everything® Pregnancy Nutrition Book
Everything® Pregnancy Organizer, 2nd Ed., $16.95
Everything® Toddler Activities Book
Everything® Toddler Book
Everything® Tween Book
Everything® Twins, Triplets, and More Book

PETS

Everything® Aquarium Book
Everything® Boxer Book
Everything® Cat Book, 2nd Ed.
Everything® Chihuahua Book
Everything® Cooking for Dogs Book
Everything® Dachshund Book
Everything® Dog Book, 2nd Ed.
Everything® Dog Grooming Book

Everything® Dog Obedience Book
Everything® Dog Owner's Organizer, $16.95
Everything® Dog Training and Tricks Book
Everything® German Shepherd Book
Everything® Golden Retriever Book
Everything® Horse Book, 2nd Ed., $15.95
Everything® Horse Care Book
Everything® Horseback Riding Book
Everything® Labrador Retriever Book
Everything® Poodle Book
Everything® Pug Book
Everything® Puppy Book
Everything® Small Dogs Book
Everything® Tropical Fish Book
Everything® Yorkshire Terrier Book

REFERENCE

Everything® American Presidents Book
Everything® Blogging Book
Everything® Build Your Vocabulary Book, $9.95
Everything® Car Care Book
Everything® Classical Mythology Book
Everything® Da Vinci Book
Everything® Einstein Book
Everything® Enneagram Book
Everything® Etiquette Book, 2nd Ed.
Everything® Family Christmas Book, $15.95
Everything® Guide to C. S. Lewis & Narnia
Everything® Guide to Divorce, 2nd Ed., $15.95
Everything® Guide to Edgar Allan Poe
Everything® Guide to Understanding Philosophy
Everything® Inventions and Patents Book
Everything® Jacqueline Kennedy Onassis Book
Everything® John F. Kennedy Book
Everything® Mafia Book
Everything® Martin Luther King Jr. Book
Everything® Pirates Book
Everything® Private Investigation Book
Everything® Psychology Book
Everything® Public Speaking Book, $9.95
Everything® Shakespeare Book, 2nd Ed.

RELIGION

Everything® Angels Book
Everything® Bible Book
Everything® Bible Study Book with CD, $19.95
Everything® Buddhism Book
Everything® Catholicism Book
Everything® Christianity Book
Everything® Gnostic Gospels Book
Everything® Hinduism Book, $15.95
Everything® History of the Bible Book
Everything® Jesus Book
Everything® Jewish History & Heritage Book
Everything® Judaism Book
Everything® Kabbalah Book
Everything® Koran Book
Everything® Mary Book
Everything® Mary Magdalene Book
Everything® Prayer Book

Everything® Saints Book, 2nd Ed.
Everything® Torah Book
Everything® Understanding Islam Book
Everything® Women of the Bible Book
Everything® World's Religions Book

SCHOOL & CAREERS

Everything® Career Tests Book
Everything® College Major Test Book
Everything® College Survival Book, 2nd Ed.
Everything® Cover Letter Book, 2nd Ed.
Everything® Filmmaking Book
Everything® Get-a-Job Book, 2nd Ed.
Everything® Guide to Being a Paralegal
Everything® Guide to Being a Personal Trainer
Everything® Guide to Being a Real Estate Agent
Everything® Guide to Being a Sales Rep
Everything® Guide to Being an Event Planner
Everything® Guide to Careers in Health Care
Everything® Guide to Careers in Law Enforcement
Everything® Guide to Government Jobs
Everything® Guide to Starting and Running a Catering
   Business
Everything® Guide to Starting and Running a Restaurant
**Everything® Guide to Starting and Running
   a Retail Store**
Everything® Job Interview Book, 2nd Ed.
Everything® New Nurse Book
Everything® New Teacher Book
Everything® Paying for College Book
Everything® Practice Interview Book
Everything® Resume Book, 3rd Ed.
Everything® Study Book

SELF-HELP

Everything® Body Language Book
Everything® Dating Book, 2nd Ed.
Everything® Great Sex Book
**Everything® Guide to Caring for Aging Parents,
   $15.95**
Everything® Self-Esteem Book
Everything® Self-Hypnosis Book, $9.95
Everything® Tantric Sex Book

SPORTS & FITNESS

Everything® Easy Fitness Book
Everything® Fishing Book
Everything® Guide to Weight Training, $15.95
Everything® Krav Maga for Fitness Book
Everything® Running Book, 2nd Ed.
Everything® Triathlon Training Book, $15.95

TRAVEL

Everything® Family Guide to Coastal Florida
Everything® Family Guide to Cruise Vacations
Everything® Family Guide to Hawaii
Everything® Family Guide to Las Vegas, 2nd Ed.
Everything® Family Guide to Mexico
Everything® Family Guide to New England, 2nd Ed.

Everything® Family Guide to New York City, 3rd Ed.
**Everything® Family Guide to Northern California
   and Lake Tahoe**
Everything® Family Guide to RV Travel & Campgrounds
Everything® Family Guide to the Caribbean
Everything® Family Guide to the Disneyland® Resort, California
   Adventure®, Universal Studios®, and the Anaheim
   Area, 2nd Ed.
Everything® Family Guide to the Walt Disney World Resort®,
   Universal Studios®, and Greater Orlando, 5th Ed.
Everything® Family Guide to Timeshares
Everything® Family Guide to Washington D.C., 2nd Ed.

WEDDINGS

Everything® Bachelorette Party Book, $9.95
Everything® Bridesmaid Book, $9.95
Everything® Destination Wedding Book
Everything® Father of the Bride Book, $9.95
Everything® Green Wedding Book, $15.95
Everything® Groom Book, $9.95
Everything® Jewish Wedding Book, 2nd Ed., $15.95
Everything® Mother of the Bride Book, $9.95
Everything® Outdoor Wedding Book
Everything® Wedding Book, 3rd Ed.
Everything® Wedding Checklist, $9.95
Everything® Wedding Etiquette Book, $9.95
Everything® Wedding Organizer, 2nd Ed., $16.95
Everything® Wedding Shower Book, $9.95
Everything® Wedding Vows Book, 3rd Ed., $9.95
Everything® Wedding Workout Book
Everything® Weddings on a Budget Book, 2nd Ed., $9.95

WRITING

Everything® Creative Writing Book
Everything® Get Published Book, 2nd Ed.
Everything® Grammar and Style Book, 2nd Ed.
Everything® Guide to Magazine Writing
Everything® Guide to Writing a Book Proposal
Everything® Guide to Writing a Novel
Everything® Guide to Writing Children's Books
Everything® Guide to Writing Copy
Everything® Guide to Writing Graphic Novels
Everything® Guide to Writing Research Papers
Everything® Guide to Writing a Romance Novel, $15.95
Everything® Improve Your Writing Book, 2nd Ed.
Everything® Writing Poetry Book

Available wherever books are sold! To order, call 800-258-0929, or visit us at *www.adamsmedia.com*.
Everything® and everything.com® are registered trademarks of F+W Publications, Inc.
Bolded titles are new additions to the series.
All Everything® books are priced at $12.95 or $14.95, unless otherwise stated. Prices subject to change without notice.